Praise for *Challenge the Ordinary*

"Dr. Henman understands what it takes to create an outstanding organization, starting with exceptional talent. At TOPGUN, we never settled for second best, which is why the name 'TOPGUN' is synonymous with excellence."

—Captain Thomas "Trim" Downing, USN, Retired,
former TOPGUN Commanding Officer

"We knew in the human spaceflight business that ordinary would never work—not in the astronaut corps nor on the flight operations teams. Only through being an exceptional organization did NASA lead the US to become the world's greatest spacefaring nation."

—Dick Covey, former Space Shuttle Commander
and retired United Space Alliance CEO

"Again, Dr. Henman offers powerful leadership lessons in her unique entertaining style. *Challenge the Ordinary* delivers a wake-up call to business leaders and provides meaningful advice on how to achieve exceptional results in today's challenging business climate."

—Jim Dale, CEO of Omega

Challenge the Ordinary

Why Revolutionary Companies
Abandon Conventional Mindsets,
Question Long-Held Assumptions, and
Kill Their Sacred Cows

By Linda D. Henman, PhD

CAREER
PRESS

Pompton Plains, N.J.

CHALLENGE THE ORDINARY
Typeset by Diana Ghazzawi
Cover design by Ty Nowicki
Printed in the U.S.A.

To order this title, please call toll-free 1-800-CAREER-1 (NJ and Canada: 201-848-0310) to order using VISA or MasterCard, or for further information on books from Career Press.

CAREER
PRESS

The Career Press, Inc.
220 West Parkway, Unit 12
Pompton Plains, NJ 07444
www.careerpress.com

Library of Congress Cataloging-in-Publication Data
Henman, Linda D.
   Challenge the ordinary : why revolutionary companies abandon conventional mindsets, question long-held assumptions, and kill their sacred cows / by Linda D. Henman, PhD.
      pages cm
   Includes bibliographical references and index.
ISBN 978-1-60163-316-3 -- ISBN 978-1-60163-470-2 (ebook)
   1. Strategic planning. 2. Organizational change. 3. Organizational behavior. 4. Success in business. 5. Leadership. I. Title.

HD30.28.H473 2014
658.4'012--dc23

2014000407

To Angela, Sherry, and Laura, three of the
most exceptional daughters a woman could ask for.

Contents

Part One

The Exceptional Organization

Chapter One

Let a Winner Lead the Way

The lyrics from the song "Step to the Rear," in the 1967 Broadway production *How Now, Dow Jones*, announced that "here's where we separate the notes from the noise, the men from the boys, the rose from the poison ivy." In this rousing musical, the characters center their lives around the stock market and saving the U.S. economy. Sounds like a familiar theme resurfacing—reality imitating art? In the world of business, separating the critical from the unimportant, the real thing from the imposter, the business where average people want to work from the exceptional organization, is no less essential.

We suspected then, but know now, that ordinary just won't work anymore. Research indicates that only a handful of star performers create the vast majority of valuable ideas for their organizations. These top thinkers, who also deliver stellar results, define the talent you'll need to create your exceptional advantage, but they don't usually perform to their maximum capacity alone. They are not free agents; rather, these highly talented, extraordinary thinkers need the structure of an organization and effective leadership to do their best work.

Leaders who choose to lead a team of these top performers need to understand that these clever—often brilliant—individuals offer more, so they expect more in return. The major-league player wants to play with other stars, not benchwarmers. Similarly, organizational stars define themselves by their excellence, so they want to associate with an organization that does too. They hold high standards for themselves, so it makes sense that they will hold their places of employment to equally high standards.

They want to work with other exceptional players in a culture that fosters their growth, formulates a clear strategy for their success, and then creates the day-to-day processes that allow them to achieve their personal goals and realize their need for accomplishment. In short, they want strong leaders who lead exceptional organizations—agile yet stable organizations that hold on to their core values while responding adeptly to the temporary nature of the global economy.

The Paradoxical Organization: Transient and Timeless

A *paradox*, from the Greek word meaning "contrary to expectation," is a statement that seems self-contradictory but may be true. It seems to conflict with common sense, but we believe it nonetheless. It contains two true statements that, in general, cannot both be true at the same time, yet it challenges us to explore the distinction between truth and plausibility. For example, if I say, "I'm a compulsive liar," do you believe me or not? Can someone be both a compulsive liar yet be telling the truth at the same time?

Throughout history, artists, poets, writers, and philosophers have used the paradox to reveal human nature—the conflicted and complicated inner world that separates us from other beasts. Oscar Wilde wrote, "I can resist anything but temptation." Robert Frost noted, "Men work together whether they work together or apart." In *Animal Farm*, George Orwell observed, "All animals are equal, but some are more equal than others."

The examples from literature show that paradoxes are more than just witty or amusing statements. They have serious implications because they sum up the totality of the work in one statement and create a meaningful and memorable way to illustrate something important. People say, "I must be cruel to be kind," often not realizing they have transcended history to offer a universal truth that Hamlet spoke to explain why he had to kill his stepfather, Claudius—the cruelty involving the murder, the kindness relating to sparing his mother the tragedy of unknowingly living with her former husband's killer. A modern-day philosopher, Yogi Berra, inadvertently emerged as the king of the paradox with such statements as "Nobody goes there anymore. It's too crowded," or the ever-popular "If you don't go to other people's funerals, they won't come to yours."

Organizations that have an exceptional advantage offer their own paradoxes: They must react nimbly to the current, ever-changing global economy while steadfastly holding to their mission, vision, and values. They must balance a "just in time" orientation with coherence. To remain the same, exceptional organizations must change adeptly and agilely, thus creating a "Ship of Theseus" or a Theseus's paradox.

The Athenian hero Theseus was probably mythical, but the ancients regarded him as a historical person, the first king to establish Athens on a firm basis as a unified city-state. Theseus, simultaneously begotten by the king of Athens and the sea-god Poseidon, appeared in several Greek tragedies, nearly always embodying Athenian ideals of humaneness and magnanimity. He also overcame insurmountable challenges, like killing the half-man half-bull monster, Minotaur, and escaping from a mazelike labyrinth with the help of Ariadne, who held the end of a thread at the entrance to the labyrinth.

After killing the Minotaur, Theseus returned to Athens, where his countrymen maintained his ship in a seaworthy condition to honor Apollo, the god to whom they had pledged their fealty for Theseus's safe return. Legend implies that the devotion to the god and the commitment to maintain the ship lasted at least until about 300 BC, but a paradox emerged—one that metaphorically mirrors the paradox that business leaders face.

The Ship of Theseus paradox raises the question of whether an object that has had all its component parts replaced remains fundamentally the same object. Through several centuries, every worn or rotted plank and wooden part of Theseus' ship had to be replaced with new, stronger timber. That prompted the philosophical question about the nature of identity: how much can something change and still remain the same?

Regardless of these issues of the originality of the ship's structure, for Athenians the preserved ship kept alive their understanding that Theseus had been an actual, historic figure—which none then doubted—and gave them a tangible connection to their divine providence. They didn't care whether it remained the same ship or not; it served the function that they needed it to.

Similarly, your organization will need to find the balance between legend and truth, originality and innovation, today and tomorrow. Most leaders build their companies based on their beliefs about the future; however, that future has shown itself to be unpredictable and fickle. Worse, should the future not turn out as expected, the requirements of breakthrough success demand implementing strategy in ways that make it impossible to adapt. Thus, the paradox. Devotion to an outdated strategy or fealty to an unrealistic vision won't help you, but a culture that has its roots in tradition will. Much as the Athenians maintained the seaworthiness of Theseus's ship, you'll want to preserve the aspects of your organization that *define* it, while replacing the worn and rotten aspects of it.

Therefore, organizations with the greatest possibility of success also have the greatest possibility of failure. That is, the same behaviors and characteristics that maximize a company's probability of notable success also maximize its probability of failure. The status quo stands firmly at odds with innovation, and the commitments of today often don't align with the reality of tomorrow. In the past, we have relied on past performance to predict the future. Now we can't. Past performance still plays a role, but only those companies that develop crystal ball accuracy in their predictions will outrun the competition. We can no longer base decisions on traditional best-practice questions such as "Does this fit with the organization's core competencies and culture?" because we don't know if the competencies and culture of today will match the challenges of tomorrow. As Yogi also said, "The future ain't what it used to be."

Five Reasons for the Paradox

1. Workforce Changes

The assumptions we once made about our workforces no longer apply. Demographic changes continue to happen so rapidly that business leaders can no longer base talent decisions on tried-and-true approaches. Gone are the days of someone entering an organization in the mailroom and rising to the CEO position. You can't assume you'll have the same talent for 30 years the way business leaders once could.

Similarly, you don't want that same talent. As your organization responds to the rapid changes happening around it and to it, you'll find that you need different kinds of specialists, depending on the nature of your products and services. "Retention" will no longer serve as a universal goal or gold standard of excellence. Instead, retention of key players and top performers will become the new battle cry and leveraging that talent an evolving strategy.

But the gods will conspire against you in your attempts. As the need for specialized talent evolves, we will see more foreign students in our graduate technology and science programs—students who intend to take their talent and education back to their countries of origin. In the near future, our public schools will continue to disappoint, and many of our students won't be able to compete for positions in our universities. Simply put, not enough people have been getting ready for the top positions.

During the recent recession, in some industries we took a four-year time-out. For example, construction ground to a screeching halt, and those who should have been preparing to take over from the retiring Baby Boomers didn't get ready. The senior people who have specialized experience, like renovating a large hospital, will be retiring. There are few on the bench who can step up.

The eminent retirement of senior Baby Boomers also means that those with the corporate knowledge and industry history won't be available for mentoring the future leaders. We will have lost a succession-planning advantage we've long taken for granted.

Adding to the confusion, researchers tell us that there has been a sharp increase in the number of companies complaining that competitors are trying to recruit their top people. Yet too few companies have changed their approaches to retaining them. Consequently, competitors have started to pirate the industry stars, a practice that was once held in disfavor.

Social media, in particular, and technology in general, have played significant roles in the poaching. In a given industry, two degrees of separation now divide the star performers from the recruiters. Penetrating today's organization and gaining information about key contributors have never been easier, and Websites like Linkedin will even supply the names of people who can do introductions. The negative implications for an organization's bench strength and leadership succession are apparent.

To our detriment, we became too reliant on human resources for recruiting and hiring. They implemented detailed, often-daunting hiring practices that take too long. Only then will you position yourself to attract the talent you'll need.

But the basic assumption that HR should be the hiring body has to change too. Now, senior executives need to identify the kinds of people and the specific people they want to hire. They need to add to their impressive list of responsibilities "Talent Magnet." All this cooks up a recipe for new, unprecedented challenges for businesses—especially those involved in cutting-edge research and development.

2. New Rules of the Road

The road that got you here won't take you into the future because today's global economy does not allow for mediocrity or outdated approaches. The rules and players have changed, and ordinary simply won't work anymore.

Advancements in technology explain many of the new rules of the road. The amount of data in our world has been exploding, and analyzing large data sets—so-called "big data"—will become a key basis of competitive analysis, underpinning new waves of productivity, growth, innovation, and consumer behavior. Now, more than ever before, leaders in every function and industry—not just a few IT or data-oriented managers—will have to grapple with the implications of big data. Big data involves data sets so large and complex that processing all of it with traditional data processing applications has become unrealistic, but the rewards provide the motivation to create pragmatic solutions.[1]

Big data can unlock significant value by making information transparent and usable at much higher frequency. As organizations create and store more information in digital form, they can collect more accurate and detailed performance statistics on everything from product inventories to vacation days. Leading companies use data collection and analysis to make better strategic decisions; others use them to develop tactics—to adjust their business levers just in time so they can precisely tailor products or services to specific customers and exact needs. Exceptional organizations will have to do both.

The challenges of big data include capturing, storing, searching, sharing, and analysis—that last one presenting the biggest challenge because big data sizes are a moving target, and the target moves constantly due to continuous improvements. Without question, sophisticated analytics can substantially improve decision-making and influence the development of the next generation of products and services.

The size of the company doesn't matter. Big companies no longer own the corner market on big data. Now, small and medium-sized companies can buy sophisticated analytic tools for very little money, and sometimes these smaller companies can absorb and exploit these technologies faster and better than larger organizations, essentially leveling the playing field. Whether the organization is big or small, it will all come down to one thing: the rate of ROI in these technologies is only high when implemented correctly.

Exceptional organizations will leverage data-driven strategies to innovate, compete, and capture value from up-to-real-time information. But then someone will have to know how to use these data to make decisions. Companies will invest enormous sums to derive insight from data, but only those few exceptional organizations that boast extraordinary talent will translate big data into big judgment.

The use of data won't be the only new rule for the road ahead. Agility and flexibility will no longer be optional. Those companies that wish to compete in the global economy will have to be willing to experiment with never-before-heard-of challenges and opportunities. They will need to steadfastly hold to their core values while remaining open to what the data tell them. They may have to address the demand for flexible work options among their employees, perhaps opening locations in new countries or involving more extensive remote working. Whatever options emerge, one thing will remain constant: those companies that define the competition will become more results than input focused. Things like "who works what hours" will become less important, while productivity will become more critical.

Strategic planning, bold leadership, decisive action—once the prerequisites of success—can now supply the ingredients for a formula for failure. Leaders must now make choices about far-reaching consequences based on a future that hasn't existed before. These successful leaders will need to learn to live in harmony with complexity, speed, instability, and ambiguity. In short, they will need to create exceptional advantages.

3. Global Tilt

The world has shifted its economic center from Western countries of the northern hemisphere to fast-developing countries such as China, India, Indonesia, and Brazil, and parts of the Middle East. These countries of the South have started to drive change that scares their Northern neighbors. New dynamics of global competition have emerged as more countries begin to seek a larger share of the jobs pie, an improved standard of living, increased financial reserves, and more political stability. But there are no clear rules for the new game.

The United States practices some protectionism in selected areas but has no coordinated economic plan, and other countries are creating their own rules as they go along. Some countries have government funding in the form of low-cost loans; others are using their country's sovereign wealth funds; in others, private equity firms are trolling for opportunities. As they are learning, economic power creates political power—not the other way around.

Leaders of exceptional organizations will start with a clear grasp of the global context, a world with no central governing body and no set of enforceable rules—a hard-earned lesson from Europe. Several things to keep in mind about this economy: it's huge, growing at a breakneck speed, interconnected, complex, unstable, and lacking in transparency. The system that affects the lives of millions of people around the world continues to be overseen by totally uncoordinated players.

Are you willing to forgo profits in the early years to win against the Southern competition? Can you convince the capital markets to live with a longer time horizon? Most leaders will answer "no." However, expansion requires commitment of people and money. Additionally, the leaders you assign or hire locally in foreign countries will have to be high-level, and you'll have to be comfortable entrusting them with significant decisions and hefty budgets.

How do you begin to think about this shift? First, educate yourself so you can understand and anticipate the global business context. Because information is readily available, there's no excuse for geoeconomic or geopolitical illiteracy. Now, more than ever, you'll need to understand trends beyond your industry and geography. Chief among these trends— trends that keep shaping and reshaping markets, society, and GDP—will be the ever-changing role of U.S. and foreign governments in economic activity. Also, changing demographics will put pressure on resources or drive markets.[2] A solid grasp of global dynamics and the ever-emerging rules in global environment will help you pinpoint those key trends that could either upend your world or create once-in-a-lifetime opportunities. Use the insight and information that experts provide, but then form your own opinions of the total system, seeing patterns at the highest level, crystallizing what it all really means.

4. Fear

Emotions and perceptions affect market movement and prosperity. Similarly, stock prices, unemployment rates, gross domestic product, and debt drive emotions and perceptions. Since 2008, fear has been the emotion that has influenced decisions from the highest levels of government to the decisions of small business owners. Collectively, we have created an economic engine that uses fear as its primary fuel, and the media supply this fuel through threats and doomsday predictions.

Twenty-four-hour news feeds need to draw audiences, and to draw audiences, those in the media require sensation. Consequently, they constantly search for the "man bites dog" story and embrace the "if it bleeds, it leads" orientation. Adding complexity to the situation, people on the other side of the globe hear news from the United States within seconds of it happening. In the new global economy, that which affects one country eventually affects others. At some point, we become immune to another "cliff" scare, but that does not imply that the stories don't hold sway. They do.

Social networking is another game-changer, though the game is still one of guessing. We know that it can spread new ideas and influence behaviors on a massive scale, in moments. Social media, cell phones, and texting have given us new ways to stay in touch but also new ways to annoy and scare each other. But all the consequences are not so mild as married Senator Weiner "sexting" a picture of himself to a young woman. Some of the social media platforms have provided outlets for information sharing that sparks protests and violence. All this combines to fan the flames of fear and causes the cycle to repeat itself.

5. Change

The fifth reason for the paradoxical organization presents its own paradox. According to the research Jim Collins presents in *Great by Choice,* the great organizations they studied were not necessarily more innovative than their less successful counterparts, and in some cases, the great organizations were *less* innovative. As the researchers concluded, innovation by itself turns out not to be the trump card we expected. More important is the ability to calibrate innovation, to blend creativity with discipline.

Great leaders do not have visionary ability to predict the future, but they can observe what has worked in the past, figure out why it worked, and build on proven foundations—all combining to decide about what changes to make when. As Collins and his team learned, dramatic change outside the organization does not mean leaders should inflict radical change on their organizations. Instead, a disciplined approach and the right cadence about change must guide them.[3]

Accuracy and agility will play a bigger part in your ability to create an exceptional organization than speed will. You will need to move quickly— probably before you think you're ready—but *pace* will prove more reliable than haste. You'll need to know when to run and when to walk. But you'll also have to understand that you'll have to jump too. Change comes more often by infliction than invitation, and Lady Luck will play her role too. The critical question won't be whether you'll have luck, but what you will do with the luck you get.

In addition to offering its own paradox, the fifth reason for overall orga-nizational paradoxes encompasses the previously mentioned four reasons. The workforce will change because the rules of the road have changed, and both of these will change because of global tilt. All of this will promote the fear that probably played a role in it starting in the first place. We now face a future that won't forgive the mistakes we've always made or the new mistakes we'll be tempted to make. Only those who steadfastly commit to creating exceptional organizations will thrive—but they will have to do so consciously and continuously.

The Four Traits of the Exceptional Organization

The economic downturn of 2009 taught us a valuable lesson that we don't want to have to relearn: we can't ever count on certainty again. Those things we always "knew" were safe bets disappointed and sometimes dev-astated us. Yet we can't afford to lose confidence, because with it goes opti-mism and success. Instead, you need a new plan that leaves little room for error. It will hinge on the strategy you select, the culture you create, a com-mitment to excellence, and the talent you attract. And it will look like this:

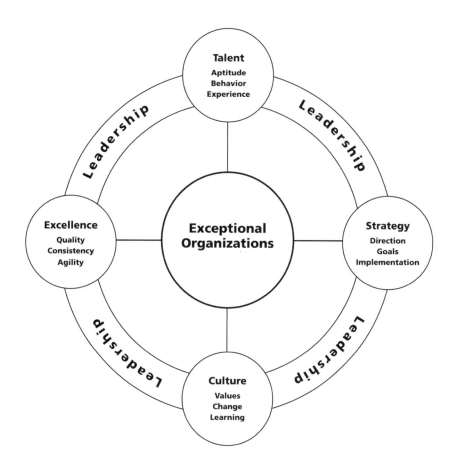

Strategy: Separating the Notes From the Noise

Traditionally, leaders analyzed customer feedback and industry data to make a decision about what the future would look like and how their organization would respond to it. Then, someone changed the rules of the game.

Today, rather than developing a single strategic commitment, leaders need to invent practical strategies, based on multiple choices that respond to different requirements of several possible futures. In short, they need to hedge their bets. Instead of imagining *one* possible future, they need to envision and anticipate several future alternatives. For each they will need to accumulate data and formulate a plan for implementation. They will need to be agile, sure-footed, and speedy—willing to change when they have to, but clear about the direction they want to go.

There are two kinds or organizations: those with a strong strategy that can respond to change and those going out of business. In other words, what got you here won't necessarily get you to the next level. The Pony Express did not become the railroad, and the railroad did not become the airlines. Vanguards in their days, at one time both the railroad and airline industries thrived. Today, however, both industries suffer from decades of bad management.

Unlike the leaders in these two industries, you will need to excel at reading the tea leaves. What opportunities and threats loom on your horizon? How can you leverage your strengths and mitigate your weaknesses to ready yourself for them? Let's take a lesson from recent history.

In 2012, the *Wall Street Journal* reported that Wal-Mart was in the midst of the worst U.S. sales slump ever, posting its second straight year of declining sales. How can this happen to America's behemoth, a store that should have been thriving as customers looked for low-cost alternatives amid an economic downturn? They misstepped. To jump-start lethargic growth and counter the rise of competitors, decision-makers veered away from the winning-formula mission: "Saving People Money So They Can Live Better." Instead, the world's biggest retailer raised prices on some items while promoting deals on others.

That wasn't the only change to its mission. A foray into organic foods didn't catch on with discount shoppers. Similarly, a push to sell trendy fashions and an attempt to cut clutter in stores to attract higher-income customers ended up alienating the company's traditional shoppers. The chain succeeded in attracting wealthier clientele but at the cost of its original customer base, those earning less than $70,000 a year, which made up 68 percent of its business. "The basic Wal-Mart customer didn't leave Wal-Mart. What happened is that Wal-Mart left the customer," according to former Wal-Mart executive Jimmy Wright.[4] The revolving door at corporate continues to spin as decision-makers scramble to go back to the mission that led to their success.

Exceptional organizations will abandon the five-year strategy and replace it with a three-year, or maybe even 18-month vision. Leaders of these companies will realize that strategies begin with ideas, not analysis. *Noise* will continue to stream into our lives through new and unprecedented sources, creating large banks of information. But those who create an exceptional advantage will separate the notes from the noise, even when that means making the necessary disruptive changes to their plans. They will learn the value of speed and agility because they will have created a culture that values both.

Culture: Separating the Duck From the Quack

Mention the words "Jeremiah Weed" to a group of veteran Air Force fighter pilots, and they will assure you they have drunk the delightful kerosene-tasting, 100-proof, bourbon-flavored liqueur. At the completion of a long week at the Fighter Weapons School, which is the Air Force equivalent to TOPGUN, or just for any reason at any bar in the Air Force, pilots will join each other in a toast to "fallen comrades." All know the tradition, yet few can recount the legend of Jeremiah Weed, much less the true story.

The true story involves the ejection from and crash of an F-4 on December 1, 1978, in the desert near Nellis Air Force Base. Major Nort Nelson, a student at the Weapons School, responded to instructor Joe Bob Phillips's scripted attack by putting his plane into a position from which he could not recover—at least in the estimation of Nelson's own instructor, Dick Anderegg. Anderegg ejected them both safely, but they lost the plane.

A year later Joe Bob, Nort, and another friend returned to the crash site, but not before stopping at the Paranaghat Bar, where they met a bearded bartender who eagerly heard the three pilots' story and engaged them in drinking games. The bartender lost.

Joe Bob asked the Grizzly Adams–looking man whether he knew how to do "afterburners." He did not. Normally, the pilots explained, this procedure involves lighting a shot of brandy and drinking the flaming liquid. The bartender apologized that the closest thing to brandy he could offer was Jeremiah Weed. The three pilots filled their shot glasses with the bourbon and demonstrated flawless afterburner technique, all three glasses returning to the bar empty, except for a small blue flame flickering at the bottom of each.

The bartender poured himself a shot and lit it—overlooking a couple of key steps in the procedure and the fact that he had a beard. Apparently, in addition to tasting like kerosene, Jeremiah Weed also has the flame-accelerant properties of it.

By the time the three pilots could beat out the flames, the bar had filled with the smell of barbequed lips and singed hair. Feeling guilty about winning the bar games and nearly immolating their new friend, the three pilots purchased a bottle of Weed and headed to the crash site.

The three decided they wanted to remember their own brush with death and to establish a custom for honoring others who have not walked away from crashes. So, on their return to Nellis, they showed the bottle to the manager of the Officers' Club and suggested she add it to the bar stock. She did. Soon Nellis fighter pilots were downing shots of Weed for no good reason except that drinking it set them apart and gave them an excuse to toast fallen comrades. As scores of other fighter pilots passed through Nellis, they saw the weapons school guys upholding the ritual, so they did too. A legend was born and a part of a culture created.[5]

As the Jeremiah Weed story illustrates, organizations learn as they adapt to the world around them and solve their problems. When something works well for a period of time, and leaders consider it valid, members of the organization begin to teach the behavior or idea to new people. Through this process, new members find out what those around them perceive, think, and feel about issues that touch the organization. Sometimes the behaviors will relate to traditions that make members of the group feel connected to one another, as the drinking tradition does; at other times, the behaviors will have more direct links to the way the organization does business. Smart leaders recognize that both hold important keys to unlocking the secrets of the organization's success.

Culture survives because of talent, but because the same talent might not stick around, you have to create a culture that is independent of talent. Sometimes star performers join an organization and work there their entire careers, but not too often anymore. More frequently, talent comes and goes, in spite of or because of the culture. In the case of the Weapons School, Nellis has been the cradle of fighter weapons and tactics since the Air Force established the Aircraft Gunnery School there in 1949 in an effort to capture the lessons and experiences fighter pilots had learned in World War II. Later the school became the Fighter Weapons School, and each successive fighter model has had its own squadron within the Weapons School. By design, talent streams through on a regular rotating basis, and the syllabus changes routinely, but significant aspects of the culture remain resistant to change, and aviators have always worn the patch on their shoulders with great pride—it separates them from those who didn't qualify to attend.

Conversely, today's organizations face an onslaught of factors that can influence and even ruin their cultures. Mergers and acquisitions often have a detrimental effect on the two individual cultures attempting to merge, leaving neither intact and none to emerge. Top performers frequently lose patience and leave the merged enterprise, causing more loss overall. Like the paradoxes mentioned earlier, culture needs to be both reliable and amoebic. It needs to hold to those things that make exceptional people proud of it while reinventing itself to be attractive to the talent you want, not just the talent you have.

Learning corporate culture doesn't involve drinking the Kool-Aid, or even the Kentucky bourbon. It's more about knowing when to raise a glass and to whom. But two components characterize all successful corporate cultures: a culture of change and a commitment to learning. When you have these in place, you can more effectively address the direction the company needs to take and do so excellently.

Excellence: Separating the Ace From the Pack

In American folklore, the feud between the Hatfields and McCoys has long served as a metaphor for bitterly warring rival parties. However, this 28-year dispute in the backcountry of West Virginia pales in comparison to the battle that rages between competence and excellence in most organizations. When people deliver pedestrian performance, senior leaders too often settle, and mediocrity reigns. Leaders of exceptional organizations—those that attract and develop exceptional performers—realize the time for errors has passed.

Excellence, the overarching requirement for exceptional organizations, defines everything else: talent, culture, and strategy. Without a clear commitment to and focus on excellence, nothing else matters.

It all starts with "who?" Your organization can be no more excellent than the least-excellent employee that holds a key position. Certainly, top performers in senior positions will hold the most sway, but at every rung of your organizational ladder, you must have the best talent for the money. Not every person needs to offer the skills, aptitude, or desire to move up that ladder, but each, from the janitor to the CEO, should represent a high standard of performance. If you accept less, you compromise excellence.

Frustration leads myriad reasons people don't perform to their potential. They simply don't know what you expect; strategy remains fuzzy, priorities change too often, or the implementation plan, if it ever existed, can't be found. Without clarity and transparency on these issues, you can't hope to attain excellence. If senior leaders fail to communicate to those who crave it, they stand no chance of attaining excellence. Clarity is the image: accountability the reflection. Once people understand the direction the company needs to take, they must be aware of the specific roles they will play in winning the race.

After "who?" comes "what?" What do we do that is world-class? If the answer isn't obvious, discover where the gaps exist between you and the competitor who outruns you. If the answer is apparent, become acutely aware of the factors that keep you in first place. This knowledge will help you maintain your best-in-class position and avoid diluting your excellence with products and services that don't support it.

People use the terms "excellence" and "exceptional" synonymously. However, the two differ. "Excellence" implies a distinction from others but not necessarily rarity. For example, one might comment that a fourth-grade pianist is excellent, but she might be one of many in her class that shares the honor.

On the other hand, "exceptional" denotes someone or something that stands apart—something extraordinary, rare, and incomparable. Mozart played the piano excellently at the age of 3, which made him exceptional. Also, he continued to improve his musicality throughout his life, distinguishing him as both brilliant and atypical. Often that which we consider excellent is also exceptional, and exceptional usually implies excellent, but not always.

In June 2013, Redmond High School in Oregon graduated 29 valedictorians because the school implemented a system that allowed all students who achieved the highest grade point average to receive the honor. Arguably, all 29 displayed enough academic excellence to earn distinction, but if 28 others shared the designation, the exceptional element faded. This example also illustrates that we have lost the ability to decide. Those 29 students may have differentiated themselves from the others in the class, but no one with decision-making authority recognized the nuances that would have allowed people to recognize the unique or singular contributions of any one of them.

College admissions boards face unprecedented challenges with this pervasive everybody-gets-a-trophy approach in high schools. Now, we see a push for a valedictorian "club" of sorts—people who took advanced placement classes and received all "As." However, traditionally the very term "valedictorian" implied exceptional achievement—even when compared to others who also accomplished excellent performance standards. It was the Most Valuable Player award high schools bestowed at the end of the game—and only one student received it, no matter how many others played well.

Imagine how we would regard the Most Valuable Player award if every player in the NFL, or even the Super Bowl, were to receive it. Certainly, we consider all players who qualify to don an NFL jersey exceptional players, if we compare them to the best high school and college players. But we don't. Instead, each year we single out two teams of excellent players to attend the Super Bowl and then from among them, decision-makers pick one and only one player to receive the award that only a handful of men have received since the league's inception. Players who receive the MVP award stand apart—they're exceptional.

People have also begun to bat the words "egalitarian" and "elite" as if they were conversational shuttlecocks. At some time, perhaps during the 1960s, the emotional meanings of these words overshadowed their earliest meanings.

"The elite" originally referred to the most carefully selected members of a group, and egalitarian doctrines maintained that all humans are equal in fundamental worth and social status. Egalitarianism then began to touch every aspect of society—expanding to include political platforms, philosophy, theology, economics, education—and, most regrettably, business.

Because nature does not endow all people equally with beauty, intelligence, talent, or drive, egalitarians eventually tried to abolish the "unfairness" of nature—to establish universal equality in defiance of facts. Because personal attributes or virtues cannot be "redistributed," egalitarians seek to deprive people of consequences—the rewards, benefits, and achievements created by personal attributes and virtues.

In the late 1960s, author and philosopher Ayn Rand attempted to explain the pernicious nature of this approach: "To understand the meaning and motives of egalitarianism, project it into the field of medicine. Suppose a doctor is called to help a man with a broken leg and, instead of setting it, proceeds to break the legs of ten other men, explaining that this would make the patient feel better; when all these men become crippled for life, the doctor advocates the passage of a law compelling everyone to walk on crutches—in order to make the cripples feel better and equalize the "unfairness" of nature."[6]

If this is unspeakable, how does it acquire an aura of morality—or even the benefit of a moral doubt—when practiced in regard to man's mind?

When something other than learning, talent, and achievement serves as a basis for favoritism, the outcome is morally repellent. The elitism I defend does not discriminate based on race, ethnicity, gender, wealth, or sexual orientation. Rather, the only differentiators are excellence and superior performance. The kind of elitists I admire and champion seek out and encourage excellence. They don't grade on the curve, hire the underdeveloped, ensure lifelong employment, or suffer fools.

This sort of elitism does not promote envy or enlarge the number of society's losers. Rather, it provides support for ideas that have shaped past progress and that will aid future advancement so that society as a whole wins—that is, it gets richer, better educated, more productive, and healthier.

Americans have stubbornly clung to the myth of egalitarianism—supremacy of the individual average person. We created that everyone-gets-a-trophy culture among our young that morphed into Cuckooland, a place where losers who lose on the basis of consequences should be shielded from thinking that their losing is deserved, and winners who win fairly should be barred from feeling comfort and pride.

Our economic recovery, and indeed global resurgence, depend on something better—better, not just different. They depend on a shift back to the notion that self-fulfillment—seductive though it may appear—must march in lockstep with a commitment to achievement.

We need to rediscover the intellectual confidence to sort out and rank competing values. Fairness is not the same as equality, and equal opportunity at the starting gun does not and should not guarantee equality at the finish line. Those who run through the tape at the finish line offer our greatest hope for thriving in the new economy. The battle between egalitarianism and elitism rages on, but now is the time to tip the scales in favor of the latter.

Businesses won't enjoy the same kind of nonsensical grading system that seems to pervade our public schools. We build our school systems for teachers, not students, and our airports for planes, not people. In business we can't lose sight of the fact that customers and markets drive businesses—not personal preferences. There will be no unionized customers who will want to avoid hurting your feelings or damaging your financial self-esteem. Only those companies that offer a systematic approach to excellence will distinguish themselves from the competition, and only those leaders who demand consistent excellence in every aspect of their organizations will classify themselves as exceptional. It all starts with the right people.

Talent: Separating the Rose From the Poison Ivy

How often have we heard "Our people are our greatest asset"? The facts tell a different story. Only *some* people are true assets. The point is to spot them, nurture them...and know when to leave them alone. These people will make the difference between surviving and thriving—between out-running your competition and tripping at the finish line.

At one time, retention of talent, any talent, was an organization's goal. Many considered a warm body with a pulse a better alternative to turnover. Then someone started tying performance to the numbers. These warm bodies, who contribute little but cost much, couldn't sustain companies through difficult economic times. McDonnell Douglas learned this in the '80s, right before Boeing's acquisition of the company, and countless airlines have experienced this, apparently with no lessons learned.

Further contributing to the paradox, you can't assume you'll have the same talent for 30 years, as leaders once could. Instead, you'll need a cocktail of characteristics to drive your business—the magic combination that I call the E^5 *Star Performer Model*: Ethics, Expertise, Excellence, Enterprise, and Experience.

This model serves as the foundation for *all* the exceptional talent you'll need in key roles. You'll find, however, that even this list won't adequately explain the stars' performance you'll need in your organization. When we examine exemplars and avatars, we find that the truly great in history offered even more, often embodying charisma, courage, passion, or an unidentifiable certain something that I call the "Je ne sais quoi" factor.

You'll also find that your future talent won't necessarily come from traditional sources. Our institutions of higher learning attract the best of the best from around the globe, but too often these stars take their education and talent back to their countries of origin. Some forward-thinking organizations have realized they need to stop that trend and recruit differently to address the organizations they hope to create in the future. That means they will have to become more attractive to the top talent still attending our universities and graduate schools. And business leaders need to play a bigger role in influencing how we educate the next generation at all levels.

Author Amy Chua attempted to offer a solution in her bestseller, *Battle Hymn of the Tiger Mom,* which stirred quite a controversy. According to Chua, raising successful children—those that we would consider stars in our organizations—involves the strict discipline that she experienced as a child and that she advocates for Western mothers.

In her estimation, play dates, sleepovers, television, and sports waste the time of a child. Only academics and music lessons—specifically piano and violin lessons—equip the child for later success. I disagree. I've coached two high potentials who had Chinese tiger moms—Don and George. Don's story has a happy ending, George's a sad one.

Don grew up in China and moved to the United States for graduate school. George grew up in the United States. Both demonstrated outstanding analytical thinking, learning skills, work ethic, and command of both English and Mandarin. Both, however, also shared a common affliction: they took themselves too seriously.

Don and George had spent their childhoods working to become adults, so they missed the rites of passage that most American kids take for granted. They didn't know how to play because they never had. They never learned the skill of influence without dominance—arguably a critical talent for negotiating how games would be played, in whose yard, and under what rules. They didn't know the value of catching fireflies, getting dirty, playing without supervision, or crafting a game from nothing. They hadn't ever played a team sport, so forget understanding the nuances of teamwork.

I approached both men the same way. I said, in essence, "You have a choice. You can run this company in a few years, or you can continue on the path you're on, and you'll be fired within a year." Both committed to improvement, but only one did.

Don worked diligently to learn the interpersonal skills he would need to mend fences. George, who believed he had right on his side, chose not to change his behavior. Don was promoted twice within a year, and George was fired before the year ended.

Chua missed the mark with her instructions. Success, especially at the top levels, depends on many lessons that we don't learn in the classroom. A good sense of humor, the ability to establish rapport quickly, responsiveness, and tolerance go further than violin lessons in acquiring leadership skills. (You'd be surprised how seldom "improve musicality" comes up when I coach executives.)

Chua got one thing right, however. She maintained that accomplishments cause self-esteem, not the other way around. Most successful people I know have accomplished much and have high self-esteem. They and their parents created an upward spiral that started at an early age. The more they accomplished, the better they felt about themselves. Whether people had a tiger or a lamb for a mother, the battle hymn they ultimately sing is up to them.

Books like Chua's highlight the different talent world we live in now and will inhabit in the future. We will figure out how to attract some of the Asian superstars who attend our schools, but then what? How will we adjust our management style and cultures to accommodate the stars' expectations? How do we teach cohesive efforts to those who have never learned them because all their lives people applauded them for solo contributions?

We have all read the diversity research that informs us that our companies will look different in the future, with women, blacks, Latinos, and Asians gaining stronger footing. We also know that as the Baby Boomers retire, new generations of X, Y, Millennials, and who knows what other designation will take over leadership roles.

Books about how to manage the different generations have started to fill the shelves in our bookstores, most ignoring the fact that exceptionalism, not generational differences, will determine how leaders need to respond to the talent needs of their organizations. Authors cram these books with advice about how you must manage and lead the people in your organization, based solely on the year of their birth. Apparently you will automatically understand all those who share your generation but remain flummoxed by those who don't.

This new, pervasive, insidious "ism" is sweeping the country, if not the world. People who would never dream of engaging in sexism or racism don't hesitate to jump on the "generationalism" bandwagon. Scores of experts have cropped up to explain how managers should handle each generation differently. But before you invest your time, consider this: Bill Gates, Bill Clinton—Baby Boomers. Tom Hanks, Michael Jordan, and Jay Leno, also Baby Boomers. Osama Bin Laden—also a Baby Boomer. Can somebody tell me what these men have in common with each other? If this much diversity exists in this short list of Baby Boomers, doesn't it make sense that uniqueness and variety exist within each generation in your organization too?

Generationalism offers the lazy executive an excuse not to appreciate the unique contributions of each person. Aside from wasting your time studying this never-proven theory, you will engage in biases that will certainly stand in the way of you identifying your stars. Top performers know no generational, gender, race, or religious lines. But they do share three traits: they are smart enough to do the job, they are driven to do it well, and they have integrity. Throughout history, all the great leaders who positively influenced the course of humankind embodied all these traits. Certainly each came from a different generation—often separated by hundreds if not thousands of years. You probably don't need to know more about each generation's preferences, but what you do need to understand is how to size people up better—how to assess top talent—because the new world we live in has no room for talent errors in particular.

Conclusion

Exceptional organizations serve as magnets to stars who, by their very nature, require superior performance of themselves and those with whom they associate. They want to feel empowered to make decisions to improve both the organization and their own lives, and they want to align their excellence with an employer that distinguishes itself through excellence. They will eagerly use "big data," but insist that it align with "big wisdom." They will offer this wisdom themselves but also demand it of those who hold sway over them.

These stars crave an action-oriented culture that responds to change and reinvents itself whenever new information or learning indicates it should, because they understand that the new world order demands more—more direction, better cultures, excellence, and star performers. In short, they want to work for companies that strive to think strategically, grow dramatically, promote intelligently, and compete successfully—both today and tomorrow. That combination will allow them to step to the front and let a winner lead the way.

Chapter Two

Strategy Guides Passion

Mythology tells us that the hero Theseus overcame insurmountable challenges, like killing the half-man half-bull monster, Minotaur, and escaping from a mazelike labyrinth with the help of Ariadne, who held the end of a thread at the entrance to the labyrinth. Scholars have offered Ariadne's actions as a metaphor for what leaders can do to help others escape the labyrinths of their own worlds: keep extensive records, and when you get lost, return to the last point of clarity and safety. Though Ariadne helped Theseus and others with her red yarn, this method will doom today's leaders to an exhaustive process that merely allows them to solve problems—not make the bold decisions about the company's future that will position them for growth and success in the new economy.

History has taught us that the prerequisites of success—courageous leadership, bold direction, clear goals, and a systematic approach to implementation—can also provide a recipe for disaster. The reason? Decision-makers must make choices with far-reaching consequences based on *assumptions* about what that future will look like. Of course, this paradox has always existed—nothing new about an inability to prophesize about the future. But one thing has drastically complicated the landscape: the future arrives much more quickly now than it used to, and many of the guests it tows along are neither invited nor welcome.

Many leaders feel unsure about their ability to create a credible strategy for growth, despite overwhelming evidence that they can—facts that prove that the best strategies come from pragmatic business leaders who are willing and able to consider alternative futures for their businesses. It won't happen automatically, however. Successful leaders will take a systematic approach in setting the direction for the organization and then develop the day-to-day tactics that will support it—all combining to create the organization's competitive advantage.

Head in Exceptional Directions

Every organization is headed somewhere. Too often, however, leaders don't consciously *choose* that direction. Instead, they react to the environment in which they find themselves. They engage in *perceived* potential, reactive decision-making, or short-term gains designed to placate shareholders and analysts. They work long hours on daunting tasks—often to no avail—because they haven't chosen the right race.

In most organizations, you'll find more people who understand how to run fast than people who can decide which race they should enter, more people with well-honed skills for producing results in the short run than visionary strategists. This happens because they start by questioning "How?" when they should have led with "What?":

- What will determine the nature and direction of our organization?
- What policies and key decisions will have a *major* impact on our financial performance?
- What decisions will involve significant irreversible resource commitment?

Visionary leaders understand that to outrun the competition, they will need to understand those things that should remain the same, those that should change, their guiding principles, and their competitive advantage. Only then will they be able to challenge the ordinary. Or, as Peter Drucker taught us years ago, "There is surely nothing quite so useless as doing with great efficiency what should not be done at all."[1]

The Timeless Advantage

Your mission forms the foundation of your timeless advantage. It should play the same role in your organization that the Holy Grail did in the Crusades. It defines your reason for being, the touchstone against which you evaluate your strategy, activities, and expectations for overcoming the competition. Without a mission, you will diffuse resources, cause individual units of the organization to operate in silos, create conflicting tactics, and confuse customers, suppliers, financiers, and employees. A mission statement answers these questions:

- Why do we exist?
- What is our business?
- Who are our customers?
- What do our customers value?

Wal-Mart's succinct mission statement, "Saving People Money So They Can Live Better," addressed all four questions, but apparently, judging from the 2012 changes, decision- makers lost the mouse pad that had those words written on it. Executives now acknowledge that they miscalculated and are adjusting their strategy. But at what cost? Analysts have been concerned that in changing direction again, Wal-Mart risked alienating whatever higher-scale shoppers it gained during its transition. In situations like this, sometimes David doesn't kill the giant; it commits suicide—an unfortunate circumstance caused by deviation from the mission.

Unlike most for-profit organizations, nonprofits are mission-driven. Therefore, they devote a great deal of thought to defining what the mission should be. They avoid sweeping statements full of good intentions and focus, instead, on objectives that have clear-cut implications for the work their members perform. The Salvation Army strives to make citizens of the rejected. The Girl Scouts help girls become confident, capable young women who respect themselves and other people, and Habitat for Humanity gives a hand up, not a hand out. Similarly, nonprofits start with the "customer" foremost in their minds—not financial gain.

Bonds—communities, societies, and those served—hold members together and define success for nonprofits. But *task* alone characterizes the successful for-profit organization. A symphony orchestra does not attempt to cure the sick; it plays music. The hospital takes care of the sick but does not attempt to play Beethoven. Indeed, as Drucker also noted, "an organization is effective only if it concentrates on one task. Diversification destroys the performance capacity of an organization." Societies and communities must be multidimensional; they are environments, but an organization is a tool. The more specialized the tool, the greater its capacity to perform its given task.[2]

The ability and willingness to differentiate your company, product, and services stand squarely at the heart of timelessness. When you build a solid foundation—your version of Theseus's ship—you'll preserve the aspects of your organization that *define* it, while replacing the worn and rotten aspects of it. When you know the difference, you'll equip yourself and others to leverage your timeless advantage but never at the expense of your transient advantage.

The Transient Advantage: The Just-in-Time Organization

The "just-in-time organization," a term largely associated with manufacturing, also describes an organization that has learned that speed is paramount—that roughly right decisions must replace accurate but slow ponderings. This type of organization has demonstrated an ability to "turn on a dime" when necessary, without losing sight of the big picture.

Henry Ford introduced the concept of just-in-time more than 90 years ago, but it has gained attention recently because of a general push to more quickly do more with less. Those companies that have adopted or adapted some form of what some call "JIT" have realized predictable benefits. They have kept inventory and the costs associated with it to a bare minimum, they've eliminated or drastically reduced waste, and they have consistently produced high-quality products with greater efficiency. But the most significant benefit has been the close relationships the approach has fostered among decision-makers, those in operations, and customers. These relationships obviously exist outside the arena of manufacturing.

The ability to respond to unexpected success can also explain transient advantage. For example, scientists at Allergan, a multi-specialty healthcare company focused on discovering, developing, and commercializing innovative pharmaceuticals, discovered a new market for its product Bimatoprost. These eye drops, originally developed to control the progression of glaucoma, also make eyelashes grow, and Latisse was born.

After seeking and obtaining FDA approval for Latisse, the drug company hired Brooke Shields to advertise the "new" product for an untapped market. Today millions of tiny, expensive bottles of Latisse have landed in the medicine cabinets of women who can afford to pay about $200 a month for darker, longer eyelashes.

Nonprofits too have changed through time as they have built on their transient advantages. For example, RAND, an outgrowth of World War

II, was dedicated to furthering and promoting scientific, educational, and charitable purposes for the public welfare and security of the United States. The aftermath of the war revealed the importance of technology research and development for success on the battlefield and the wide range of scientists and academics outside the military that made such development possible.

RAND developed a methodological approach called *systems analysis*, the objective being "to provide information to military decision-makers that would sharpen their judgment and provide the basis for more informed choices." As RAND's agenda evolved, systems analysis served as the methodological basis for social policy planning and analysis across such disparate areas as urban decay, poverty, healthcare, education, and the efficient operation of municipal services such as police protection and fire fighting.

Today, RAND's work continues to reflect and inform the American agenda. While one part of RAND works to define the emerging epidemic of obesity among Americans, another has presented lessons learned from the military response to Hurricane Katrina that can be applied to future military disaster-response efforts. While one division analyzes standards accountability under No Child Left Behind, another details ways to reduce the terrorist threat from regions with weak governmental control. Across a broad range of subjects, RAND research is characterized by its independence, objectivity, nonpartisanship, high quality, scientific rigor, interdisciplinary approach, empirical foundation, and dedication to improving policymaking on the major issues of the day.[3] RAND has not lost sight of its original mission, yet it continues to act as a just-in-time source for analysis and information.

The Seven Secrets for Balancing Timelessness and Transiency

Business authors and theorists have traditionally advised leaders to "stick to the knitting," whereas other voices have chimed in "turn on a dime." Obviously, getting the balance right is critical, but how can a business leader harmonize the two voices to create beautiful music?

1. Stay close to the customer. RAND and others serve as shining examples of what can and should happen when business leaders listen to and heed the advice of their best customers— not all customers, just the best ones. Anticipate their needs, feel their pain, and devise the solution before they need it. No

one told Steve Jobs what to invent or what the "next best thing" would be.

2. Develop an EOC orientation. Strategists often refer to VOC or Voice of the Customer. While the VOC remains important, the EOC, or Eye of the Customer, also plays an important role. Proactive decision-makers look at the world through their customers' eyes. Latisse would quite literally have lost its competitive advantage if they had not looked through the eye of the customer.

3. Reward entrepreneurial behavior. Recognize individuals at all levels of the organization, and listen to their feedback.

4. Have an exit strategy for products, customers, and services that no longer support both your timeless and transient advantages.

5. Budget quickly. Don't tie yourself to a one-to-three-year strategy that relies on budget decisions that may have to change. Instead, budget quarterly, and assign control of money decisions to a disinterested group or individual that doesn't run a division or business. Also, don't set up a "spend before the end of the fiscal year or you won't get it next year" mentality. Reward those who return money.

6. Put your smartest people in charge of risky decisions. The smartest, not necessarily the hardest-working, people should make the decisions related to innovation and risk. The last thing you want is an idiot with initiative deciding the future of your business. Balance experimentation, which takes time, with analysis, which happens quickly.

7. Make feedback to senior leaders seamless, fast, and laudatory. Remove roadblocks in the chain of command and replace them with easy access.

We have long taken business advice from business magnate and investor Warren Buffet. Now is the time to weigh that wisdom with country/western singer Jimmy Buffet's observation that "I didn't ponder the question too long. I was hungry and went out for a bite." Only those hungry leaders who can figure out how long to ponder will balance their timeless and transient advantages to use them as the foundation of their strategic principles and competitive advantages.

Turn Your Strategic Principle
Into Financial Results

Results start with a strong strategic principle, a shared objective about what the organization wants to accomplish. The strategic principle guides the company's allocation of scarce resources: money, time, and talent.

The strategic principle doesn't merely aggregate a collection of objectives. Rather, this simple statement captures the thinking required to build a sustainable competitive advantage that forces trade-offs among competing resources, tests the soundness of particular initiatives, and sets clear boundaries within which decision-makers must operate.

Creating and adhering to a concise, unforgettable action phrase can help everyone keep an eye on the ball at all times. Wal-Mart used its mission statement, "Saving People Money So They Can Live Better," to develop its strategic principle: "Low prices, every day." This succinct phrase should have challenged Wal-Mart's 2012 decision to sell trendy fashions to attract higher-income customers, but it didn't, and they paid the price for the mistake.

A well-thought-out strategic principle pinpoints the intersection of the organization's passion, excellence, and profitability, or in the case of not-for-profit organizations, its unique contribution. As you can see from the graphic, success lies at the intersection of the three.

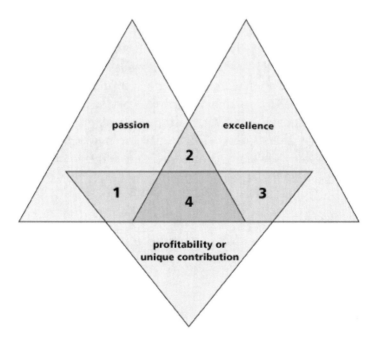

If your organization operates in Section 1, you will probably experience some short-term success, and star performers will find themselves drawn to work for you—initially. People who can do the work they feel passionate about and engage in work that rewards efforts with large monetary compensation can often stay in the game for the short run. But if you aren't the best—and the clever in your organization will quickly figure out that you aren't—the competition will soon surpass you.

Passion and excellence without profitability, or Section 2, won't even allow you a short run. This undisciplined orientation—to do what you like and are good at—without consideration of the market, won't provide anything other than some short-lived fun, which should last right up until the time your bills come. You won't find too many virtuosos in these kinds of organizations for very long, if at all.

Section 3 offers a recipe for burn-out. You can work hard at something you're good at and that makes you significant money, but you won't excel at it for long unless you feel some passion for it. Star performers don't dip their professional toes into the water; they show up to make waves. If they don't feel passion for the work, they won't do either.

The sustained success of exceptional organizations lies in Section 4, the intersection of passion, excellence, and profitability. These companies have high-quality products and services that consistently encourage them to develop newer and better offerings. Only here can your organization thrive as you work diligently to produce a product or service that your competition can't match.

When companies face change or turmoil, the strategic principle acts as a beacon that keeps the ships from running aground. It helps maintain consistency, but gives managers the freedom to make decisions that are right for their part of the organization. Even when the leadership changes, or the economic landscape shifts, the strategic principle remains the same. It helps decision-makers know when to develop new practices, products, and markets. When they face a choice, decision-makers will be able to test their options against the strategic principle by simply applying the three-part litmus tests:

1. Are we passionate about this work?
2. Can we do it better than our competitors?
3. Will it make us money?

When designed and executed well, a strategic principle gives people clear direction while inspiring them to be flexible and take risks. It offers a disciplined way to think about decisions, strategy, and execution, and challenges people to play an ever-evolving better game. Top performers embrace both change and risk, but they do their best work when they understand the parameters within which they must work. These allow star performers to act as agents for and champions of change, rather than as mavericks.

Your Competitive Advantage

The mission and strategic principle—both cornerstones for organizations that challenge the ordinary—don't usually pose the most difficult issues. Threats to the strategy lie not in figuring out what to do, but in devising ways to ensure that, compared to others, you *actually do* more of what everybody knows you should do—that is, leverage your competitive advantage.

We don't improve primarily because rewards remain in the future; we experience the disruption, discomfort, and needed discipline more immediately. My work with countless companies has taught me that the necessary outcome of strategy formulation does not involve analytical insight—although it is an indispensable first step: It requires *resolve*. People have to make up their minds that they want a different future than the one they have and steadfastly commit to making the changes that will bring about that ideal state—that set of circumstances that aligns the strategy with tactics to create your competitive advantage. With this mindset, leaders consciously sacrifice some of the present rewards to achieve a better tomorrow. Drawing from the work of Tregoe, here's how this balance looks:[4]

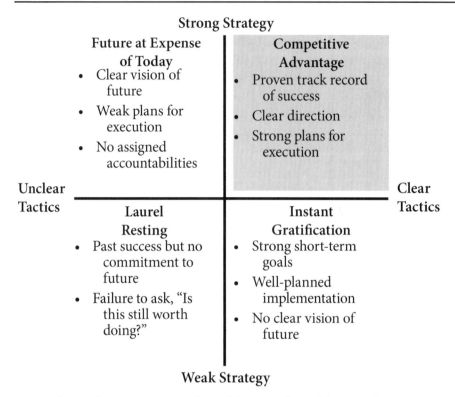

Each quadrant represents desirable or undesirable ways for companies to operate.

The Competitive Advantage quadrant represents an organization that has established a competitive edge that includes a strong strategy and the clear tactics to support it. Based on a proven track record, this company has identified those decisions that have led to success in the past and that promise success in the future. By responding to customer needs, developing talent, implementing effective operations, and defining sound financial objectives, this organization has acknowledged what it must do to beat the competition and has identified ways to implement this strategy.

Companies that operate in this quadrant continuously seek ways to build on their capabilities. Leaders adapt well to change and eagerly experiment with new approaches and novel ideas. They don't readily settle for "okay," but instead challenge themselves and others to constant improvement, and they differentiate themselves as the places virtuosos want to work.

A company that has clarified its competitive advantage commits itself to excellence, the foundation of strategy. High-performance organizations that have stood the test of time and promise to continue productivity in the future provide examples of this. When a commitment to excellence exists, passion and profitability often follow.

Organizations operating in the *Instant Gratification* quadrant often succeed in the short term. Despite current profitability, they lack a strong strategy. They engage in effective operations that have accounted for their success in the past, but success in the future remains doubtful. Often hospitals and manufacturers operate in this quadrant. In the long run, rivals take over, but for a period of time, these companies can stay afloat with hard work. Companies like this frequently offer good products or services and are passionate about what they do, but they lack excellence or profitability.

Members of these organizations frequently resist discussions of strategy because what they're doing seems to be working. In these situations, I often encounter a significant commitment to lean processes, Six Sigma, or Total Quality Management, all tactics for driving a strategy. The leadership makes solving immediate problems their primary focus, and strategy formulation seems like a distraction from that priority. Investing the time to engage in a strategy formulation process will lead them to fewer wasted hours and distracted efforts in the future, but for an organization accustomed to instant gratification, the future seems too far off and too abstract.

Most failed companies get buried strategically, not tactically. They may have been making the best horse-drawn buggy in the world when they went under. They may have had strong day-to-day tactics, but they picked the wrong direction or chose too many directions simultaneously. In other words, the problem usually doesn't lie in an inability to produce a quality product or service; it's knowing what customers will want more of in the future.

The *Future at the Expense of Today* quadrant depicts a company that has invested the time and energy to write and develop a strong, clear strategy. However, they have failed to formulate the ways they will execute. Some of the high-tech companies and pharmaceutical manufacturers offer examples of how a company might operate in this quadrant. This kind of situation most often occurs when leaders have left the strategy-setting session with no accountabilities for each initiative. When no one has a vested, personal interest in the outcome, you put tactics, execution, and implementation at risk, not to mention your overall success.

The challenge of the leader is to offer a disciplined approach—an intellectual framework to guide decisions and serve as a counterweight to the quick and easy fix of unfettered growth. This requires an examination of which industry changes and customer needs the organization will respond to and which ones it will reject. Deciding which business you will turn away can play as important a role as determining which business you want.

Laurel Resting organizations struggle tremendously. Most of the major airlines fall into this quadrant. At one time they may have had some clear direction, perhaps some strong leadership and committed employees who developed the processes and systems for driving the business. But, for whatever reason, these best practices have eroded. Apparently no one has asked recently, "Is this still worth doing?" Usually companies that operate in this quadrant for very long don't stay companies for very long.

If your organization is operating in quadrants other than the *Competitive Advantage* one, you must first rid yourself of the strategies and tactics that no longer produce results, to begin sloughing off the decisions of yesterday in order to make the pivotal ones for tomorrow. And you have to harness the resolve to delay gratification. (Working in the *Competitive Advantage* quadrant usually hurts in the short run.)

Real strategy lies not in figuring out what to do but in devising ways to ensure that, compared to others, we actually do more of what everybody knows we should do. The single biggest barrier to making change is the feeling that "It's okay so far." Too often leaders settle for the status quo—or good—rather than demanding exceptional. These kinds of leaders destine themselves and their organizations to hire good, maybe even very good, performers. But they won't attract stars. Virtuosos want to play for the best team, not the good one.

Successful strategy cannot be what "most of us, most of the time" do. It has to involve everyone's commitment to making it happen. You can't achieve a competitive advantage through things you do reasonably well most of the time. Everyone has to resist the temptations that will steer you off course.

Usually we know what we should do. Figuring out the obvious is not difficult. *Doing* what needs to be done, however, isn't always easy. No mysterious cure lurks unnoticed and undiscovered. We all know what we have to do to improve. But the discomfort happens *now* when we deprive ourselves of the things we want, so we postpone the improvement.[5]

St. Louis–based Enterprise Rent-A-Car offers one of the most compelling examples of a company leveraging its timeless, transient, and competitive advantages. After World War II, Jack Taylor, a decorated Navy fighter pilot who served on the USS *Enterprise*, from which today's company takes its name, returned to his hometown and started his business. He soon discovered that you uncover your best opportunities by listening to your customers.

Jack didn't set out to build a rental car company. Enterprise began as an automobile leasing business with a different name. Through time, his leasing customers asked for loaner cars while their vehicles were in the shop. Jack began offering daily rentals. From an initial investment of $100,000 and just seven cars, Enterprise has grown to a $15 billion global powerhouse with more than 74,000 employees in more than 7,000 locations. Through the years, Taylor and those that he has hired have stuck to their mission "to fulfill the automotive and commercial truck rental, leasing, car sales, and related needs of our customers and, in doing so, exceed their expectations for service, quality and value."

How many times did we hear that Hertz was number one but Avis tried harder? Avis attempted to play leapfrog with the unicorn of the rental car business and created no advantage. Enterprise knew better.

Enterprise didn't try to get you out of the airport faster. That was Hertz territory. Even though they did try harder and give better customer service than all the others, they didn't tout that. Instead, they told you they would pick you up. But Enterprise might have ignored its current competitive advantage if they had not listened to the employee who suggested the concept.

They became number one in supplying replacement cars to people who have had an accident. Now they have built a successful business by partnering with insurance companies, and by the way, they will also get you out of the airport fast now too. But that isn't how it all began.

Who is the unicorn in your industry? Are you trying to emulate, duplicate, or imitate it? If so, you will probably always take second place and never discover, much less leverage your transient advantage. Whether you are an independent consultant or an executive in a large organization, my guess is you've spent too little time analyzing your unique contribution.

Instead of trying to leap over or chase the competitor in front of them, leaders who have learned to leverage their transient advantage change the game to one they can win. Customer responsiveness explains much of Enterprise's success, but not all of it. Decision-makers at Enterprise also responded to the voice and eye of the customer because they also listened to a frontline employee who helped steer the company into the rental car business in the first place and a consultant who came up with the idea for its now defining "We'll Pick You Up" service.[6]

What can you do that no one else does as well? Who would miss you if you went away? The answers to these questions will give you a sense of your competitive advantage, that which separates you and makes you better. Instead of trying to leap over or chase the competitor in front of you, change the game to one you can win, and then make sure you have a solid plan to decide what has to happen to implement the strategy.

The Feud Between Strategy and Decision-Making

The best leaders get most of the important calls right. They exercise good judgment and make the winning decisions. All other considerations evaporate because, for the most part, at the senior-most echelons of any organization, people won't judge you by your enthusiasm, good intentions, or willingness to work long hours. They have one criterion for judging you: do you show good judgment? Therefore, leveraging your strengths in this arena and avoiding the hidden traps of individual and group decision-making define two of the surest ways for you to improve in your own decision-making and to influence the effectiveness of your team.

When group members make effective decisions, they can do so because they have used time and resources well, resulting in correct, or at least well-thought-out, conclusions that they can easily carry out. Problems, however, can interfere with this process. Here are some to look out for.

The Groupthink Trap

In 1972, social psychologist Irving Janis first identified "groupthink" as a phenomenon that occurs when decision-makers accept proposals without scrutiny, suppress opposing thoughts, or limit analysis and disagreement. Historians often blame groupthink for such fiascoes as Pearl Harbor, the Bay of Pigs invasion, the Vietnam War, the Watergate break-in, and the *Challenger* disaster. Groupthink, therefore, causes the group to make an incomplete examination of the data and the available options, which can lead the participants to a simplistic solution to a complex problem.

The decision-making that led to the *Challenger* disaster illustrates how each of these causes of groupthink can lead to a tragic outcome. The *Challenger* blasted off at an unprecedented low temperature. The day before the disaster, executives at NASA argued about whether the combination of low temperature and O-ring failure would be a problem. The evidence they considered was inconclusive, but more complete data would have pointed to the need to delay the launch.

Cohesion and pressure to conform probably explain two of the primary causes of the groupthink. The scientists at NASA and Morton Thiokol felt the pressure of their bosses and the media to find a way to stick to their schedule. Because the group discouraged dissenters, an illusion of unanimity surfaced, and the collective rationalization that allowed the decision-makers to limit their analysis led to their favoring a particular outcome—to launch on time.

Due to an extraordinary record of success of space flights, the decision-makers developed an illusion of invulnerability, based on a mentality of overconfidence. After all, NASA had not lost an astronaut since the flash fire in the capsule of *Apollo 1* in 1967. After that time, NASA had a string of 55 successful missions, including putting a man on the moon. Both NASA scientists and the American people began to believe the decision-makers could do no wrong.[7]

Any one of the causes of groupthink can sabotage decision-making, but in the case of the *Challenger*, they created a tragic outcome by displaying most of the symptoms. When you're in the throes of groupthink, you can't always see or understand what's happening. That's why you need to take steps to prevent it before it rears its ugly head.

The Failure to Frame Trap

When you or your organization faces a significant decision, as the senior leader, one of your primary responsibilities will be to frame the problem for yourself and others. Like a frame around a picture, this can determine how we view a situation and how we interpret it. Often the frame of a picture is not apparent, but it enhances the artwork it surrounds. It calls attention to the piece of work and separates it from the other objects in the room.

Similarly, in decision-making, a frame creates a mental border that encloses a particular aspect of a situation, to outline its key elements and to create a structure for understanding it. Mental frames help us navigate the complex world so we can successfully avoid solving the wrong problem or solving the right problem in the wrong way. Our personal frames form the lenses through which we view the world. Education, experience, expectations, and biases shape and define our frames, just as the collective perceptions of a group's members will mold theirs.

People who understand the power of framing also know its capacity to exert influence. They have learned that establishing the framework within which others will view the decision is tantamount to determining the outcome. As a senior leader, you have both the right and responsibility to shape outcomes. Even if you can't eradicate all the distortions ingrained in your thinking and that of others, you can build tests like this into your decision-making process and improve the quality of your choices. Effective framing offers one way to do that.

The Complexity Trap

Too often, people seek unnecessary perfection in the place of pragmatic success. Part of the problem involves an often-unspoken belief that the simple is somehow unintelligent, primitive, or embarrassing. That's an overly complex view.

Remember Occam's Razor: The easiest answer is usually the best. I could tell you more, but let's keep this simple. Effective framing can help you embrace "Occam's Razor," a principle attributed to the 14th-century English logician and Franciscan friar that states "Entities should not be multiplied unnecessarily." The term "razor" refers to the act of shaving away everything that stands in the way of the simplest explanation, making as few assumptions as possible, and eliminating those that make no differ-ence. All things being equal, the simplest solution should win.

The Status Quo Trap

Fear of failure, rejection, change, or loss of control—these often un-founded fears cause decision-makers to consider the wrong kinds of infor-mation or to rely too heavily on the status quo. According to psychologists, the reason so many cling to the status quo lies deep within our psyches. In a desire to protect our egos, we resist taking action that may also involve responsibility, blame, and regret. Doing nothing and sticking with the sta-tus quo represents a safer course of action. Certainly, the status quo should always be considered a viable option. But adhering to it out of fear will limit your options and compromise effective decision-making.

The Anchoring Trap

A pernicious mental phenomenon related to over-reliance on the status quo, known as "anchoring," describes the common human tendency to rely too heavily, or to "anchor," on one piece of information when making deci-sions. It occurs when people place too much importance on one aspect of an event, causing an error in accurately predicting the feasibility of other options.

According to research, the mind gives disproportionate weight to the first information it receives, to initial impressions, and preliminary value judgments. Then, as we adjust our thinking to account for other elements of the circumstance, we tend to defer to these original reactions. Once some-one sets the anchor, we will usually have a bias toward that perception.

Most people are better at *relative* than at absolute or creative thinking. For instance, if I were to ask you if you think the population of a city is more than 100,000, instead of coming up with a number of your own, your mind will tempt you to use 100,000 as a relative frame of reference.

To avoid falling into the anchoring trap, don't reveal too much informa-tion. Once you give your opinion and shape information, others will tend to defer to your senior leadership position and echo your values and ideas. When this happens, you lose the opportunity to think about the problem from a variety of perspectives.

The Sunk Cost Trap

Adherence to the status quo and anchoring closely align with another decision-making trap: the predisposition not to recognize sunk costs. The sunk-cost fallacy describes the tendency to throw good money after bad. Just because you've already spent money or other resources on something, doesn't mean you should *continue* spending resources on it. Sometimes the opposite is true, yet because of an illogical attachment to our previous decisions, the more we spend on something, the less we're willing to let it go, and the more we magnify its merits.

Sunk costs represent unrecoverable past expenditures that should not normally be taken into account when determining whether to continue a project or abandon it, because you cannot recover the costs either way. However, in an attempt to justify past choices, we want to stay the course we once set. Rationally we may realize the sunk costs aren't relevant to current decision-making, but they prey on our logic and lead us to inappropriate choices.

The Inference and Judgment Trap

Facts are your friends. When you face an unfamiliar or complicated decision, verifiable evidence is your most trusted ally, but also the one many senior leaders reject. Instead of steadfastly pushing for definitive information, they settle for the data others choose to present, seek information that corroborates what they already think, and dismiss information that contradicts their biases or previous experience. When guesswork or probabilities guide your decisions, or you allow them to influence the decisions of others, you fall into the trap of too little information or the wrong kind of information.

Facts are your friend, but they are scarce allies. Inferences and judgments, which can be more influential and pervasive, tend to dominate discussions and drive decisions. To the untrained ear, the inference can present itself convincingly as a fact. Inferences represent the conclusion one deduces, sometimes based on observed information, sometimes not. Often inferences have their origin in fact, but a willingness to go beyond definitive data into the sphere of supposition and conjecture separates the fact from the inference.

Flawed decision-making explains many of the tragic mistakes organizations have made in the name of strategy. In spite of the leadership team's best efforts at the off-site two-day strategy-setting meeting, the company just doesn't move forward. Or it moves forward in the wrong direction or at the wrong speed. More often, however, the organization enters the right competition but trips during the race.

Implementation: The Scene of Many Accidents

A breakthrough product, dazzling service, or cutting-edge technology can put you in the game, but only rock-solid implementation of a well-developed strategy can keep you there. You have to be able to deliver—to translate your brilliant strategy and operational decisions into action. Of course it all starts with a clear mission, a strong strategic principle, and a well-formulated strategy that leverages the competitive advantage. Clear strategy leads the process; great performance completes it. If you're like many executives, however, in an effort to improve performance, too frequently you address the *symptoms* of dysfunction, not the root causes of it. You focus your attention and that of others on what's going wrong instead of why it doesn't work. That explains the problems developers had with the Comet.

Those who led the jet age had clear strategy: both the United States and the United Kingdom wanted to win the race in the sky to offer the first jet service across the Atlantic Ocean. But differences in implementation decided the winner.

Once begun, the competition for dominance in the air progressed quickly. Less than 50 years after the Wright Brothers flew at Kitty Hawk, Great Britain launched the Comet, the first commercial jet plane; but the glory was fleeting. The revolutionary Comet suffered from a curse—a catastrophic, inexplicable flaw, and an unknown Seattle company put a new competitor in the sky: the Boeing 707 Jet Stratoliner.

The race culminated in October 1958, between two nations, two global airlines, and two rival teams of brilliant engineers. This Anglo-American competition pitted the Comet, flown by the British Overseas Airways Corporation (BOAC), against the Boeing 707, flown by Pan American World Airways. Until 1958, more people crossed the Atlantic Ocean aboard ships than on airplanes. Fewer than one in 10 American adults had ever been on an airplane. (Today nine out of 10 adults has flown.)

But the race began well before 1958. In the autumn of 1952, Juan Trippe, the head of Pan American, the dominant U.S. international carrier, decided not to wait for American manufacturers to give him what he wanted. He ordered three British Comets, with an option for seven more. Eddie Rickenbacker, the World War I U. S. flying ace and head of Eastern Airlines, made an even more audacious announcement. He would pay $100 million for 35 Comets, but he wanted all of them by 1956. *Fortune* magazine called 1953 "the year of the Coronation and the Comet." *Time* called the Comet "the new queen of the airways," but the pronouncements came too soon—seemingly condemning the Comet's chance to win the race.

In January 1954, the Comet roared down the runway at Rome's airport and climbed through 26,000 feet. Shortly after, the Comet blew apart, instantly killing everyone on board. Rumor blamed sabotage for the explosion over Italy, but this hadn't been the Comet's first brush with disaster. Previously, a Comet had broken apart just six minutes after takeoff from Calcutta's airport, killing 43 people. Authorities concluded the plane had been taken down by a vicious thunderstorm.

Two other Comets had suffered serious damage in incidents involving pilots struggling with sudden, unexpected rolling of the plane just after takeoff. Yet no one wanted to blame the plane. Soon all seven of the remaining Comets in the BOAC fleet were put back into service. Sixteen days later, another Comet blew apart in the skies over the Tyrrhenian Sea, killing all on board. Sabotage and thunderstorm theories aside, clearly the Comet had a mysterious flaw that speed and ambition—the banes of effective implementation—had caused the designers to overlook.

Even though the Comet later went through arduous revisions, the British aviation industry never fully recovered from the Comet disasters and never regained its jetliner supremacy, its early inroads short-lived. The 707 became the leading plane of the Jet Age, and until the advent of jumbo jets, more than a decade later, the majority of people who crossed oceans did so in a Boeing 707.

Bill Allen, the CEO of Boeing, was smart, ambitious, and systematic in deciding to jump into the jet airliner business. The company decided to pursue military contracts for large, four-engine jet tankers that could provide aerial refueling and cargo services. Consequently, it developed an important advantage: a huge wind tunnel in Seattle that could be used for aerodynamic testing near the speed of sound. Boeing engaged in endless hours of testing on countless variations to find the secrets of successful jets.

Allen courted Pan Am, United, and American presidents. (Eisenhower would end up flying in a 707 as soon as 1959.) Through his methodical leadership approach (he would consistently go around the room of engineers to hear everyone's perspective), Allen came to the conclusion that would enable the company to demonstrate a prototype jet to the armed services and the commercial airlines in the summer of 1954. Under Allen's 25-year tenure as its leader and his strict commitment to execution of a clear strategy, Boeing grew from $13.8 million to $3.3 billion.

Historians might also argue that Boeing had a "second-mover advantage," meaning the second to experiment has the benefit of learning from the first mover's failures. They could argue, too, that the Comet was the most spectacular aircraft ever built but would have to admit that its failure was equally spectacular—costing more than a hundred lives.[8]

Clearly, implementation, not strategy, caused British aviation to fail. Strategy formulation involves asking "what?" Execution is a systematic process of rigorously discussing "how?"—questioning, tenaciously following through, and ensuring accountability. It includes linking the organization's mission, vision, and strategy to execution, creating an action-oriented culture of accountability, connecting the strategy to operations, and robust communication. When you implement effectively, you get smart answers to these questions:

- How do we position products, compared to our competitors?
- How can we translate our plan into specific results?
- How do we consistently monitor both performance and results?
- How can we attract the right kinds of people to execute our plan?
- How can we build strong relationships with our customers and business partners so that they will act as brand ambassadors and challenge us to improve?
- How do we make sure our activities deliver the outcomes to which we've committed?

In other words, the heart of implementation lies in three core constructs: strategy, people, and operations. To implement the strategy successfully and get answers to these questions, you'll need to address all three.

Implementation involves discipline; it requires senior leader involvement; and it should be central to the organization's culture. Done well, implementation pushes you to decipher your broad-brush theoretical understanding of the strategy into intimate familiarity with how it will work, who will take charge of it, how long it will take, how much it will cost, and how it will affect the organization overall.

My experience has shown that execution fails for one of 10 reasons:

1. Senior leaders never truly commit to the strategy (what needs to happen), so they make decisions on tactics (how things should happen), confusing activity with results.

2. The CEO starts the victory dance on the 20-yard line, glad the team has played the game of formulating the strategy, overlooking the fact that they haven't actually won the game.

3. No one individual "owns" an objective.

4. Individuals leave the strategy formulation session without a plan for and commitment to a time line for achieving the objectives.

5. People concentrate on contingent (What now?) actions instead of preventive (Don't let that happen.) actions.

6. Leaders don't set priorities.

7. Leaders don't tie rewards and consequences to achievement of objectives.

8. Pressing day-to-day problems trump critical threats to the strategy.

9. Leaders don't serve as avatars and exemplars.

10. Leaders don't balance risk and reward.

Conclusion

Strategy discussions have changed since Peter Drucker and those of his ilk began challenging business leaders to think about and lead the direction their companies would take. But the truly important things about strategy have remained the same. Strategy formulation still requires the willingness and ability to make the tough choices about what to do and what not to do. You still need to define where you want to compete, how you intend to win, and how you plan to leverage your advantages—the timeless, transient, competitive, and exceptional advantages that have consistently helped you outrun the competition up until now.

In mythical times, Ariadne enjoyed a proven track record of success. She and only she could save the potentially doomed from her half-brother, the half-bull. But while important things have remained the same since Drucker offered his sage wisdom, much has changed since Ariadne saved her lover, Theseus. We now know that traditional approaches and mere problem-solving won't be enough, even when you have a goddess working on your behalf.

Chapter Three

Culture Informs Behavior

We use the word "culture" fairly arbitrarily, citing it to explain why things don't change, won't change, or can't change. We talk about the culture of a society or country, school cultures, business cultures, culture clashes, and emerging cultures. A powerful force, culture anchors strategy and creates the environment where the best people can do their best work. It's that subtle yet powerful driver that leaders strive—often futilely—to influence. Leaders who aspire to challenge the ordinary realize they need to pay more attention to the culture they help create so they can understand it, guide it, and tie it to their strategies for growth.

What Do We Mean by "Culture"?

Legends tend to have differing adaptations; the truth has no versions. Both influence—either intentionally or unintentionally—the cultures we build. Corporate culture—the pattern of shared assumptions that the group has adopted and adapted over a period of time—develops in much the same way as legends and traditions do. Edgar Schein offers this model for understanding the factors that influence culture:[1]

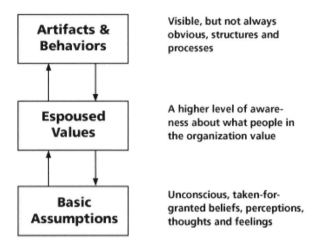

Artifacts include all the phenomena we see, hear, and feel when we encounter a group. They include the visible products of the groups, such as the physical environment, language, technology, products, clothing, manner of address, stories, and observed ritual.

Observing artifacts and behaviors is easier than understanding them, however. For example, the Egyptians and Mayans both built visible pyramids, but the meaning of the pyramids differed in each culture—tombs in the former and temples as well as tombs in the latter. Someone not schooled in both cultures might understandably reach the wrong conclusion. In organizational cultures too, an outsider evaluating artifacts poses myriad problems because we tend to assess in terms of our own backgrounds, not always seeing what lies in front of us and not coming to the same conclusions as those in the organization do.

For instance, an informal organization where people wear jeans, call each other by their first names, and walk around frequently, might seem ineffective or nonprofessional to the outsider. On the other hand, a formal organization with everyone wearing business suits, sitting at desks, and not talking to one another may seem to lack innovation. Any observer will see the same artifacts and behaviors, but attaching the correct judgment to them won't always be accurate or easy. That's why we have to dig deeper to discover the values and assumptions that explain how and why a culture exists.

Values: The Foundation of Your Legacy

Espoused values reflect those perceptions that leaders consider "correct." Over time, the group learns that certain values work to reduce uncertainty in critical areas of the organization's functioning. As the espoused values continue to work, they gradually transform into an articulated set of beliefs, norms, and operational rules of behavior. Eventually these values become embodied in an ideology or organizational philosophy that serves as a guide for dealing with ambiguity or difficult events.

When a solution to a problem works repeatedly, people start to take it for granted. The hypothesis, supported only by a hunch, comes gradually to be treated as a reality. Basic assumptions become so taken-for-granted that no one challenges them. Therefore, they influence behavior, even when people don't mention them.

Learning all these nuances doesn't happen automatically. Sometimes organizations engage in "on-boarding" in an attempt to teach newcomers these inter-workings of the company. More often, however, that which defines the heart of the culture will not be revealed. Only as the new people gain permanent status will they be allowed to enter the inner sanctum and share the secrets.

Two problems. First, some people never navigate to the inner sanctum, and second, the journey takes too long. Star performers tend toward impatience. They want to know immediately what will be expected of them, by whom, and under what conditions. They will want to hit your ground running, eager to do a great job. Distractions related to navigation to the inner sanctum will just annoy and de-motivate them. (Distractions annoy and de-motivate everyone, for that matter.)

Corporate values describe the principles and standards that guide an organization's ethical and business decisions. Organizations typically list things like leadership, integrity, quality, customer satisfaction, people working together, a diverse and involved team, good corporate citizenship, and enhancing shareholder value. Though all of these are laudable, which would a successful company *not* value? A list of ideals that *any* organization would promote doesn't really distinguish your company from any other, and you're not likely to have any arguments about the importance of embracing these ideals. But how? How do you translate value on paper into value in practice?

Leaders in exceptional organizations realize their espoused values should address the thorny issues and provide a compass for navigating uncharted seas, even when the price of doing so is significant. Instead of writing these on a plaque in the foyer, leaders *live* these espoused values and expect others to as well. These values mean something and serve as criteria for making business decisions. They decide they will fire their most valued, high-potential person for a violation of these values. They grapple with the tough questions and develop a list of standards that serves as more than a nice poster; these values will serve as the bedrock of their strategy and give them the guidelines about how and what to change.

Change Orientation:
The Will to Welcome Uncertainty

As stated earlier, "culture" represents that set of beliefs that govern behavior. We create it as we go along, sometimes consciously, often unconsciously. When companies embrace a change orientation, they consider innovation as part of the culture, not a process or project that they engage in for a given period of time. People innovate and change when they see a benefit—when they perceive that the change will improve their condition, not when someone else wants it.

For example, two of the biggest cultural changes in the United States during my lifetime have been smoking and littering cessation. In the 1950s, we thought nothing of dumping an entire bag of garbage on the parking lot as we left the Burger Palace. Similarly, until relatively recently, to enjoy a meal at a nice restaurant, a patron had to secure a "non-smoking" reservation or settle for "first available." In both examples, people changed because they perceived an improvement—to their environment in the first case and to their personal health in the second.

Conversely, U.S. culture has not been able to reduce speeding violations, except through coercion. Now some municipalities have installed cameras that record unsuspecting motorists speeding. Several days after the infraction, the driver receives a ticket in the mail, along with a lovely picture of the car and driver. Arguably, this coercion influences drivers to slow down when they visit that area again, but in the short run, the cameras don't reduce speeding violations.

Force doesn't foster meaningful change in organizations either. People change when the pain of staying where they are overcomes the fear of change. Sometimes, however, people don't perceive the pain before significant damage has occurred. Like insidious heart disease, symptoms of impending destruction may go unnoticed. The job of senior leaders is to build a culture of change, one that supports the long-term strategy of your company.

Truly great companies understand the difference between what should never change and what should be open to change—between what is sacrosanct and what is not. A well-conceived change effort, therefore, needs to protect core principles, the enduring character of an organization—the consistent identity that transcends trends, technology, product line, or services. Core principles provide the glue that holds an organization together through time.

Throughout history we can see examples of how people captured and exemplified their fundamental beliefs. The Declaration of Independence, the Uniform Code of Military Justice, and the Bible all offer examples of how people have written and adhered to their core creeds. Even when the organization grows, diversifies, or changes location, these beliefs provide enduring tenets and a set of timeless principles. Successful leaders don't confuse, and don't let their direct reports confuse, a change in operating practices with a change in core ideology.

It doesn't happen easily, however. The root of culture is "cult," a testament to the kind of thinking that can often guide decision-makers to adhere to a mindset that no longer works. But just as senior leaders can encourage cult-like thinking, they can stimulate a culture of change. A change in operating practices or strategy does not constitute a desertion of all that is "holy," but only those organizations that create a true culture of change can help their people understand the difference. Once again, history offers examples.

We don't ordinarily remember Ulysses S. Grant as someone who cowered easily. After all, under Grant's leadership, the Union Army defeated the Confederate military, effectively ending the Civil War with the surrender of Robert E. Lee's army at Appomattox. That hard-won victory came at a price, however, when Grant faced formidable adversaries like Lieutenant General Nathan Bedford Forrest. One of Grant's friends reported that this particular southern general "was the only Confederate cavalryman of whom Grant stood in much dread."

What caused Grant's anxiety? A cavalry and military commander, Forrest distinguished himself as one the war's most unusual figures. Less educated than many of his fellow officers, Forrest had amassed a fortune prior to the war as a planter, real estate investor, and slave trader. He was one of the few officers in either army to enlist as a private and be promoted to general officer and division commander. Possessing a gift for both strategy and tactics, Forrest created and established new doctrines for mobile forces, earning him the nickname "The Wizard of the Saddle."[2]

We remember Forrest for the *New York Tribune*'s erroneous quote that Forrest stated that his strategy was to "git thar fustest with the mostest." He actually said he "got there first with the most men," a less colorful but more accurate explanation of Forrest's success. Forrest didn't realize at the time that he had defined the characteristics of a culture of change—and he did it before the pain of remaining the same overcame his fear of change.

Exceptional organizations follow Forrest's example. They change *proactively* rather than *reactively,* and they do so quickly—not necessarily in accordance with a three-to-five-year strategy. Of course, leaders of exceptional organizations keep the mission and vision of the company in mind as they make decisions and force tradeoffs, but they do so at the speed of change—not the pace of the typical glacier.

You won't get there first with the most or strike fear in the hearts of your competitors if you insist on adhering to the accepted, ordinary rules of the industry or your company's status quo position. Just because "we've always done it that way" doesn't mean you should do it that way in the future. As I always ask my clients, "If you weren't already doing that, would you decide now to do it?" Playing in a bigger game does not require you do more of what you're already doing; it demands *thinking* bigger. Breakthrough growth demands actively changing rules, mindsets, and habits. Fortunately, exceptional performers have both the capacity and desire to change all three.

While we're embracing change, let's not categorically jump on a pioneering bandwagon. As our history books also teach us, pioneers often ended up dead. The first people to cross the ocean, expand to the western United States, or explore outer space often met with unfortunate outcomes. The same happens in business. In the book *Will and Vision,* the authors found that just 9 percent of pioneers ended up the final winners in their market. Gillette didn't pioneer the safety razor; Star did. Polaroid didn't lead the way with the instant camera; Dubroni did. According to the authors, 64 percent of pioneers failed outright, and others took innovation to the finish line.[3]

So what's a business leader to do? Get there first with the most? Or let the other company innovate while you rest on your laurels? The answer is neither, but a combination of both. Along with a picture of General Nathan Bedford Forrest, the smart leader should put a picture of Custer at his last stand.

Innovation and change can cripple you as surely as change aversion can. The gold lies in a culture that embraces well-thought-out change but balances it with a realization that the status quo and traditional approaches offered some redeeming qualities. Success related to a culture of change relies on the people making the decisions. Those who take a disciplined approach to creativity but marry it to discipline stand to win. Those who carelessly bet on the wrong horse just because it's a new horse stand to lose.

Psychology teaches us that during uncertain times, most people look to established authorities for the answer. The patient who receives disturbing lab results turns to the authority—the physician—for guidance. When we want to make a big financial investment, we ask financial experts. When our kids act up, we seek the advice of our parents or friends. We *perceive* expertise, often without irrefutable evidence that it exists.

These are ordinary responses, but successful leaders don't settle for the ordinary. They observe and react. They consider conventional wisdom, the opinions of trusted advisors, and thought leaders in the field. But then they go beyond.

You can start building a change culture by replacing large-scale, amorphous objectives with results-driven goals that focus on quick, measurable gains. An empowered employee at the lowest possible level of the organization should "own" each goal for which he or she will be held accountable, and you should be flexible enough to react quickly to market shifts or new market opportunities. That's how agility happens.

Steering an aircraft carrier presents many more challenges than turning a speedboat. Therefore, organizations that attract the best talent need to resemble a harbor full of agile speedboats, not a port for a monolith. The formula for building this harbor is simple: reinvent, reengineer, and become the architect of your organization's future. You'll know you have the formula right when you see leaders continuously seeking new opportunities and overcoming challenges, delegating both decisions and tasks, people showing obvious commitment to continued improvement, and everyone showing a burning passion to succeed. When you get the formula right, a culture of change—where your best people will do their best work—can't help but follow. These questions will help you determine whether you have a change-oriented culture:

- How prepared are you to make decisions you can implement immediately?
- Will people buy leader-only decisions?
- How do you evaluate risk?
- How willing are you to give up the comfort of the status quo?
- How have market changes demanded change of you?
- What speed do you prefer? Your people? The market demand?

To remain competitive and exceptional, a culture has to be one of incentive, tolerance, reward, experimentation, high risk tolerance, and a focus on the behaviors required to create that culture, not quick victories. Many organizations demanding more "innovation" simply want faster problem-solving, which will only return things to the status quo.

By definition, problem-solving involves the process of finding a solution to something that needs to change or a deviation from what you expected to happen. It requires a multistage process for moving an issue or situation from an undesirable to a more advantageous condition and typically involves a process for answering the following questions:

- What changed, when, and why?
- What is the tangible evidence that you have a problem?
- How can you measure the magnitude of the problem?
- What caused the change?
- Is this change or deviation consequential enough to spend time resolving it?

Once you have the answers to these questions, you can start to evaluate alternatives and to overcome the obstacles that stand between them and a satisfactory resolution. There are many ways to do this, but too many organizations engage in ongoing problem-solving, usually returning things to the status quo and seldom really embracing innovation and change. Growth necessitates more. It entails a change of mindset—a commitment to innovation and improvement. As former British Prime Minister Harold Wilson once said, "The only human institution which rejects progress is the cemetery." The formula is simple: reinvent, reengineer, and become the architect of your organization's future. But you can't do any of these without learning as you grow.

The Learning Environment: Your Laboratory for Exceptional Ideas

Innovation stands squarely at the heart of a learning culture—with rigidity and fear as its arch enemies. Fear causes us to build silos that serve as our fortresses. When we fear, we go into protection mode, but reinvention prevents fortress-building. Star performers don't need shielding, so they resent fortresses. They adapt and adopt quickly and want an organization that does too. If you wait to react, it may be too late. As the senior leader, your job is to build a culture of change, one that supports the long-term strategy of your company. To do that, you'll need to encourage learning.

The term "learning culture" confronts yet another paradox. Culture acts as a stabilizer, a traditional force, a way of making things predictable. How then, by its very nature, can a culture become learning oriented, adoptive, and innovative? How can a leader stabilize both perpetual learning and change?

A learning culture must contain a core shared assumption that the appropriate way for an organization to improve involves proactive problem-solving and learning. If the culture reflects fatalistic assumptions of passive acceptance, learning will become more and more difficult as the rate of change in the environment increases. Therefore, leaders must ultimately make the *process* of learning—not any given solution to any specific problem—part of the culture. As the problems you encounter change, so will your learning methods. In a learning culture, leaders don't imagine that truth resides in any one source (themselves) or method. Rather, they find truth in experienced practitioners in whom they place their trust; they experiment and live with errors until a better solution is found.

As Peter Senge noted, as the world becomes "more complex and inter-dependent, the ability to think systematically, to analyze fields of forces, to understand their joint causal effects on each other, and to abandon simple linear causal logic in favor of complex mental models will become more critical to learning."[4] Leaders of learning cultures recognize the limitations in their own wisdom and experience, relying heavily on the best thinking of their top performers. In this scenario, alignment occurs among leadership style, culture, and virtuoso needs.

Learning organizations expect failure. They realize that if failure doesn't happen, the company isn't pushing hard enough. We will remember Steve Jobs for his enormous successes, but what about the Lisa? Setbacks didn't stop Jobs, and they won't hinder successful leaders in the future either. These leaders learn from their mistakes—all the while keeping their own motivation high so that they can encourage others to go through the inevitable pain of learning and change. They control their own emotions to manage anxiety—theirs and others'—as learning and change further characterize the culture of their organizations. They also do the following:

- Refuse to settle for mediocrity in themselves, their direct reports, the company's products and services, customer loyalty, or financial gain.

- Create the intrinsic/extrinsic cycle. Make information that is implied, inherent, and basic open, clear, and unambiguous. Similarly, make overt, unequivocal knowledge fundamental and essential.

- Recognize what's valuable to the organization, provide a central source for information and learning, and have someone appointed to determine who else in the organization needs the knowledge.

- Make knowledge digestible. Understand that if people can use it quickly and easily, they'll internalize it. These leaders don't have someone create a PowerPoint show or print a three-ring binder that will gather yet more dust on every topic that comes down the pike.

- Realize that knowledge training must appeal to the self-interest of the user. They should address speed and facility (ease of use), clearly define rewards (increased revenues, customer satisfaction), and consequences (accidents, loss of profits, personal firing).

• Identify sources of innovation and replicate them.

In general, leaders committed to learning discover where they've been successful by deconstructing successes so that those in the organization can replicate them. They understand *why* they've had great success, not just that they've had it. Additionally they find out what they and others can do to identify what has to happen to drive the organization to a higher level—not more volume, but more profit. They also eagerly examine failure and cause/effect relationships—not to assign blame, but to learn.

Although the aviation industry has had more than its share of business problems, they provide a shining example of what other companies can do to advance learning. For example, after an airliner crashes, there are no industry secrets. Airlines willingly reveal lessons learned. Everyone in the industry shares the common goal of making air travel safer, so individual airlines and the FAA require recurrent training. The airlines don't overlook chances to learn from their own mistakes or those of others. They continually and consistently set new best practices and commit the necessary resources to make sure they keep pace with relevant changes. Imagine how this practice and dedication to learning would help non-aviation industries that would commit to examining how changing markets, demographics, and perceptions may affect their organizations. All action and learning starts with a clear decision to make them part of a culture.

Indecision: The Culture Killer

Excellent decisions are the coinage of the organizational realm. When senior leaders consistently make good decisions, little else matters; when they make bad decisions, *nothing* else matters. Any student of organizational development will tell you that a pivotal decision—or, more likely, a series of pivotal decisions—literally separated the businesses that flourished from those that floundered. Every success, mistake, opportunity seized, or threat mitigated started with a decision.

Success doesn't happen without decisions, but neither do mistakes, except when the decision involves indecision—a kind of decision not to decide. When you play the toughest game you can play in the most competitive league you can enter, you will have mishaps and missteps, but indecision doesn't have to be among them. However, the culture of too many organizations conspires against success. Decisions—good, bad, or decent—get stuck in the entrails of the organization, much as flotsam and jetsam accumulates on an untended beach. Companies create their own bottlenecks and harm themselves in ways that the competition never could. They become their own strongest competitors—the enemy within.

Leaders who aspire to create action-oriented, learning cultures recognize where and how bottlenecks occur in their organizations, and they understand the role they need to play in helping those in their chains of command assume decision-making responsibility. Here's what they think and believe:

- **All decisions are not created equal.** Day-to-day implementation decisions should stay with the person who has responsibility for carrying them out. But the high-stakes decisions—those that affect the strategic direction of the company—have to remain at the senior level.

- **Action trumps theory.** Few decisions require 100 percent accuracy and precision. That's why I advise clients to move on an idea when they're 80 percent ready. The value of attaining the other 20 percent usually doesn't justify the time and opportunities wasted. A decent decision that you put into action will give you more ROI than a brilliant idea that remains unexecuted or slowly implemented.

- **Consensus is overrated.** Although laudable in the abstract, holding out for universal agreement consumes too much time. Successful leaders usually learn the hard way to seek consensus only when they need the input of others in the group to make the decision and their ultimate support of it. Otherwise, consensus-building can create an obstacle to action and a formula for lowest-common-denominator compromise.

- **Accountability saves the day.** Ultimately, one person has to own the decision. One and only one person needs to serve as the single point of accountability—the person who has the right to make the decision, the ability to decide, and the power to commit the organization to act on it. This person should have a proven track record for solving unfamiliar problems, an awareness of relevant trade-offs, a bias for action, and a keen ability to anticipate consequences—both positive and negative.

The person who owns the decision-making rights and responsibilities will want to ask these questions:

1. Who else needs to contribute to this decision?
2. Who has to agree?
3. Who should be notified?
4. Who will carry it out?

Effective decision-making does not happen by accident. In most cases, executives have made a conscious, well-thought-out effort to make an effective decision. They have gained information to understand the problem that necessitates the decision; they have examined and evaluated numerous choices; and they have settled for nothing less than stellar data. Then, they did the courageous thing. They opted for the best, not the safest or most popular course of action—decisions that set a clear tone at the top of the organization.

Communication: Setting the Tone at the Top

Communication and information-sharing form the foundation for a strong organizational culture. Therefore, leaders who aspire to strengthen their cultures need to create a multichannel communication system that allows everyone to connect with everyone one else. This doesn't mean that you must immediately purchase the latest technology for immediate access to each person. It also doesn't imply that, in the interest of collegiality, everyone should be copied on every e-mail, an insidious invention of the devil that slows work across the world. It does mean that every need-to-know person stays in the loop and anyone must be able to communicate with anyone else, and everyone involved assumes that telling the truth is both desirable and expected. Of course, this kind of communication network can exist only when high trust exists among all participants and when leaders lead the way by trusting employees to have both the skill and motivation to improve.

Effective communication stands at the core of a change-oriented, learning organization, and an awareness of differing perceptions creates the core of that communication. People respond differently to messages because of the diversity of perceptions. Assumptions that do not take into account perceptual differences often lead to erroneous conclusions and trigger inappropriate behavioral responses. Such assumptions may directly cause conflict and unwarranted hostility.

For example, if the compliance officer imagines that the VP of sales is pressuring her for a quick turnaround on a decision because "he only cares about selling, not quality," she may respond unfavorably. Similarly, if the VP of sales sees compliance as the "business prevention unit," he may become defensive.

Our perceptions create the lenses through which we view the world; most conflicts occur when these world views differ. I'm reminded of an old joke about two elderly Southern gentlemen, Early and Floyd, who, while sitting on the veranda one evening sipping their mint juleps, notice a little frog who says to Earl, "Sir, I am a beautiful maiden whom a wicked witch has cursed by trapping me in this hideous amphibian's body. But if you were to kiss me once, I would spring forth and remain your devoted love for the rest of your life." Earl thinks for a minute, scoops up the little frog, and puts her in his pocket. In disbelief Floyd exclaims, "Earl! What are you doing? She is a beautiful maiden!" Earl shrugs and answers, "Floyd, at my age, I'd rather have a talking frog."

When we start with the realization that the Earls of the world would rather have a talking frog, we can choose the words we use to communicate our own perceptions. Words give us the ability to represent the world through symbols, a skill that allows us to make sense of our world and gives us the tools we need to transmit perceptions from one person to another. Our choice of words helps to shape our reality, and our perception of reality influences our choice of words. The very words that empower us to create meaning with one another, however, can also create barriers between us because each of us assigns words the meaning we want them to have. The word itself doesn't have a universal meaning, even though millions of pages of dictionaries exist for the sole purpose of helping us develop common reactions to words. Instead, words provide our code for transmitting our ideas to others. As people who have found themselves in heated, inane arguments will tell you, words can quickly turn into pesky little rascals that can be used in more than one way.

For instance, consider this newspaper headline: "Safety Experts Say School Bus Passengers Should Be Belted." Probably the safety experts were advocating the use of seat belts, but based on the words alone, can we be sure? Intentionally or unintentionally, words can cause roadblocks to understanding.

For example, psychologist Dr. Richard Wiseman conducted research through The LaughLab at the University of Hertfordshire in the UK, which attracted more than 40,000 jokes and almost two million ratings. The following joke won:

> Two hunters are out in the woods when one of them collapses. He doesn't seem to be breathing and his eyes are glazed. The other guy whips out his phone and calls the emergency services. He gasps, "My friend is dead! What can I do?"
>
> The operator says "Calm down. I can help. First, let's make sure he's dead." There is a silence, then a shot is heard. Back on the phone, the guy says "OK, now what?"[5]

The dissimilar coding and decoding of words provides grist for the humor mill, but these mistakes don't serve us well when we attempt to send a message in earnest.

Words give us the means for sharing ideas and expressing emotion, but they can also serve as barriers. Certainly, the hunter and the emergency service operator experienced a barrier to effective communication. The reasons for these barriers? We act as though meaning resides in words like some kind of chemical compound. Just because a thought makes perfect sense in our heads doesn't, in any way, imply that anyone else will understand that idea in exactly the same way that we do.

Instead, words are arbitrary mixtures of letters that represent concepts. Because concepts differ, and because people assign symbols to concepts in different and often unpredictable ways, misunderstandings occur. So while we have no guarantees that communication will ever occur in the way we intend it to, we can learn ways to control the way a conversation goes and avoid the fate of the hunter's friend.

First, be receiver-oriented and use specific language the receiver will understand. Although seemingly self-evident, not everyone can follow this directive. For example, yesterday I learned of yet another useless, vague term a client has decided to use. Human resources at a major hospital chain has determined that "at risk" employees will receive feedback about their performance issue and then "an initial reminder" about the problem. If the trouble persists, the employee will receive "an advanced reminder." In my opinion, a "reminder" is a pop-up on your computer screen, a bing on a cell phone, or a piece of string on the wrist, not a veiled threat of termination.

HR, apparently in an attempt to act receiver oriented, wants to steer leaders away from dirty words like "reprimand" or "warning." This sort of wrong-minded nuttiness does not represent receiver orientation. The receiver garners no benefit from politically correct but nebulous terminology.

On the one hand we need to be sensitive; on the other hand, we can't sanitize our language to the point that we don't understand each other or that we don't represent reality. Fortunately, the use of specific language can help us strike that important balance.

People who use *concrete* language—exact precise words—rather than *abstract* language or jargon avoid confusion and let others understand exactly what they're talking about. For instance, recently my youngest daughter took a job with a video game company, even though she majored in criminal justice in college and had no real technical training for the position. When she received an assignment that she didn't understand, her brain routinely said, "You can't do this," but her pride said, "Oh, yes you can."

Finally one day, her intrapersonal communication pattern backfired. Her boss asked her to troubleshoot a game, especially the HUD, to see if she could find the problems. Thinking that a HUD was a small German car, and having too much pride to ask for clarification, she spent the morning scouring the game trying to find the little car to see if she could discover the trouble in the game. Only after expressing her frustration to a coworker did she realize she should have been looking at the Heads Up Display.

Many industries and organizations have their own acronyms and jargon, and for the most part, these don't cause communication breakdowns because people encode and decode them similarly. However, when communicating to a new person or someone outside the organization these kinds of words can prove troublesome.

In general, abstract words are unclear because they are broad in scope. They tend to lump things together, ignoring uniqueness or even subtle differences. Vague and nonspecific, abstract words describe things that cannot be sensed through one of the five senses. Words like attitude, communication, loyalty, commitment, thorough, high-caliber, improvement, and reliable all leave much room for interpretation

Conversely, concrete words describe things that we can talk about in behavioral terms or perceive by using one of our five senses. They clarify the sender's meaning by narrowing the number of possibilities and tend to decrease the likelihood of misunderstanding.

A critical element of an action-oriented, learning culture, precise language helps you move ideas to action. On the other hand, if you engage in inaccurate or vague message-sending, action and learning stall. In their eagerness to please, people will do *something*, but not necessarily what you had in mind.

I experienced this reality in a training session, ironically focused on better message-sending. I asked the participants to turn to a certain page and then gave them the instructions of what they needed to do. Unfortunately, I had neglected to put on my reading glasses before making the assignment, so I read the wrong page number. Dutifully the participants went to the page I had assigned and attempted to do what I had asked them to do. No one mentioned that my instructions made absolutely no sense, and no one called my attention to the fact that I had sent them on an impossible mission.

They worked together for the allotted time and then came together as a large group to debrief. After one or two minutes, I realized that things weren't adding up. Quickly I concluded that they had gone to the wrong page, or the right page from the instructions, but the wrong page as far as making sense. Keep in mind, I had absolutely no power over them, and in the low-threat environment of a training session, they had no reason whatsoever to feel intimidated about asking me for clarification. Still, they didn't. They did what they thought I wanted them to do and wasted valuable time.

Leaders who want to establish the kind of culture that will position them to create an exceptional advantage have to assume the onus for making sure others have decoded the message in the way you intended it to be decoded. You can do this in two ways. Encourage questions in general, and ask specific questions in particular situations. For example, you might inquire, "Do you see any roadblocks to getting this done?" If I had done that in the training session, someone might have said, "Yeah, it doesn't make any sense." That would have been a valuable tidbit of information.

Concrete words stress observable, external, objective reality. They focus the receiver's attention on the thing or action being described, rather than on anyone's personal reaction. Conversely, judgmental words showcase evaluation and emphasize personal reactions. They direct the receiver's attention to the *emotion* rather than to a dispassionate portrayal of the event, often prompting a defensive reaction. For example, stating "You have missed the past three reporting deadlines" distinctly describes what the sender wants to convey. "Your missed deadlines haven't shown consideration for the others on your team" puts the focus on the sender's emotions, not the message.

Concrete language also helps you stick to the facts, avoiding inferences, another source of problems. By definition, statements of fact include only what we observe and cannot be made about the future. Inferences, on the other hand, go beyond what we see and can concern the past, the present, or the future. Facts have a high probability of accuracy; inferences represent only some modest degree of probability. Most importantly, facts bring people together; inferences, like judgment, create distance and cause disagreements.

Nonverbal communication also plays a role in strengthening or weakening organizational culture. Even less precise than the most exacting of verbal language, nonverbal communication is vague, unintended, continuous, and more highly prone to misinterpretation. Yet, research indicates that we trust it more than we do verbal communication. When a discrepancy between the words we say and the nonverbal message we display exists, the receiver will often trust the authenticity of nonverbal displays of feelings more than the verbal explanation of them.

For example, Dan, an extremely gifted and focused engineer in a highly technical Fortune 500 company, had trouble connecting with people and experienced high turnover in his department. I had spoken to Dan on the phone and was very impressed with his verbal ability and responsiveness, so I couldn't imagine why he had retention issues. Then I met Dan in person and resolved all questions. Dan wore a constant frown and look of discontent. Even when he talked about something he enjoyed, the frown persisted.

Rather than telling Dan about my observations, I decided to show him. I asked him to prepare a two-minute role-play conversation that he might have with a direct report. We videotaped the interaction, with me playing his direct report. When I played it back, I turned down the volume and asked Dan to *hear* with his eyes. He watched himself scowl and glower for two full minutes. When I turned off the tape, I asked him to forget that he knew the nature of the discussion and to guess what the speaker had been doing. He said, "It looks like I'm trying to explain quantum physics to an oyster" (a little engineering humor). Dan had no idea that his nonverbal demeanor interfered with his effectiveness. In other words, his *intentions* had very little to do with the reality that he alienated people with his facial expressions and glares. Once he understood, he corrected the problem and retrained himself to look interested, not intimidating and scary.

In the workplace, we use communication to enhance performance, produce better outcomes, and foster strong relationships—all constructs of action-oriented, learning cultures. But it isn't so easy. Flawed technique can quickly turn a meeting into a fruitless argument and set the tone for future discord.

Conclusion

So often I encounter an executive team that seems to have it all—the whole six-pack. But they lack the plastic thingy that holds it all together. Culture is that plastic thingy. Leaders who hope to create exceptional organizations realize they must act as culture managers—the people who help to create the environment where star performers can consistently and consciously challenge ordinary standards, protocols, and performance.

These leaders set the tone at the top, and lead the never-ending journey to discover new and better ways to solve problems and adapt to the world around them. When something works well over a period of time, and leaders consider it valid, these vanguards lead the charge to teach behaviors, values, and ideas to new people and to reinforce them with existing employees. Through this process, people find out what those around them perceive, think, and feel about issues that touch the organization.

Chapter Four

Excellence Defines Results

While many critics might suggest that modern Western culture has lost touch with excellence, the facts tell a different story. The winners in the organizational survival game—recently redefined by the economic downturn—have reinvented the standards for us and let us know what to expect.

In the early 1920s, a revolutionary cultural movement, known as Surrealism, began with the goal of resolving the previously contradictory conditions of dream and reality. Surrealist works feature the element of surprise, unexpected juxtapositions, and non sequitur. One noted Surrealist, René Magritte, painted a series of pipes entitled "Ceci n'est pas une pipe." (This is not a pipe). Magritte wanted those who viewed his painting to distinguish between a picture of the thing—the pipe—and the actual thing.

In the same way, strategy, culture, and talent are not the company. They certainly paint a credible picture of some of the vital elements of the organization, but ceci n'est pas une organization, and the picture is not the thing. To resolve the contradictions between dream and reality, leaders need more. They need ways to respond to the element of surprise, the unexpected concurrences, and the illogical turns of events a global economy can provide. Setting the bar for their industries—a bar that encompasses a focus on quality, a commitment to consistency, a concentration on the customer, and the ability to do it agilely—are sure ways to begin.

Quality: The Advantage for Outgunning the Competition

Most companies continue to struggle in their attempts to identify and develop excellence in their products, services, and talent. They eagerly pay top dollar for what they want instead of getting the best for the dollars they pay. The decision-makers at the U.S. Navy Fighter Weapons School (TOPGUN) don't have that problem, however. After interviewing Captain Thomas "Trim" Downing, USN, Retired, a former TOPGUN Commanding Officer, I understand why.

TOPGUN "hires" students with a specific mission and clear criteria in mind. The mission is to develop, refine, and teach aerial dogfight tactics and techniques to selected fleet air crews who then return to their parent fleet units to relay what they learned to their fellow squadron mates—in essence becoming instructors themselves. The list of criteria remains constant and simple: the chosen few represent the best of the best eligible aviators. Distinguishing themselves with exceptional talent, they exude passion for both flying and teaching others and continually evidence their commitment to making themselves and others better. The aviators whom TOPGUN invites back to instruct represent the absolute best and most professional the Navy and Marine Corps can offer. The aviators, the instructors, the mission, the tactics, and the techniques all combine to create a culture of excellence where there's no room for error.

By the time a seasoned pilot returns to command TOPGUN, he has accumulated decades of leadership experience and thousands of flight hours. When Downing took the helm of TOPGUN in 2004, he had been flying fighters nearly 20 years. Having attended TOPGUN as both a student and instructor, he knew both the joys and challenges that awaited him.

Leading talent like a squadron of TOPGUN instructors isn't all good news—but most of it is. According to Downing, who had experienced leadership in a variety of scenarios, leading those whose job involves teaching other top performers brings great job satisfaction. When exceptional people join together, one can only expect excellent results. Having experienced the high morale of the instructors during his own TOPGUN instructor tour, it didn't take Downing long to recognize the extraordinary level of cohesion and esprit de corps that developed among the instructors in his own chain of command. They spent long hours together at work but then also planned their weekends together, involving their wives and children in weekend ski trips and parties. They were a proud group, fiercely protective of their reputation for stellar performance, and they didn't suffer substandard performance lightly. Fortunately, they seldom had to.

There have been exceptions. Since its inception in 1969, fewer than 500 pilots have earned the right to wear the TOPGUN Instructor name tag. The vast majority returned to operational units to represent both themselves and their TOPGUN training for what it had been: a rare opportunity both to learn and to teach cutting-edge skills and excellence.

When top performers have problems, as Downing learned, they can cause long-term damage to themselves, their families, and/or the organizations, but he could usually spot minor problems early. Sometimes this involved his recognizing an instructor who was at risk for burnout. The job required long hours and intense focus, but because both brought such satisfaction, sometimes the instructors would jeopardize their work/life balance. Perfectionism also hounded some. In their attempt to make everything perfect, these instructors could make themselves and everyone around them miserable.

But among the instructors, all extremely talented individuals themselves, was the "cardinal sin" of arrogance that could potentially have devastating results—and stand at cross purposes with excellence. As commander, his job was to keep the instructors "humble," a daunting task when you consider that these are the best fighter pilots in the world, in an environment that not only encourages individual excellence but demands it. In other words, Downing had to address arrogance while simultaneously trying to instill self-confidence. "Internal arrogance," as Downing called it, involved an instructor becoming so confident that he decided that the rules only applied to lesser pilots, or he was so focused on the high-end tactics that he forgot the basics. Both can lead to mishaps.

The "external arrogance" was both more damaging and more deadly. When the instructors developed the "I don't have anything else to learn" mentality, they lost their own edge and their ability to teach others effectively. They also caused significant damage to the TOPGUN reputation, and sometimes caused others to pay the ultimate price.

When one such student attended TOPGUN, the instructors immediately recognized his stellar flying ability; however, they differed about whether he should be invited to return as an instructor. Those in his favor won but ultimately rued their decision when he brought embarrassment to the program by causing a fratricide incident in 2002. In any organization, left unchecked, arrogance can cause the extraordinarily gifted to become extraordinarily dangerous. In a flying organization, that danger can be fatal.[1]

TOPGUN best practices teach several important lessons to those who wish to create exceptional organizations. First, start with outstanding talent in key positions, and make no exceptions. The best of the best expect to work with other superior performers. When you form this kind of organization, you can look forward to your top talent developing loyalty and esprit de corps because they take pride in associating with those who share their excellence. However, to be a truly elite organization, these stars have to believe that they belong to something greater than themselves. Downing frequently reminded his team that they "stood on the shoulders of giants," those who had gone before them to set the standard of excellence that the current generation had not only the privilege and obligation to uphold but also to perpetuate.

Second, when you establish a culture of excellence and high expectations, the culture becomes self-perpetuating. Each generation of new managers understands what top talent looks like, so hiring, development, and retention improve. Tie talent decisions to a clear strategy, and you have a success formula.

Third, there's no substitute for raw talent, but taken singly, it doesn't offer much. You must also assess the person's ethics and commitment to developing others. When talent, character, and behavior come together, decision-makers can rest assured that they will receive the top talent for the dollars they pay.

Apple represents an example of the importance of talent. Steve Jobs, arguably the most gifted technology genius ever to allow us to benefit from his brilliance, drew talent to him like a magnet. According to the various accounts of his personal style and leadership approach, he was no day-at-the-beach to work for. He would reportedly blast people in front of their peers, engage in tirades, and generally serve as a tyrant. Yet, he had no attrition problems. Whereas highly trained, enormously gifted talent ran screaming from the other tech companies, Jobs retained some of the best and brightest in the industry. He created evangelists for his products. People believed in him, Apple, and the team that reported to Jobs. Since

Jobs' death, Apple has continued to remain strong, and the talent has stayed in Apple's doors. Why? The self-perpetuating nature of excellence and high expectations. The best Navy pilots want to go to TOPGUN, and the best technology prodigies want to work for Apple. It all depends on the right culture.

Excellence, the overarching requirement for exceptional organizations, defines everything else: talent, culture, and strategy. Without a clear commitment to and focus on excellence, nothing else matters.

Certainly, you won't want to pay to have *the* top person in the industry in every position. You'll go bankrupt before you can hire for the critical roles. Not everyone who works at Naval Air Station Fallon represents the level of excellence that the pilots do, but from the guard at the gate to the commander of TOPGUN, you notice a sincere desire to do things well. If you accept less, you compromise excellence.

A goal, strategy, intention, or plan to be excellent is not the answer. Rather, an *understanding* of what you can be the best at holds the key. (Refer to the "strategic principle" in Chapter Two.) This awareness will force the trade-offs when you face decisions about allocation of resources—human and financial. Stick with what you know—and what you can do at a world-class level. That's what senior leaders did when they faced an unprecedented wrestling match with Mother Nature in 1991.

On June 15, 1991, the second-largest volcanic eruption of the past century, and by far the largest eruption to affect a densely populated area, occurred at Mount Pinatubo in the Philippines. The eruption produced high-speed avalanches of hot ash, gas, giant mudflows, and a cloud of volcanic ash hundreds of miles across.

The eruption took everyone by surprise, yet no military members lost their lives in the evacuation of 15,000 people from Clark Air Force Base, due largely to the excellence of those whom former Air Force historian C.R. Anderegg dubbed "The Ash Warriors." We rely on the military to deliver excellence in the face of enemies, foreign and domestic, but we seldom think of them combating the forces of nature. Yet, when any organization challenges itself to deliver excellence, it can respond to disasters, regardless of their source.

When an Air Force installation faces an emergency, typically the duty of crisis action team commander falls to the installation's vice wing commander, in this case, then-Colonel Anderegg. Although he had no training in volcanology, and limited experience in crisis management, Anderegg successfully led the Ash Warriors in their valiant race against time and Mother Nature's nasty attempts at harm. Anderegg, the Ash Warriors, and the senior leaders of the 13th Air Force may have had little experience in fighting volcanoes, but they had one other distinguishing attribute that they had practiced repeatedly: quality performance.

I spoke with Anderegg about his role and that of the Ash Warriors in managing crisis. He said that three critical issues helped them answer the daunting question: "How do we evacuate 15,000 people in six hours?"[2]

The first answer was confidence in leadership. The Ash Warriors had spent their careers learning that when you have faith in your leaders, the most overwhelming tasks can be accomplished. Anderegg relied on Major General Studer, the commander of the 13th Air Force, and those in Anderegg's chain of command depended on the officers and NCOs who gave the orders. People didn't waste time asking, "Why should I trust you?" They had confidence.

When you commit to excellence, the word gets out. Those in the organization have seen your track record and know they can expect the same stellar performance from you now that you've always delivered. If you haven't built this reputation before the crisis, however, you gamble about the reaction your people will have. Virtuosos possess self-confidence, so they expect to feel confident about those who lead them.

The second factor that influenced their ability to achieve the daunting task of evacuating so many people with the unforgiving clock ticking away their opportunities involved training—an ongoing, consistent commitment to standardized processes. As Anderegg pointed out, Air Force personnel don't spring forth fully formed and ready to face adversity. The Air Force creates them. Although they had never faced the perils of an erupting volcano, the Ash Warriors had confronted hurricanes and typhoons. They knew their own jobs and the specific skills related to crisis management. Those oft-practiced skills helped them rise to the challenge of evacuating Clark.

In business organizations, unwelcome surprises happen too, often in the form of a crisis. When your people understand their jobs and have received the requisite training to do them well, when the unexpected happens, they will have the ability to transfer these experiences to the new situation. The learning curve becomes less steep, even when the stakes rise. If the nature of your business makes certain kinds of crises more likely, you're remiss in not training people adequately to face worst-case scenarios.

The third part of Anderegg's answer addressed discipline. Through confidence in the leadership and training, military personnel develop the discipline to ask themselves, "What is *my* part?" instead of "Why should I do this?" Through their military experiences, the Ash Warriors had learned others' expectations of them. They had practiced responding to different scenarios and had actually faced other catastrophes. Their discipline ensured they would follow through on their commitments and duties, even when those evolved minute-to-minute as the volcano's activities progressed.

Bureaucracy stands at cross purposes with discipline, which in turn compromises excellence and the action orientation you want to create, especially in a time of crisis. Bureaucracy exists to compensate for incompetence and lack of discipline—two things that would have handicapped the Ash Warriors in their efforts to evacuate the base and possibly have cost them their lives. Certainly the Air Force advocates a clear chain of command, but no confusion exists about who should make what decision. That has all been worked out well ahead of the crisis, so decision-making, accountability, and expectations remain clear, no matter what happens.

Many companies build the bureaucratic rules to justify the existence of those who influence rule-making and to manage the small percentage of people who simply can't or won't do their jobs. When you tie a culture of discipline to a commitment to attract and retain the best and brightest in your industry, a magical alchemy of action and results occurs.

But discipline by itself won't produce excellence. Numerous organizations throughout history have exhibited tremendous discipline as they marched in lockstep precision to ruin. You need a *system* of discipline that is characterized by quality and agility. That means people understand that implementation of the strategy holds the key to everyone's success, and interdependence coexists symbiotically with rugged self-reliance. People depend on others when task completion requires teamwork, but they also know how and when to make and carry out decisions independently. They understand the structure for getting work done—excellently.

When organizations face hiring and promotion decisions, too often they weigh experience disproportionately against excellence. A pattern of this kind of decision-making eventually jeopardizes the confidence employees must develop in their leaders. If you further exacerbate the situation with little training, you can't hope to develop excellence.

Sometimes the crisis you face will present unprecedented challenges, just as the eruption of Pinatubo did. The Air Force had no experience in evacuating a military base that was under siege from a mountain, because it had never happened before. But they did have the leaders of the 13th Air Force, Dick Anderegg, and the Ash Warriors—all examples of quality by any measure.

Consistency: The Antithesis of the "One-Hit Wonder"

We most often use the term "one-hit wonder" to describe music performers who have had a single success. Sometimes these one-hit wonders produced novelty songs such as Jeannie C. Riley's 1968 number-one hit "Harper Valley PTA." In spite of the song gracing the charts in the '60s, hardly anyone today would admit to thinking the hit represented true quality. And because Ms. Riley never produced another top-seller, we can also agree she didn't offer consistency.

Quality of people, training, service helps to explain the ongoing success of TOPGUN and the Ash Warriors' triumph over Mother Nature, but we should also consider the consistency of the two examples. TOPGUN doesn't produce superior aviators once in a while; they do it with every class, year after year. Similarly, members of the Air Force routinely and constantly train to meet expected and unexpected enemies—human and environmental. In both examples, the groups started with quality and then learned to replicate success.

In subsequent years, Riley enjoyed moderate chart success with country music, but she never again duplicated the success of "Harper Valley PTA," which missed, by one week, becoming the *Billboard* Country and Pop number-one hit at the same time. She began recording gospel music during the late 1970s, but she never produced another hit. Producers of one-hit wonders often don't know how to create something else because they never understood why the first success happened.

Consistency of performance involves starting with a high-quality offering and then understanding not only that you've been successful but *why* the success occurred. In Riley's case, the success might have been because of timing, the novelty of the song, or mild curiosity of pop fans about country music. Judging from its short-lived success and inability to pass the test of time, Riley didn't start with a quality song, so even if she had deconstructed her achievement, finding a consistent way to duplicate it might have proved impossible.

Contrast Riley to Elvis or the Beatles. They too introduced a new "sound" for their time, and both enjoyed consistent places on the pop chart, and in the case of Elvis, on the country and gospel billboards too. Not everyone became a fan of Elvis or the Beatles, but millions found quality in their work, so the stars repeatedly replicated their successes on several continents for several generations of music fans. Having passed the test of time with flying colors, even today, Beatles reviews and Elvis impersonators still grace the stages in Las Vegas.

Quality may be in the eye of the beholder, but the consistency to reproduce success clearly lies in the eye of the consumer. For example, in 1959, Mattel introduced the Barbie Doll, an immensely popular toy that has enjoyed more than 50 years of steady sales. The doll experienced immediate and wide-sweeping success, perhaps because it was the first toy to have a marketing strategy based extensively on television advertising. So in addition to Barbie being an iconic toy—that is, not a baby doll—she launched a new method for reaching future buyers and set the stage for most other toys that followed.

Someone buys a Barbie doll every three seconds somewhere in the world. More than a billion have been sold and more than a billion fashions have been produced for Barbie and her friends. And Barbie has had more than 130 careers in her lifetime, including that of fighter pilot. (Perhaps channeling TOPGUN quality and consistency?)[3]

Mattel offered further evidence of its ability to consistently produce excellence with the Cabbage Patch kids in the early 1980s. Mattel didn't create these dolls; instead, they bought the rights to them from Coleco, who began mass production in 1982. Coleco went bankrupt, and Mattel took over—ever vigilant for an excellent product that would carry on the toy maker's traditions. American Girl dolls and their related clothing and accessories came on the scene in 1986, released by Pleasant Company. In 1998, Pleasant Company became a subsidiary of Mattel, adding yet another rung to the toy maker's ladder of excellence.[4] Through its history, Mattel has modeled excellence in both its quality of toys and its consistent commitment to leverage the newest trends. But none of it would have happened if decision-makers had lost sight of the customers and what they wanted.

Customer Focus: Impressing the Ultimate Judge

At some time during the recent history of the Olympics, people in the United States began to talk about "pleasing the Russian judge." When our athletes competed in events that involved a significant level of subjective scoring—boxing, figure skating, gymnastics—often the panel of judges from all over the world would award top scores to a particular American athlete, but the Russian judge would score the event significantly lower. These notorious skewed evaluations both harmed the U.S. athletes and positioned the Russian competitors for better chances at medals. When an athlete managed to impress one of these Russian judges, people remarked that "he even impressed the Russian judge," high praise based on the herculean feat of astounding the ultimate judge.

In your business, you too face an ultimate judge: your best customers—not just any customers, or even most customers—your *best* customers. Each organization will define "best" in a different way, considering volume of purchase, potential for repeat sales, current and future buying power, or a host of other variables. Agreement about criteria for defining "best" *within* the organization is critical; concurrence among others in the industry much less so.

These ideal customers will play the role of Russian judge in your future. They will be difficult and sometimes impossible to please. They will seemingly request the unreasonable, and by virtue of their ability to take their business to your competitor, appear to skew their evaluations, often changing their criteria over time. But they will do one other critically important thing: They will let you know what a gold-medal-winning product or service looks like. If you let them, they will become both your harshest judges but also your most trusted source of information about what you must do to win the gold. These will help you do that:

1. Give them what they want, not what you want them to have or what you think they need. Too often, very good companies fail to become excellent because they offer what *they* think customers want instead of actually asking what their best customers

prefer. For instance, this year I've spent more nights in hotels than the average nomad has spent in a tent in her lifetime. Most of the hotels have been high-end hotels, but a few have been more moderate chains, like the Marriott.

The price of a night's stay has little to do with excellence or customer service—at least customer service that I find important. Sure, they knock on the door or call the room about every 10 minutes to ask if everything is okay or to rearrange my stuff, make my bed, and hide candy around like the hospitality Easter Bunny. But one of the most expensive ones didn't have my room ready at 5 p.m. because the customer service supervisor hadn't "checked it" and couldn't possibly take the word of housekeeping that the room was ready. I didn't consider waiting in the lobby for 45 minutes excellent, or even adequate, customer focus.

Several of the most expensive hotels charged extra for internet. One added imaginary room service charges to the bill. And one called the room 10 minutes after the posted checkout time to see if I planned to vacate, even though another "customer service associate" had agreed I could have a late check-out.

At one downtown Chicago high-end location, the hotel had no hair dryer, no extra blankets, no spare box of Kleenex, and no additional rolls of toilet tissue. Would it spoil some vast eternal plan if a hotel that charges $400 a night would also add $4 worth of paper products to the experience and throw in free internet?

I know that the employees at this hotel have had extensive training in customer service because they all sounded alike in their speech patterns and all handed me anything written with the type facing me. The man who checked me in even came out from behind the desk to give me my key envelope with the flap open and the numbers facing me. This highly ingrained gesture occurred five minutes after I had witnessed their doorman exchanging insults with a cab driver and 10 minutes before I couldn't connect to the internet in my room. I tried calling for customer service, but the battery on my room phone had died.

2. Don't settle for satisfied. If you want to distinguish your company from your competitors, your goal shouldn't be to "satisfy" your customers; it should be to wow them. "Satisfying" customers keeps them from complaining, but it won't necessarily bring them back for more.

    In his book, *The Hidden Wealth of Customers,* author Bill Lee offers compelling logic for taking customer focus so far beyond satisfaction that your best customers will prospect for you while also speeding product adoption and long-term loyalty. As Lee pointed out, there are more of them than us, they have more credibility with other customers, some understand your other buyers better, and they associate with each other (their peers) more than they do with us.[5] But these kinds of customers don't rave about you or even refer you to their colleagues unless you have gone far beyond satisfying them. These Russian judges, who can act as your most effective but least expensive sales force, will demand excellence.

3. Abhor unfair practices. Whenever an author of a business book looks for examples of best practices, we usually end up once again using Southwest Airlines as the gold standard for customer service excellence—no small thing when you realize Southwest does business in an industry characterized by an anti-customer focus. One of the reasons for their success—among an impressive list of many—has been their refusal to engage in unfair practices that harm their customers or at least separate them from their money. Changing flights or cancelling a trip on all other major airlines usually involves both a "penalty" for the change and a higher ticket for the new flight. Given a choice, therefore, fear of unexpected events and emergencies have caused customers to book their flights on Southwest, even when another carrier would be more convenient. For many years, Southwest has been the only major carrier that has remained profitable, staying out of bankruptcy and merger threats. Any money they might have gained through these unfair "penalty" practices has more than remained in their coffers. Similarly, Southwest doesn't charge to check a bag. Arguably, a competitor could point out that charges for bags are not unfair because bags require bag handlers who

have to earn a salary. Fair enough. But Southwest's continued commitment to surpass "satisfied" has led them to make decisions that abhor unfairness and to embrace excellence. And it's paid off.

4. Don't charge for the inconsequential. Southwest has shown us the value of avoiding extra charges, because they don't charge for things that don't cost them. The key strokes required to change a flight, especially a flight that the customer changes online, cost the airline nothing. The additional charges associated with hiring more baggage handlers to manage the free bags people can check on Southwest add negligible expenses when compared to the good will created among their customers.

Hotels continue to charge for internet service, however. Odd and contradictory as it seems, lower properties in a chain like the Marriott don't charge for the service, but the high-end, expensive ones in downtown areas do. These hotels, which customers would otherwise consider excellent, give themselves a black eye when they nickel-and-dime their "guests." If managers realize they need to charge for a service, just include it in the price of the room. No one who pays in excess of $400 for a hotel room will object to paying $414.

5. Hire humans who speak good English to answer your phone. Call me a Luddite, but I like talking to people, not machines. We remember the Luddites as the 19th-century British textile artisans who protested against newly developed labor-saving machinery. The machines of the Industrial Revolution threatened to replace the artisans with less-skilled, low-wage workers, leaving the skilled workers without work, which sparked the protest.

Today, excellence suffers when organizations allow machines to do the work that humans once did, and should still do, especially when that work involves some sort of technical assistance. Last week I experienced so many technical difficulties with a company that creates some of the assessments I use that I made the decision to switch. Psychologists regard this particular assessment very highly. Quality most definitely defines its excellence. For years, this testing company has done the requisite research and updated the validity studies to ensure they offer *the* best quality instrument. Yet, I will join the ranks of my fellow assessment psychologists who have abandoned its use because of poor customer service.

Specifically, the company has decided to offer an online version of the test, which keeps pace with the industry—a smart and necessary update. However, they failed to get all the bugs out of the system in the first place, so the quality suffered. Then, they neglected to create the systems that would guarantee they could consistently deliver stellar results. Sometimes the online version worked, sometimes it didn't. But we never knew until the person had completed the assessment. Finally, they failed to provide a human being to help me determine what we could do to solve the problems. I'm still waiting for a return call from a human, and the problem happened four days ago. In all fairness, I did receive a message earlier in the week from a man who left a message on my voicemail, but his accent was so pronounced that I have no idea who he was or what he suggested.

6. Return calls and e-mails within four hours. Unless you're sitting alert at NASA or performing intricate brain surgery, you can return phone calls in a timely fashion. Yet, the number of complaints I hear about unanswered calls and e-mails shocks me. In some form, the sender of the e-mail or the voicemail probably represents an internal or external customer. Whatever the case, the failure to answer in a timely fashion does two things. First, it sends the message that you simply don't care about this person, the issue, or the priority that person holds in your life. Second, you impede progress. Usually a caller or e-mailer has a specific questions or request for information. If you don't provide it, you affect that person's ability to move forward.

7. Don't change what people like. The only thing worse than not giving people what they want is taking away something they once had. The airlines, once again, offer the most grist for the mill. They once offered bag checking as a part of the ticket. Then they began restricting the number of carry-on bags a person could have, which led to more checked bags. Of course, the airlines incurred a cost because they had to hire additional

baggage handlers, so they wanted to pass along the cost to the customer. Why not just raise the cost of a ticket by $25? Any day you fly Southwest, you will notice both full planes and jam-packed overhead bins. People don't abuse the free checked-bag feature at Southwest. In fact, they don't even use it unless they have to. For obvious reasons, most people prefer to keep their bags with them.

Taking away something people once liked will cause customers to turn from you, but so will changing a once-appreciated product or service. Frequently, companies will realize they can't continue to offer the same standard of quality at the same price, but instead of raising the price, they cut the quality. Or, they raise the price for existing services at the same time they offer new customers a lesser rate. Phone and cable companies have grown notorious in these practices. We all know the outcome. Each company of this kind has begun scrambling for new business. Almost daily, I receive a marketing piece from AT&T. They once had me as a customer, but their ongoing violation of customer focus left me realizing I won't go back to them, in spite of their formidable efforts.

In business you don't have the daunting, if not impossible, task of pleasing the Russian judge. You have the realistic job of focusing on the ultimate judge—your best customers. Though still not easy or simple, this commission is practical and attainable. If you abandon it, however, and settle for a "satisfied" customer, it won't be long until your competitor figures out the "wow" factor and starts to offer it. Just ask decision-makers at any of Southwest's competitors.

Agility: The Guns, Germs, and Steel of the Organization

In Jared Diamond's *Guns, Germs, and Steel,* the author takes the reader on a whirlwind tour through 13,000 years of history on all the continents. In addition to weapons, disease, and tools, the author discussed the origins of empires, religion, writing, and crops—and the role of each in the differing developments of human societies. He also directly and indirectly offered some observations and recommendations about what leaders can do to influence the cultures they create and the organizations they aspire to lead.

He started with the overarching question "Why did wealth and power become distributed as they are, rather than in some other way?"[6] He posits that societies developed differently on different continents because of differences in continental environments, not in human biology. He uses the series of tribal wars, known as the Musket Wars, among New Zealand's indigenous Maori people between 1818 and the 1830s to explain how European guns spread among tribes that had previously fought one another with stone and wooden weapons. He noted that these wars illustrate the main process running through the history of the last 1,000 years: human groups with guns, germs, and steel, or with earlier technological and military advantages, who had discovered ways to feed their warriors, excelled at the expense of other groups, until either the latter groups disappeared, or everyone came to share the new advantages.

After the book's release, Diamond began receiving notes from business people, including Bill Gates, and economists pointing out the possible parallels between the histories of entire human societies and the histories of groups in the business world. The author began to question how we can account for the success of one company over another, even in the same industry.

He concluded that, if your goal is innovation and competitive ability, you don't want either excessive unity or excessive fragmentation. Instead, you want your country, industry, or company to be broken up into groups that compete with one another while maintaining relatively free communication.[7]

Diamond used beer to demonstrate his theories about the role of competition in success. As he noted, Germans make wonderful beer. People throughout the world tout the quality of German beer, and the Germans produce it consistently throughout the country. But they don't do it efficiently.

The German beer industry suffers from small-scale production. There are a thousand tiny beer companies in Germany, shielded from competition with one another because each German brewery has virtually a local monopoly, and their laws shield them from the competition of imports. Conversely, the United States has 67 major beer breweries, producing twice as much as Germany does. The average U.S. brewery produces 31 times more beer than the average German brewery. Also, most German beer is consumed within 30 miles of the factory where it was brewed. There's no competition; there are just a thousand local monopolies and no agility.[8]

A commitment to excellence demands a quality product that you can consistently produce, but it also requires agility in approach to beat competitors. The organizational equivalents, therefore, to guns, germs, and steel are technology, talent, and crystal balls. You'll certainly need the big data mentioned in Chapter One. These will constitute the guns and steel of your organization. But more importantly, you'll need people to make sense of this information, looking at historical contexts to anticipate future needs. Then, these same people will have to create the crystal balls that will foretell several likely futures and the probable events that will cause these events.

Agility expert Amanda Setili draws from years of experience as a McKinsey consultant and founder of Setili and Associates. She helps her clients position themselves in the market and suggests leaders do three things to increase their agility:

1. Observe opportunities. Setili advises clients to stay close to their customers—to immerse themselves in the customer experience and even to shop the competition's products. Look for changes and listen for clues.

2. Make decisions—not one decision to become agile, but a series of decisions that will leverage your competitive advantage and driving forces. Get your best people in the room and have them look at your products and services through a different lens. Think about assigning two teams: one to brainstorm ideas for new products and another to play devil's advocate. Think about alternatives for dramatic change.

3. Stay agile while implementing. According to Setili, the readiness for change is just as important as the ability to change. Setili likened corporate agility to a tennis match.[9] The best players literally stay on their toes; they don't rest on their heels. Organizations that can do the same position themselves in the market to respond nimbly to sudden, even unexpected changes. They don't merely run the race faster on the track others build or in the direction their competition has decided to run. Alert to both opportunities and changes, agile organizations *respond*

to what customers need and *define* for competitors what race they will enter. They can do all this because they started with a foundation of excellence built on quality, consistency, and customer focus.

Conclusion

Why do some organizations hit the ground running, while others trip over their own shoelaces? The answer lies in their organizational DNA—the constructs of an exceptional organization: strategy, culture, excellence, and talent. Exceptional organizations serve as magnets to star performers who, by their very nature, require excellent performance of themselves and those with whom they associate. They want to feel empowered to make decisions to improve both the organization and their own lives, and they want to align their excellence with an employer that distinguishes itself through excellence.

These stars crave an action-oriented culture that responds to change and reinvents itself whenever new information or learning indicates it should. They want to "fly" for TOPGUN, not a failing airline. In short, they want to work for companies that strive to think strategically, grow dramatically, promote intelligently, and compete successfully—both today and tomorrow. That combination will allow them to step to the front—to separate the duck from the quack and the ace from the pack.

Part Two

The Individual

Chapter Five

Star Talent Creates Your Future

Today's economy does not allow for mediocrity. If companies don't have the best people delivering their products and services, their competition will. Peter Drucker pointed out decades ago that the ability to make good decisions regarding people represents one of the last reliable sources of competitive advantage because very few organizations excel in this arena. Now, more than ever, the single most important driver of organizational performance is talent—but not just any talent—*stars*. Only those organizations that comb the planet for the experts, prodigies, and geniuses can hope to lead their industries into the future. Average and ordinary simply won't be enough—but neither will high potentials.

Understanding stars and virtuosity does not involve binary thinking—that is, one either is or is not a star. When compared to other high school players, by all objective criteria, we might consider an outstanding high school baseball player a great athlete. However, when contrasting him to college, minor league, or major league players, the evaluator might reach a different conclusion.

You have probably already spotted the "high potentials" in your organization. These people have shown consistently over time that they can be counted on to deliver results. Perhaps they even represent the best your company has ever employed. In other words, when playing in the league they've always been in, they set themselves apart from the average employee. You're glad to have them, and you'd hire them again without hesitation. The question I ask my clients who have an aggressive growth strategy challenges some different thinking: "They got you *here*, but can they get you *there*?" In other words, their top performance exists *on a continuum*. They may be the best you've ever had, but do they represent the best your competition has ever had or will have? Here's a way to think of this:

High Potentials	Stars
Ethical	Beyond reproach
Highly talented	Expert
Highly skilled	Excellent
Disciplined	Enterprising
Generally experienced	Experienced in critical areas

Maybe your high potentials are good enough to keep you in the game. And maybe not. Some of your high potentials may well have the potential to one day claim virtuoso status. They may have the raw talent, a commitment to excellence, and the resolve to develop both themselves and your organization. But you need to see evidence. You need to see proof that they can learn quickly and advance rapidly, both in terms of responsibility and skill acquisition. Only then can you be optimistic that you have the right people.

Stars distinguish themselves and exemplify the *E⁵ Star Performer Model*: Ethics, Expertise, Excellence, Enterprise, and Experience. They force people to take them seriously. They don't raise the bar—they set it for everyone else. They serve as gold standards of what people should strive to be and attain. If you were to scour the world, you'd be hard-pressed to find people who do their jobs better. You wouldn't hesitate to hire them again, and you'd be crushed if you found out they were leaving.

Because they are thought leaders, others look to these virtuosos for guidance and example. Often they consider them edgy and contrarian, but they seldom ignore them. Virtuosos chafe at too much supervision or tight controls—fortunately, they need neither. They constantly search for the new horizon and welcome the unforeseen challenge. No synonym for the word "virtuoso" exists. Some might substitute "artist," "expert," or "musician," but these don't suffice. Many can lay claim to these titles and still fail the virtuosity litmus test. By definition, few virtuosos exist. If you're fortunate to have a team of them, recognize them for who they are, and use your influence to help them make beautiful organizational music.

Ethics: Doing Well by Doing Right

Even though some could claim that exceptionalism and virtuosity can exist independently of any moral compass, in business, ethics forms the foundation of both. Arguably, a great talent, such as Hemingway, can offer universal appeal for generations, even though many found him generally to disregard the rules of civility during his lifetime. Yet few would yank his widespread accepted title of literary virtuoso. Therein lies the imperfection of the metaphor. Business simply won't countenance this sort of breakdown. Although somewhat abstract and ethereal, for the purpose of this discussion, let's assume ethics underpins all that defines a true virtuoso.

Aristotle helped us understand this point of view more than 2,000 years ago. According to him, the chief good for man is happiness, which, according to his philosophy, consists of rational activity pursued in accordance with virtue. Therefore, living well demands *doing* something, not just *being* in a certain state or condition of integrity. It consists of those lifelong activities that *actualize* ethics and—as we now understand—create stars.

Aristotle insisted that ethics involves more than a theoretical discipline: we ask about the "good" for human beings, not simply because we want to have knowledge, but because we will be better able to achieve our good if we develop a fuller understanding of what it is to flourish. Aristotle maintained that the study of ethics should seek to influence *behavior*. Therefore, what do stars actually do to demonstrate their ethics?

In business, the difficult and controversial question arises when we ask whether certain goods are more desirable than others. For example, years ago I knew a consultant, Tim, who had the answer. Tim, who was based in St. Louis, routinely flew to New York to visit several clients. The agreement between Tim and these clients involved their paying his travel expenses. Therefore, Tim bought a roundtrip first-class ticket, per the agreement, and billed each of the three clients for it. He didn't divide it among the three— he billed each separately for it and pocketed the difference. Legal? Probably. Ethical? No, but then I don't recall anyone accusing Tim of either integrity or virtuosity.

Although Tim did what was good for *him*, ethics involves a search for the *highest* good, and Aristotle assumes that the highest good, whatever it turns out to be, has three characteristics:

1. The action is desirable for itself.
2. It is not desirable for the sake of some other good.
3. All other goods are desirable for its sake.

Obviously Tim's decision to profit from the price of an airline ticket doesn't pass Aristotle's test. But it had other consequences.

Tim ran a boutique firm that employed other consultants who knew of his practices. Can anyone express surprise that they started emulating their boss's behavior?

In addition to "massaging" his own expense reports, Tim took other shortcuts to drive the business. He routinely demanded the selling of services, even when that compromised the best interest of the client. He told clients what he thought they wanted to hear, even when what they needed to know differed. He required his direct reports to follow suit. Also, he frequently discussed highly confidential, guarded information with those who had no need to know.

The direct reports began to claim meals they could have eaten but didn't, tips they should have given but didn't, and expenses they might have incurred but hadn't. Sometimes the firm passed these costs on to the clients, but eventually Tim learned he too had suffered from the unethical culture he had created.

Three other things happened. First, clients began to hear of the unethical practices, which caused him to lose business in the short run and suffer damage to the firm's reputation in the long run. Second, Tim eventually found himself spending an inordinate amount of time policing the behavior of his direct reports. Instead of building a business, he squandered his time reviewing expense reports and monitoring the elevators at 4:30 to make sure no one left early. Third, Tim lost the stars he had hired. He had a stable of thoroughbred stars that left him one by one through the years, simply because they wanted better for themselves and the clients they served. They wanted to work in a place that deontologically matched their personal commitment to doing the right thing.

Deontology, from the Greek *deon*, which means "obligation" or "duty," is the ethical position that judges the morality of an action based on the action's adherence to rules—choices that are required, forbidden, or permitted. This school of thought posits that some acts are *inherently* ethical or unethical, irrespective of legality, pragmatics, or common practice. For example, some people consider torture wrong, regardless of the legality of it or its use to obtain critical intelligence. These people support a deontological view. Others consider torture generally wrong but, when not taken to extremes, necessary for national security. Philosophers commonly contrast deontological ethics with consequentialist ethics—that is, the rightness of an action is determined by its consequences.

Stars embrace the deontological school and evidence this in their behavior. You don't have to check their expense reports, because even if they could get away with padding it, they wouldn't. You don't have to worry about them embarrassing the company with inappropriate behavior in their personal lives, because they self-regulate. They don't believe that two wrongs ever make a right, and they don't look for the moral loopholes because they wouldn't jump through them anyway. Perhaps Bernie Madoff could have ranked among the financial stars of the world had he used his innate talent differently and embraced this school of ethical theory.

As Aristotle noted thousands of years ago, opinions vary about what benefits human beings. Many excuse behaviors that would ordinarily seem wrong, but when done for the betterment of the organization, can be forgiven. (One might note that Aristotle never had a sales quota.) Similarly, legal loopholes allow for wrong-minded logic. Philosophers since Aristotle have tried to explain ethics in more practical terms, but I embrace the three criteria he posited.

Integrity is a not a raincoat you put on when the business climate indicates you should. It is a condition that guides your life—not just a set of protocols. Stars don't acquire their ethical foundations solely by learning general rules. They also develop them—those deliberative, emotional, and social skills that enable them to put their understanding of integrity into practice in ways that are suitable—through practice. Similarly, stars understand that they can't "teach" ethics to others by requiring their signatures on a statement. Instead, they *exemplify* and model ethics in their personal and professional lives.

At a visceral level, stars understand Hemingway's observation that "What is moral is what you feel good after. What is immoral is what you feel bad after." (His life indicates he understood this intellectually, as many of us do, but failed to weave this knowledge into his day-to-day behavior, a tendency we also share.) Going beyond awareness actually to practice integrity is one of the things that separates the virtuoso from other top performers.

Expertise: The Raw Data of Talent

Some might argue that ethics should not be included in a discussion of virtuosity. As mentioned previously, we often consider people world-class, with no regard to conduct outside the arena of their excellence. However, no one would suggest compromising on expertise, because it literally defines what lies at the heart of virtuosity. To better understand the nature of expertise, I offer four critical constructs: intelligence, talent, knowledge, and consistency of performance, which also transitions us to a discussion of excellence. (Experience should be considered a fifth construct, but in this discussion, I will address it separately.)

Although the ranking of these five might differ, depending on the nature of the virtuoso, in business, the most crucial forecaster of executive success is brainpower, or the specific cognitive abilities that equip us to make decisions and solve problems. Three main components define this leadership intelligence: critical thinking, learning ability, and quantitative abilities. Of these, *critical thinking* is the most important and the least understood.

Dispassionate scrutiny, strategic focus, and analytical reasoning form the foundation of critical thinking. These abilities equip a person to anticipate future consequences, to get to the core of complicated issues, and to zero in on the essential few while putting aside the trivial many. As I pointed out in *Landing in the Executive Chair: How to Excel in the Hotseat*, you can often evaluate a person's critical thinking based on their pattern of decision-making:

- Does this person understand how to separate strategy from tactics, the "what" from the "how"?

- Can this person keep a global perspective? Or does she or he become mired in the details and tactics? "Analysis paralysis" has caused more than one otherwise top performer to allow opportunity to slip away.

- Do obstacles stop this person? Or do they represent challenges, not threats? The ability to bounce back from setbacks and disappointments frequently separates the strong strategist from the effective tactician.

- Can he or she create order during chaos? Stars keep problems in perspective and realize that very few things are truly as dire as they first seem.

- Does this person have the ability to see patterns, make logical connections, resolve contradictions, and anticipate consequences? Or is she or he unaware of trends?

- What success has this person had with multitasking? Often the ability to handle a number of things at once implies good prioritizing and flexibility.

- Can this person think on his or her feet? Or does this person miss opportunities because of an inability to respond? Quickness, however, does not guarantee effective critical thinking skills. Some people rush to make mistakes; others take their time and then err.

- Can this person prioritize seemingly conflicting goals? Is this person able to zero in on the critical few and put aside the trivial many when allocating time and resources?

- When facing a complicated or unfamiliar problem, can this individual get to the core of the issue and immediately begin to formulate possible solutions?

- Is this person future-oriented and able to paint credible pictures of possibilities and likelihoods? The key question remains, "Can this person solve complicated, unfamiliar problems?"

- How do unexpected and unpleasant changes affect this person's performance? If his or her analytical reasoning is well-honed, organized, systematic decision-makers can respond favorably to change, even if they don't like to.

- When in a position of leadership, does this person serve as a source of advice and wisdom? Can she or he act as an effective sounding board to others who struggle with complex issues?

Most people can learn to follow a protocol or set of procedures. Give them a check list, and they can execute the plan. They know how to run fast, but sometimes they don't know which race to get in. Often these individuals are valuable employees, maybe even top performers. But they aren't stars.

General learning ability is the second most important aspect of leadership intelligence. When leaders can acquire new information quickly, they do not lose valuable time moving through the pipeline. They size up the new leadership situation, learn about their people, learn about products and processes, and then immediately act on this knowledge. When this happens, the organization responds by moving the new leader's idea to action. Reading ability, vocabulary, and fundamental math skills form the foundation of learning ability. Often, but not always, educational success is an accurate predictor of how quickly someone will learn in the organization. Certainly, ongoing learning teaches people about their own learning styles, so they become more proficient at acquiring new information and skills.

Although critical to success at the top levels of most organizations, not every turn in the leadership pipeline requires quantitative abilities. Knowing what the numbers mean and using them to make sophisticated business decisions equips an individual to make budget or profit and loss assessments. Superior development of these skills allows a person to evaluate the nuances of mergers, acquisitions, and risk-taking ventures as they analyze strategy. Numerical problem- solving, critical thinking, and proficient learning define the basics of business acumen.

In my more than 35 years of consulting, I have found that, without question, natural intelligence is the most important component of expertise in the business arena and the single most significant differentiator at the upper echelons of large organizations. Stanford psychologist Lewis Terman recognized this when he pioneered his IQ tests in the early 1900s. In his opinion, nothing about an individual is as important as IQ, except possibly morals.[1] I echo the observation and sentiment, but I also recognize the observations of "IQ fundamentalist" Arthur Jensen, who observed that IQ levels, beyond those that would qualify an individual for admission to graduate school (about IQ 115), become relatively unimportant in terms of success. In other words, IQ differences in the upper part of the scale—above 115—have fewer implications than the thresholds below that.[2]

To give a frame of reference, most successful professional football players are big guys, but beyond a certain weight, you don't see increased skill or excellence. Like the size of NFL players, intelligence has a threshold. You have to be smart enough to do the job well—but not appreciably smarter than that. Stars don't lack leadership intelligence; they have enough. But they also embody what psychologists call "practical intelligence" or "emotional intelligence." They know what to say, when, and to whom. They understand their own emotions, fears, and motivations and those of others.

In a general discussion of virtuosity, talent and intelligence would be separate. Some individuals may have exceptional talent for music, art, acting, or some other activity but not exceptionally high IQs. However, once again, in the business arena, the most sought-after talent will usually be so closely linked to cognitive abilities that separating them seems impossible. But there are exceptions. I have tested world-class salespeople who earned modest scores on all the cognitive assessments. They didn't even score well on the sales knowledge tests! But put them in front of a customer, and they sell. Therefore, when asked to assess a salesperson, I tell clients the one and only reliable piece of data is track record. Do they have a talent for selling? If they do, little else matters. If they don't, *nothing* else matters.

Excellence: Consistency of Performance

Although required, expertise is not enough. Even when people possess world-class talent, they must practice and hone their skills routinely and religiously. For example, renowned pianist-turned-conductor Vladimir Ashkenazy said that if he misses a day of practice, he notices. If he misses two, his wife notices. If he misses three, the audience notices. Ashkenazy, like most stars, realizes the unmistakable link between practice and excellence.

Of the five constructs of star performance, excellence poses the most challenges for understanding it and attaining it. What makes us excellent?

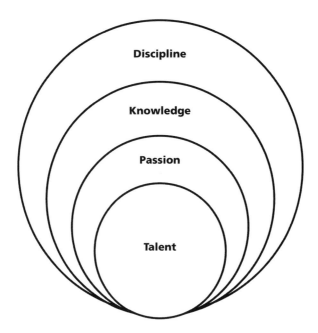

Talent stands firmly at the foundation of excellence, but awareness of the talent has to occur, too. Unknown potential does us little good if we leave it in the realm of the unidentified. That's why exploration of a variety of activities and subject matter is so important for children. They may possess enormous reserves of untapped talent that lie dormant for a lifetime. That doesn't happen to the stars that shine on our stages and in our organizations. Through whatever process and help from others, they identify the strengths that set them apart.

It all starts with talent—the natural ability or aptitude to do something well. People who possess talent often initially take it for granted, even asking themselves, "Can't everyone do this?" Eventually they realize they can deliver consistent stellar performance every time they attempt the activity, and not everyone else can. Further, once they have identified the strength, they don't abandon it. Instead, their passion spurs them to find ways to use it in ever-evolving new ways.

Passion serves as a kind of magnetic field around the activity or pursuit. Stars feel themselves *pulled* to learn about and participate in things related to their talents, while they simultaneously feel repulsion for some that aren't. For example, a linguist might have looked forward to English class but dreaded science. He might have found the study of literature fulfilling but the study of botany burdensome. Stars literally crave the thing for which they feel passion. Sometimes this hunger to know about a subject will unveil a talent early in one's life, but sometimes the talent surfaces later—along with the zeal to develop it.

After they recognize their talent, they acquire knowledge—the content and context for using it. They *learn*, either by themselves or from others, what they need to know to grow their innate abilities. A would-be virtuoso may have the inborn talent of perfect pitch, but unless and until someone shows her how to hold a cello, she will never gain the knowledge and skills that will make her the world-class cellist she dreams of becoming. Even though it all involves hard work, stars acquire new skills quickly and adeptly because the process usually feels painless and enjoyable—which circles back to fueling the passion they feel for their talents.

Then, they organize their lives so they can apply their excellence—they hone the skills and practice what they're already good at. They develop the discipline to practice, but they realize practice only makes perfect if you practice perfectly, and no amount of practice will help the person who lacks talent.

Athletes know this, but those of us in business often overlook it. Sports greats work with coaches every day who watch them, videotape them, give them feedback, and constantly strive to improve on already nearly perfect performance. Also, athletic coaches don't waste their time attempting to develop talent where it doesn't exist. Instead, they concentrate their coaching efforts on those who have exhibited the raw ability to become excellent.

And it all happens with a disciplined approach to practice that allows the athlete to attain virtuoso status before the age of 30.

Some would-be greats have the talent, passion, and knowledge to attain virtuoso status but fall short because they lack discipline, which means they lack an ordered approach to developing their talent. Maybe they simply don't know what they would have to do to improve. Perhaps they don't have a teacher or mentor who could shine the light into the darkness to illuminate the path they will need to take to reach their goal of greatness.

But that usually doesn't explain the breakdown. Most people understand what they need to do to change and improve, but they lack the resolve to do it. They don't develop the habits that would ensure their continued advancement because that would cause a disruption to their current lives. The rewards of virtuosity lie in the future, but the disruption and sacrifices happen today.

Tempting though it may be, we should not confuse excellence with perfection. Achieving excellence certainly demands a disciplined approach to development of talent and passion and the ability to deliver a stellar performance most of the time, but it does not require perfection: accuracy, precision, exactness, and care, yes—but not perfection. If a virtuoso defines perfection as the goal, three things happen. First, the person never achieves the goal because it's unrealistic. Second, along the path to perfection, the star performer can lose motivation, and frustration will set in. And finally, the star will lose valuable time and squander precious resources trying to accomplish something that won't appreciably augment his or her efforts. Star athletes learn these lessons quickly.

In a June 2, 2010, American League baseball game in Detroit, Detroit Tigers pitcher Armando Galarraga nearly became the 21st pitcher in Major League history to pitch a perfect game. Facing the Cleveland Indians, Galarraga retired the first 26 batters he faced, but his bid for a perfect game vanished when first-base umpire Jim Joyce incorrectly ruled that Indians batter Jason Donald reached first base safely on a ground ball. Galarraga finished with a one-hit shutout in a 3–0 victory. The following week decision-makers in the world of baseball opted to deny pitcher Galarraga his "perfect game," even though the video confirmed the out, and umpire Jim Joyce admitted his bad call on what should have been the final out of the game.

Unlike others who might have been in his situation, Galarraga accepted the injustice with poise and got the next batter out. Joyce personally apologized for his mistake, and the Detroit fans gave the umpire a standing ovation the next day. Also, in a show of good sportsmanship, Galarraga shook hands with Joyce.

Galarraga, by all objective criteria, had been perfect; conversely, Joyce had been flawed. Both men, however, showed a laudable level of good sportsmanship in the face of adversity. Probably neither man thought that game his finest hour—Galarraga because of the profound injustice of losing a much-coveted distinction, and Joyce because of his own limitations—but both gave the rest of us a lesson in the importance of stellar sportsmanship, and both illustrated that our goal should be success, not perfection.

If we make perfection the goal, we will never experience triumph, and we'll seldom be satisfied. Stars thrive on achievement and accomplishment because both bring satisfaction. Through my coaching experience with would-be perfectionists, however, I've learned this: They think they're right. "What could possibly be wrong" they ask me, "with making things precise and demanding accuracy?"

Good question. The major problem with perfection is loss of time. It simply takes too long to make things perfect. You can quickly become mired in the details and suffer analysis paralysis.

For example, I once worked with a top performer named Cheryl, a card-carrying perfectionist. She did outstanding work, but she never met a deadline that I'm aware of. Flawless and exacting, her reports reflected the *enormous* amount of time she had spent writing each as though it would vie for the next coveted spot on the *New York Times* bestseller list. She wrote and rewrote. She edited. On business trips she called her assistant to change a "happy" to a "glad." She spent an inordinate amount of time trying to make each report a work of art that everyone would admire for decades to come. (A handful of people read these reports before filing them away, never to be read again.)

I suggest she was not a star because she overlooked opportunities to build the business through accomplishing more work. And she annoyed clients when she didn't meet the deadlines. Also interesting, her office resembled the aftermath of Three Mile Island. Instead of nuclear waste, however, she covered every surface with papers, files, and assorted debris. (Apparently perfectionism does not have universal demands.)

The goal of stars and those who lead them, therefore, needs to be success, not perfection. If you try to make everything perfect, you sacrifice results and efficiency. Brain surgery and launching the shuttle demand nearly perfect performance every time. For most of us, however, 80-percent right is good enough. The time and missed opportunity you'll invest to get the other 20 percent won't usually give you a strong return on your investment. Stars understand that "finished" trumps "perfect" most of the time, so they move into the future more quickly than others.

Stars have what I call a "future tense" lens. They see benefits in the future, so they eschew instant gratification for the sake of the long-term, enduring pleasure their talent promises. They have reason to believe they will be *great,* so they don't settle for reasonably good performance—but neither do they insist on perfection. Because their progress has been constant and predictable, they develop optimism that fuels their discipline. When they do face a setback, they have the resilience to bounce back and recommit to their systematic, disciplined approach to excellence. Their disciplined approach to developing their excellence also marks them as those who are enterprising and resourceful.

Enterprise: Setting the Bar

In *Outliers,* Malcolm Gladwell introduced "the 10,000-Hour Rule" which he formulated after studying the work of Anders Ericsson. Ericsson followed the lives of professional musicians and contrasted them to those non-professionals who had started playing an instrument at the same age. The research showed that the professionals steadily increased their practice time every year until, by the age of 20, they had reached 10,000 hours. No "natural" musicians floated to the top with less practice.

Is the "10,000 rule" a general imperative for success? Will we find stars of every stripe proving it? Generally speaking, yes. Those whom we would consider stars in business have usually worked in their area of expertise at least five years. If these people worked a 40-hour work week 50 weeks a year, they would have "practiced" approximately 2,000 hours a year, thus supporting the rule.[3]

If you work hard, you will succeed at some level. If you don't, you won't. In my thousands of hours of coaching, I have found that hard work and integrity account for success in many industries all the way up the ladder—until you reach the top rung. At that top rung, the hard work has to remain steady, but then talent and expertise start to play a bigger role. Innate talent leads to excellence, but as Gladwell pointed out with his 10,000-Hour Rule, excellence doesn't happen without dogged determination.

As I've repeatedly noted, leadership intelligence accounts for success at the upper echelons of any organization, but no one succeeds without a strong achievement drive. Certainly the talent to zero in on best uses of time helps prioritize what needs to be done and the critical nature of some tasks, but without a clear bias for action, movement through the pipeline cannot occur.

The willingness to work hard and a high-energy, go-getter attitude define "enterprising." A competitive spirit, a "can do" attitude, self-discipline, reliability, and focus further augment it. Personality assessments can help identify achievement drive in new hires and internal high-potentials, but observation provides the surest way to know if a person has what it takes to get the job done.

Largely because of their passion to apply their talent and expertise, stars eagerly embrace challenges and overcome obstacles. Their motivation clearly starts at their core and doesn't respond well to external things like pep talks, incentive programs, and charisma. Resourceful and determined, stars *invent* rather than respond to the environment around them. They want to do their best work, so they don't readily take "no" as any kind of answer. By experimenting with novel approaches and eagerly embracing innovation, they develop the experience to understand what kinds of efforts will engender the most dramatic growth and change.

Experience: The Yesterdays That Define the Tomorrows

When I advise clients on hiring and promotion decisions, a recurring challenge I face involves helping them evaluate experience. Most senior leaders tend to over-value it, especially when the person has "just what we need" in terms of previous employment and industry experience.

By my definition, stars offer enough experience to claim expertise and to succeed, but when I encounter true virtuosity, I think of experience differently. I don't want to see a resume that chronicles 15 years of experience, when 10 of those years really amounted to one year 10 times. Similarly, a long list of jobs that showed no advancement in skills and leadership doesn't impress me.

On the other hand, Captain Sullenberger rose to fame when he successfully landed U.S. Airways Flight 1549 in the Hudson River on January 15, 2009, saving the lives of 155 people. In 2009, Sullenberger was a senior captain with more than 19,000 hours of flying time that he had accumulated in his more than 30 years of flying experience. In interviews and writings after the crash, Sullenberger credited his vast experience in both flying and safety for his ability to do what had to be done on that January day. Could he have done it with 2,000 hours of flying time? We'll never know. If you were to put a group of military and commercial pilots in a room and ask them this question, two things would happen: First, you'd have a fierce debate on your hands. Second, you still wouldn't have a definitive answer. The disagreement doesn't address whether or not stars need experience. The question remains: "How much is enough?"

Stars bore easily, so they move quickly through the ranks and separate themselves from other high potentials with their sheer hunger for knowledge, opportunity, and challenge. They also demonstrate self-awareness, which is a key construct of experience. They accept their talents and weaknesses with equal degrees of equanimity. They know they can't excel at everything, so they isolate those talents that will define their success and concentrate on situations that will allow them to flourish.

Consider John. In 2005, a member of the board of directors of a St. Louis publicly traded, $1.5 billion company called me to help them in their selection of a new CEO. They had narrowed the field to two candidates: Dan and John. Of the two candidates, Dan offered more impressive experience, but in a more general sense, he was the weaker candidate. I told the search committee that John was the better of the two candidates, even though he didn't offer the experience Dan did. I went one step further and said that if John didn't accept their offer, they'd have to re-open the search because, although experienced, Dan didn't have the leadership skills to run this company. They kept telling me more about Dan's experience. I finally said, "Guys, here's what I know about experience. Age does not always bring wisdom. Sometimes age comes alone." In Dan's case, that's what had happened. Reluctantly, the board hired John, and a competitor hired Dan and summarily fired him six months later.

When John took the helm in November of 2005, the stock sold for $19. Almost overnight it doubled and then quickly tripled. In a little more than three years, the company had expanded in North America, Europe, and Asia.

John succeeded for several reasons: He had 16 years of *different* experience, not one year 16 times; he's a brilliant strategist; he's self-aware, ethical, enterprising and excellent—in short, a virtuoso. Experience plays a major role in defining virtuosity, but it appears at the top of the pyramid for a reason. To identify stars in your chain of command, weigh the other criteria more heavily, and don't exaggerate the role of experience. Realize its major function is to help you recognize a mistake when you make it again, and ideally, to make fewer of the ones you've made before.

Conclusion

We seem to understand, at least intellectually, that we will excel only by leveraging strengths, not by mitigating weaknesses. Of course, we should try to minimize weaknesses, but only to the point that they no longer undermine our strengths. In other words, working on a weakness will help us prevent failures, but it won't ensure virtuosity.

This commitment to leveraging strengths won't happen automatically, however, because our understanding of the concepts tends to be more intellectual than applicable. Too frequently we focus on pathology and weakness, not health and forte. For instance, psychologist Martin Seligman found more than 40,000 studies on depression but only 40 on joy, happiness, or fulfillment. Fear, depression, and anxiety can mask talent and retard the development of excellence, but overcoming them won't create it.[4] To understand and attain virtuosity, we need to spotlight those things that cause it, not the ones that stand in its way. Only then will we be able to develop it—in ourselves, in those who count on us, and in our organizations.

Chapter Six

Exemplars and Avatars

The word "avatar" has evolved through the ages from the description of Hindu gods that descended from heaven to live among us to a more modern-day definition that includes computer representations of our alter egos or contrived characters. In either sense, the definition describes that which can go beyond human constraints, those earthly bonds that limit our talent and excellence. Star performers don't represent deities in human form, but they do set a gold standard that suggests humans have the capacity to excel well beyond the shackles we have placed on ourselves.

In Chapter Five, I expanded the traditional definition of *virtuoso* beyond the boundaries of music to include business leaders, vanguards, artists, medical researchers, military leaders, and thought leaders. The E^5 *Star Performer Model* helps us understand how these five general factors form the very essence of virtuosity. But more needs to be said. We also need to look at some of the specific traits that have distinguished virtuosos throughout history—those things that set them apart from the also-rans. Sometimes these fall into neat categories like passion, charisma, and courage. But at other times, uniqueness creates the outliers.

Once we understand the traits of these exceptional people, their origins, and their resilience, we can make better decisions about those whom we should include in our mental pantheon—and, more importantly, we can learn to identify and develop those who cross our paths who embody these laudable traits. The pantheon we aspire to create won't be a burying place or shrine. On the contrary, it will be a hall of fame for those we collectively wish to know better.

Traits of Virtuosos

Several years ago, I asked a graduate class to identify the top five leaders of all time. A student mentioned Elvis. In the hallowed halls of academia, one doesn't expect to see "Elvis" on a list with Lincoln, Churchill, and Martin Luther King. The student offered compelling reasons that Elvis should be on the list, however, asking when we last saw a Churchill impersonator packing in the Vegas crowds. To his credit, the student had mentioned "the ability to influence" as one of the key criteria for distinguishing oneself as a leader.

Though I still wouldn't call Elvis's influence leadership, that student challenged my thinking about leadership and about exceptional performance. I began to recognize some of the traits that we associate with those who distinguish themselves throughout history, and I started calling this particular one the "je ne sais quoi" trait—the characteristic we recognize when we see it but can't always name specifically. Elvis had it; others do too.

Je Ne Sais Quoi

Elvis Presley, born on January 8, 1935, in Tupelo, Mississippi, never received formal music training or learned to read music. Early in his career, he failed an audition for a local vocal quartet, the Songfellows, because, as he told his father, "They told me I couldn't sing." This uneducated man who couldn't sing would go on to become a cultural icon, widely known by the single name Elvis and often referred to as the "King of Rock and Roll" or, simply, "The King."

Even though Elvis never ran a company, led troops into battle, or reformed social injustice, he did one thing far better than most: he influenced. Decades after his death, his estate makes more money than it ever did when he was alive, his birthday celebration at Graceland sells out each year, and the popular stage show *Million Dollar Quartet* continues to reign in many cities.

I consider influence a certain "je ne sais quoi" trait because we don't know why it occurs, but we can't deny its power—the ability to sway opinions, taste, and attitudes. It doesn't necessarily involve pressure or dominance. Influence involves inducing others to change their behaviors without the exertion of control or the authority that comes with positional power.

Elvis reported to his father that the Songfellows didn't think he could sing, but millions of us held a different opinion. His velvety voice dominated the pop, country, folk, and gospel charts for most of his life, and his recordings continue to sell. Certainly he exemplifies the E^5 *Star Performer Model*, but that alone doesn't explain his exceptional success.

Sinatra had the magical something before Elvis, and the Beatles had it after. Elvis topped the charts until the British "Fab Four" invaded the United States and the world. The strongest-selling band in history, we can consider them a virtuoso team—even though, singly, Paul McCarthy and John Lennon would match the virtuoso criteria. On February 9, 1964, the group performed live on *The Ed Sullivan Show* and changed forever the face of rock and roll. Approximately 34 percent of the American population viewed the program, the largest audience that had ever been recorded for an American television program. The next morning the media reported that consensus in the United States was generally against the group.[1] That evaluation was both short-lived and inaccurate. Within two days, Beatlemania had captured the U.S. audience and established forever its influence and dominance on pop culture.

Former *Rolling Stone* associate editor Robert Greenfield compared the band to Picasso as "artists who broke through the constraints of their time period to come up with something that was unique and original in the form of popular music. No one will ever be more revolutionary, more creative and more distinctive."[2] On the heels of Beatlemania, the group became icons of the 1960s counterculture, catalysts of sorts for bohemianism and activism in various social and political arenas.

Explaining virtuosity status for Mozart, Chopin, Beethoven, and other classical icons requires no imagination. They clearly and profoundly support the model. But once in a while, a person or group emerges whose influence doesn't stand up to the virtuoso litmus test. We simply can't explain why we collectively chose Sinatra, Elvis, or the Beatles. But even non-fans cannot deny that we did.

Sometimes others—like Walt Disney—choose a person who will influence us, and we accept their offering. Such was Disney's choice to laud Davy Crockett, the celebrated folk hero, soldier, politician, and "king of the wild frontier," who was born August 17, 1786. During his 50 years on earth, he served in the militia of Tennessee, represented Tennessee in the U.S. House of Representatives, served in the Texas Revolution, and gave his life at the Battle of the Alamo. He was also a virtuoso that we'd probably have forgotten about if not for Disney's influence.

Crockett didn't start life as a star, however. The fifth of nine children, he failed at school and eventually ran away from home at the age of 13 to avoid his father's wrath. Crockett became famous in his own lifetime for larger-than-life exploits popularized by stage plays and almanacs. But not until after his death did the yarn-spinners credit him with brazen acts of mythical proportion.

By the late 19th century, however, we had largely forgotten Crockett. Walt Disney rekindled the legend in a 1950s TV show, which also introduced the celebrated coonskin cap. Most Baby Boomers think of actor Fess Parker as the face of Davy Crockett. Every kid on my block, and perhaps across the nation, could sing "The Ballad of Davy Crockett," which included a claim that Crocket "Kilt him a b'ar when he was only three."

Historians agree Crockett died at the Alamo March 6, 1836, but the agreement ends there. Some say he surrendered during the battle and that Santa Anna demanded his immediate execution. Others maintain that Crockett's body was found in the barracks surrounded by Mexican corpses, with Crockett's knife buried in one of them

Perhaps more myth than fact, and details notwithstanding, the historical David Crockett proved a formidable hero—a rough-hewn representative of frontier independence and virtue. In this regard, the motto he adopted and made famous epitomized his spirit: "Be always sure you're right—then go a-head!" We can include Crockett in a discussion that addresses the unexplainable traits of virtuosos, but at least as far as the Disney portrayal of him goes, I suspect charisma also played a role in his fame.

Charisma

When we refer to leaders as charismatic, typically we mean they personify a special quality of leadership that captures the imagination and inspires unswerving allegiance and devotion. Media commentators regularly describe charisma as the "X-factor," the enigmatic character of a person that suggests a combination of its two central meanings: compelling charm and divinely conferred power or talent—a spiritual gift. The term retains a mysterious, almost elusive quality that we reserve for those virtuosos that seemed inexplicably blessed with grace, favor, and influence. Benjamin Franklin serves as an example.

Benjamin Franklin, one of the Founding Fathers of the United States, a noted polymath, author, printer, statesman, postmaster, scientist, musician, inventor, satirist, civic activist, and diplomat, earned his place in history as a charismatic bon vivant. A leather-aproned shopkeeper who dined with kings, Franklin taught us that leadership, charisma, and good humor can march hand-in-hand to have far-reaching effects during and after a person's lifetime.

An ambitious urban entrepreneur who climbed the social ladder to claim his place in history, Franklin has winked at us since he first claimed prominence on America's historical stage. Franklin kept a twinkle in his eye as he offered his best political and pragmatic thinking to help us understand and accept profound truths that we might otherwise have rejected.

He was the only man who shaped all the founding documents of America: the Albany Plan of union, the Declaration of Independence, the treaty of alliance with France, the peace treaty with England, and the Constitution. He did so as he helped invent American's unique style of homespun humor, democratic values, and philosophical pragmatism.

We continue to experience both Franklin's influence and inventions today, perhaps because he continually reinvented himself. America's first great publicist, he was, in his life and writings, consciously trying to create a new American archetype. In the process, he carefully crafted his own persona, portrayed it in public, and polished it for posterity—all without the help of 24-hour news feeds.

He formed a dislike "of everything that tended to debase the spirit of the common people," all the while trusting the hearts and minds of his fellow "leather-aprons" more than he did those of any inherited elitism. Ironically, he personified intellectual elitism and intuitively embraced democracy. [3]

Passion

No discussion of avatars and exemplar would be complete without a nod to Steve Jobs, an American businessman, designer, and inventor. Best known as the co-founder, chairman, and chief executive officer of Apple, we remember Jobs as a pioneer of the personal computer revolution—the person who influenced forever the entire consumer electronics field.

Steve Jobs was not a model boss or human being, tidily packaged for emulation, however. Driven by demons, he could force those around him to fury and despair. But his personality, passion, and products were all interrelated, just as Apple's hardware and software tended to be, as part of an integrated system—a system propelled by a binary view of the world. Colleagues referred to this as the "hero/shithead dichotomy." You were either one or the other, sometimes in the same day. In Jobs's world, the same held true of products and ideas—"the best thing ever" or "shitty, braindead, or inedible." Stories of his tantrums, including rows with Bill Gates, have long dominated the halls of Apple, his bad behavior even prompting those who worked for him to establish an annual award for the person who best stood up to him during the previous 12 months.

Jobs could trace both his success and failure to the same root element: the refusal to accept that the bounds of reality and politeness applied to him. He and his team did the impossible because Jobs didn't realize it was impossible. Obsessed by perfection and compulsion, he wanted precision and excellence, and he didn't let a little thing like civility get in his way.

Like so many virtuosos, Jobs did not have an auspicious start. Plagued with boredom and social awkwardness, he had a hard time making friends and staying focused on the schoolwork that he found too easy. His parents agreed to promote him one grade, even though his test scores indicated he could function several levels above that. But even the single promotion exacerbated his social clumsiness. He and a select group of friends ameliorated both the boredom and low social astuteness with drugs and pranks. On one occasion, he and another friend put up "Bring Your Pet to School Day" posters throughout the school. The chaos the following day, with critters of every stripe running amok at the school, proved more the exception than the rule, however. Usually his pranks involved electronics—wiring microphones to eavesdrop on private conversations, for example.

His business beginnings did not hold any more promise than his academic ventures did, at least not initially. Starting Apple with his friend Steve Wozniak in 1975, the two men converted Jobs's father's garage into their manufacturing facility. The Apple II took the company from Jobs's garage to the pinnacle of a new industry. Restless and impatient, Jobs set a course that would take him on a wild ride for the next decade.

Throughout 1984, Jobs took a roller coaster ride with his sometimes-up/sometimes-down technologies, ideas, and sales. But his relationships remained on a predictable merry-go-round rotation. New people joined the spiral of quickly deteriorating associations, but few exited the ride. Finally, facing a disgruntled board who called for his resignation, Jobs left Apple in 1985 and founded NeXT, a computer platform development company specializing in the higher-education and business markets.

In a strange twist of fate, Apple purchased NeXT in 1996, and as part of the deal, Jobs was named Apple advisor. As Apple floundered, Jobs took control of the company and became interim CEO in 1997. Jobs's leadership saved Apple from near bankruptcy, and the company once again enjoyed profitability by 1998.

During the next decade, Jobs oversaw the development of the iMac, iTunes, iPod, iPhone, and iPad, and directed the establishment of Apple Retail Stores, iTunes Store, and the App Store. The success of these products and services, which provided several years of stable financial returns, propelled Apple to become the world's most valuable publicly traded company in 2011. Many commentators regard the reinvigoration of the company as one of the greatest turnarounds in business history.

Jobs provides a riveting story of the roller-coaster life and searingly intense personality of a creative entrepreneur whose passion for perfection and ferocious drive revolutionized six industries: personal computers, animated movies, music, phones, table computing, and digital publishing. He stands as the ultimate icon of inventiveness and applied imagination. He built a company where leaps of the imagination combined with remarkable feats of engineering.

Steve Jobs launched a startup in his parents' garage that he built into the world's most valuable company. He didn't invent many things outright, but he mastered the art of putting together ideas, art, and technology in ways that defined the future.

Not always nice and occasionally not very smart, he was a genius. His imaginative leaps were instinctive, unexpected, and magical. His insights came out of the blue, wherever that is. We will remember him as the greatest business executive of our era, and history will place him in the virtuoso hall of fame, "a Muse of fire, that would ascend the brightest heaven of invention" (*Henry V*).[4] Arguably, Jobs' passion drove him to succeed, but he started with a rare combination of abilities.

Raw Talent: Accept No Substitutes

Critics of Elvis and the Beatles would argue that they displayed nothing beyond mediocre musical ability—that is, no real talent or expertise. Their fans would dispute that claim, but even the most ardent among them could not convince a jury that Elvis displayed half the singing talent that an average operatic tenor contemporary of theirs, whose name we have forgotten, exhibited at every performance. However, both the pop musicians and the operatic tenors had raw talent: about that we can agree. In this case, maybe we can't put our finger on what separates those we consider exceptional from talented others. But sometimes we can—for example, in the case of Walt Disney.

In 1966, rumor suggested Walt Disney had been frozen at the time of his death—cryogenically preserved to await the day when science could revive him and cure his disease. Nothing could have been further from the truth. In fact, Disney started a fire in the entertainment world that continues to burn decades after his death. *The Saturday Evening Post* hailed him as the "world's most celebrated entertainer and possibly the best known non-political public figure." Perhaps no single figure so dominated American—and indeed, even global—popular culture as Walt Disney. Each year during his life and since his death, millions view a Disney movie, visit his theme parks, watch his television shows, listen to his recordings, buy his products, and read his books. He has held sway in much that has touched our lives, inspiring millions of people and affecting billions of dollars.

We cannot measure Disney's influence as a film producer, director, screenwriter, voice actor, animator, entrepreneur, and philanthropist by numbers or encomia, however. We can only understand it in terms of how profoundly he reshaped American culture and consciousness. In the late 1920s, he began reinventing animation, gradually turning it from a novelty that emphasized movement and elasticity into an art form that accentuated character, narrative, and emotion. During his lifetime, he received four honorary Academy Awards and won 22 Academy Awards from a total of 49 nominations, including a record four in one year, giving him more awards and nominations than any other individual in history.

Disney distinguished himself by being one of the first to use television as an entertainment medium, with *Zorro, Davy Crockett, The Mickey Mouse Club*, and *Walt Disney's Wonderful World of Color*, among his most notable works. He also changed the shape of American recreation with his Disneyland parks, re-conceptualizing the amusement park as a full imaginative experience—a *theme park*—rather than a series of diversions, shows, or rides.

In short, he redefined *pretend* in ways that had never existed before. Disney, more than any other American artist, described the terms of wish fulfillment and demonstrated on a grand scale how fantasy can empower us—how we can learn, in effect, to live within our own illusions and even to transform the world into those illusions. "When You Wish Upon a Star," his television theme song, served as Disney's anthem and guiding principle. He made his own dreams come true and recast the world to be nearer his heart's desire, modeling for us the very essence of entertainment, the promise of a nearly perfect word that conforms to our wishes.

Like most virtuosos, Disney seldom dabbled. Those who knew him grew accustomed to his intensity about that which intrigued him. Largely self-educated, he focused entirely on things that mattered to him—like animation. A man of contradictions, he was both nostalgic with his small-town, flag-waving patriotism and futuristic in his forward-thinking television programs that helped shape attitudes about technological change.

We can trace much of Disney's success to his ability to wring every possible profitable squeal and squeak out of such assets as the Three Little Pigs and Mickey Mouse—first by diversifying into wide variety of activities, then by dovetailing them so all worked to exploit another. Disney and his team didn't do anything in one line without giving thought to its likely profitability in other lines.

We will remember Disney as an entertainment virtuoso whose influence went beyond his initial area of concentration. He advanced film and television, but he also encouraged space exploration, urban planning, and historical awareness. In short, he demonstrated how one person can assert his will on the world and wish upon a star—the leader of the club that he made for you and me.[5]

Einstein's raw talent presented itself in the form of brilliance. Brilliant rather than engaging, few would characterize Albert Einstein as "charismatic." In fact, his nonconformist personality, his instincts as a rebel, his curiosity, passion, and aloofness cast him in a very different light. Instead of winning over his followers with the methods Benjamin Franklin and those of his ilk had used, the German-born theoretical physicist started a revolution in physics by developing the general theory of relativity. Many regard Einstein as "The Father of Modern Physics" and the most influential physicist of the 20th century. Best known for his mass–energy equivalence formula, $E = mc^2$, he also received the 1921 Nobel Prize in Physics "for his services to theoretical physics, and especially for his discovery of the law of the photoelectric effect," which was pivotal in establishing quantum theory within physics.

What made him a genius? His biographer Walter Isaacson posits that Einstein's brilliance sprang from the rebellious nature of his personality. His success came from questioning conventional wisdom and marveling at mysteries that struck others as mundane. This led him to embrace a morality and politics based on respect for free minds, free spirits, and free individuals.

Lest we get carried away and start to believe that rebellion alone will define greatness, let us call to mind the plethora of people in the 1960s who rebelled against virtually everything and simply annoyed people in the process. Many who attempted revolution merely ended up being revolting.

Conversely, Einstein ushered in the modern age by questioning conventional wisdom. He published more than 300 scientific papers, along with more than 150 non-scientific works, and his great intelligence and originality have made the word "Einstein" synonymous with genius.

When President Eisenhower eulogized Einstein, he declared, "No other man contributed so much to the vast expansion of 20th century knowledge." The *New York Times* ran nine stories and an editorial about Einstein's death, declaring, "The most thoughtful wonderer who appeared among us in three centuries has passed on in the person of Albert Einstein."[6]

Einstein requested cremation for his remains, except his brain. That organ journeyed to numerous labs and held the attention of laudable brain specialists. Compared to other genius brains in the study, the scientists found some notable but not profound variations and finally concluded that the relevant question was how Einstein's mind, not brain, worked.

He was a loner with an intimate bond to humanity, a rebel immersed in reverence. As his biographer Isaacson noted, this "imaginative, impertinent patent clerk became the mind-reader of the creator of the cosmos, the locksmith of the mysteries of the atom and the universe."[7] It all started with his raw talent, but it didn't end there.

How to Grow a Virtuoso

Clearly, the world needs more virtuosos, but they don't seem to spring forth, fully formed from the La Brea Tar Pits. Nature or nurture, something happens early in life to cause these exceptional creatures to roam the earth.

In 1968, sociologist Robert Merton explained the origins of exceptional people when he formulated the theory of "cumulative advantage," also known as the "Matthew Effect" because of its foundation in the gospel: "For to all those who have, more will be given, and they will have an abundance; but from those who have nothing, even what they have will be taken away."

We've seen countless examples of this theory in practice. Successful people seem to engender more success. Superlative students get the finest teachers. The most gifted athletes receive the best coaching. The rich get richer, and the poor get poorer. Certainly, I'm the first to give Lady Luck her due, and I value the role opportunity plays in the lives of the greats. If Beethoven had been born in the wilds of Africa, with no piano in sight, civilization might have been robbed of one of the great musical geniuses of all time. Similarly, if Michelangelo's family had owned a bakery, perhaps we'd now have a world-class torte that bore his signature instead of the Sistine Chapel. But none of this paints a credible picture of how virtuosos come to walk among us.

To better understand the process, I recently interviewed former space shuttle commander and retired United Space Alliance CEO Dick Covey. Covey, a former Air Force "brat," had no special advantages in his childhood, such as private schooling or tutoring. Rather, like most military kids, he attended whatever school happened to be where his dad happened to land—some good, some not quite so good.

Although advanced in his studies, he was not what a teacher would call a "good" student—but not because he couldn't learn. On the contrary, teachers found him challenging because he learned so fast that he quickly became bored with the pedestrian pace of the high school classes in northwest Florida. He did have direction and focus, however. He had read everything written about Alan Shepherd and knew he wanted to be an astronaut.

At the suggestion of his father's friend, Covey applied to and was accepted by the Air Force Academy. When he entered in 1964, he immediately enrolled in an accelerated math and science program to prepare him for eventual graduate work at Purdue in astronautical and aeronautical engineering. Had he not enrolled in this program immediately after entering the Academy, he would not have qualified. From an early age, he received and heeded sound advice, and he constantly thought ahead.

Covey received a master's degree in seven months and then began undergraduate pilot training in March 1969. Even though he had never flown and competed with scores of those who had, he graduated first in his class for academics and second overall, behind a student who entered pilot training with 1,700 hours. After graduation, he took more training to learn to fly three fighters in as many years.

After completing 339 combat missions in Southeast Asia and accumulating more than 1,000 hours of flight time, Covey applied to test pilot school—the path he had determined would lead him to the Astronaut Corps. His dreams came to fruition when NASA selected him from thousands of applicants to fill one of 15 slots.

During his 16 years with NASA, Covey had the opportunity to hire those who would follow in his footsteps, so during the interviewing process he began to develop a sense of what separated the good from the great. Although all applicants had proven their skills as pilots and test pilots, the demands of flying in the Astronaut Corps often uncovered things that separated those who would be successful from those who would not make the grade.

Sometimes an inability to learn at an extremely fast pace caused the astronaut to falter, but more commonly those who didn't make it exhibited what Covey called "poor judgment." Sometimes this poor judgment showed up in their professional decision-making or behavior, but more often it became evident in their personal lives. Although one could argue that personal lives and professional lives should be separate, Covey said he asked himself, "If your judgment is so poor in that situation, and you put yourself and the Astronaut Corps in that compromising position, how can I trust you to make good decisions in other circumstances?" No one wanted bad press for the people or the NASA mission.

Occasionally a personality trait or tendency stood in the way of success for the astronaut. Quirky behavior or a "me first" orientation were death knells for the relationships that formed a critical part of the teamwork demanded of the astronauts. As Covey pointed out, when you spend long periods of time together working under intense constraints, you have to believe in your team members.[8]

Each industry and league within the specific industry defines the specifics of virtuosity, but one thing remains clear. Those who learn quickly, give others reason to trust them, and exhibit strong character, overcome the major hurdles that impede the advancement of the good performers. Covey had some of the elements of cumulative advantage. He was born with brains, his father had smart friends who could give him sage advice, and he was the right gender (in his era, only males were allowed into the Air Force Academy, fighter squadrons, and NASA).

When botanists find a rare orchid, they scrutinize the characteristics of the superior seed and then research the environmental constructs that led to the exquisite flower: soil conditions, weather, temperature, moisture, and so on. Similarly, when we encounter the human equivalent, we should examine the salient factors that led to the development of the virtuoso.

Nature or nurture? The answer doesn't matter. By the time people enter a profession, the die has been cast. Whether you're making a hiring or promotion decision, you can infer candidates' potential for stellar performance from their track record of performance and good judgment, because the best predictor of future behavior is still past behavior.

Covey's high school teachers may have found him challenging, but I doubt many found his success surprising. He identified an objective, listened to wise advice, delayed reward, and then committed himself to those who would develop his greatness. Does the credit for a bumper crop go to the plant or the farmer? Probably both.

The Role of Resilience and Courage

Ordinarily, the definition of a term states what it *is* rather than what it *is not*. However, trying to find agreement among researchers about the definition of "resilience" is akin to asking poets to share one opinion about the word "love." Researchers do agree, however, about what resilience *is not*. It is not sickness; it is not pessimism; it is not failure to adapt. For the purpose of this discussion, therefore, I will define resilience as "the capacity to cope with and recover from adversity." It implies an ability to "bounce back."

What constitutes resilience? It all starts with how we communicate within ourselves. Those who have studied trauma victims tell us, and my research on the Vietnam POWs confirms, believing in something "bigger" helps. This form of faith creates a sort of unifying pattern that organizes a person's deepest convictions about him- or herself and others, and it involves an individual's firmest core understanding of truth. It is the canvas upon which the artist paints, the unseen order the artist "sees" but that others see evidence of.

Why can some people bounce back from adversity while others languish? Why can some leaders help those around them find the path through the crisis when others can't? To find the answers, I decided to study heroes, courageous people who had overcome some sort of significant adversity and emerged healthy and hardy. I wanted to draw from the experiences of these exemplars in order to advise leaders about ways they can help themselves and others weather the storms that inevitably affect organizations. To find these answers and to better understand how resilient people handle adversity, in 1995, I moved to Pensacola to study the repatriated Vietnam prisoners of war at the Robert E. Mitchell POW Center. I found answers— surprising answers.

February 12, 2013, marked the 40th anniversary of the repatriation of 566 Vietnam POWs—Operation Homecoming. Researchers had reason to worry about this group because evidence from prior captivity situations indicated high incidences of post-traumatic stress disorder: 50 to 82 percent among WWII POWs, and 47 to 90 percent among Korean War POWs. Because of these staggering numbers, in 1976 the Navy began a study of 138 Vietnam POWs. In 1996, during the 20-year follow-up, the researchers found that only about 6 percent of the Vietnam POWs in the study had received a diagnosis of PTSD. We expected better results. We didn't anticipate how good.

The data are astonishing when comparing the Vietnam group to the other captivity situations, but the statistics held other surprises too. To give a frame of reference, at any given time, about 1 to 4 percent of the population in a metropolitan area experiences symptoms of PTSD caused by violent crime, natural disasters, or other traumas. In other words, this group of POWs, whom the captors imprisoned, tortured, isolated, and beat, had no significantly higher incidence of PTSD than average people in the average city in America. How can that be?

The study participants told me that four main forces in their lives helped them remain resilient:

1. A belief in God.
2. Patriotism, a belief in America even as she fought an unpopular war.
3. Dedication to each other.
4. A sense of humor.

These men personified the importance of never losing altitude, airspeed, and ideas at the same time—a popular expression among aviators. Even though their captivity indicated that they had obviously run out of all three in a literal sense, in a metaphorical or psychological sense, they sustained all three: to maintain their perspective, build relationships, and creatively solve unfamiliar problems.

Research tells us that we want power and authority over our futures. When we perceive control in our lives, we feel optimistic and secure. When we don't, we feel persecuted. We start to feel undermined, overwhelmed, and immobilized—powerless.

Even though their captors *victimized* them, the Vietnam POWs didn't consider themselves victims and never developed a victim's mindset. Instead, they took control of the few things they could control. Their captors told them when, what, and if they could eat, and when they could shower, sleep, and use the toilet. They had no authority over the everyday things we take for granted. But they had power in a few areas: their humor perspective, their commitment to one another, and their involvement in a well-defined structure. In short, they built a culture of honor and responsibility—a system influenced by their values and cemented through their behaviors.

Laura Hillenbrand's bestseller *Unbroken* offers another example of courage-defining exceptional behavior and outcomes. She recounts, on a May afternoon in 1943, an Army Air Forces bomber crashed into the Pacific Ocean and disappeared, leaving only a spray of debris and a slick of oil, gasoline, and blood—and a young lieutenant, Louis Zamperini, the plane's bombardier, stranded in a life raft. So began one of the most extraordinary odysseys of the Second World War.

In his early years, Zamperini had been a sneaky and incorrigible delinquent, often breaking into houses, fighting, and fleeing his home to ride the rails. A change happened in his teens, however. He began to channel his defiance into running, discovering an extraordinary talent that carried him to the Berlin Olympics and within sight of the four-minute mile. But when war came, the athlete became an airman, beginning a journey that would lead to his doomed flight and a war against the elements.

Zamperini survived the crash of the plane, but ahead lay thousands of miles of hostile open ocean, deadly leaping sharks, a foundering raft, thirst, hunger, starvation, enemy aircraft, and eventual incarceration in a Japanese POW camp.[9] Driven to the limits of endurance, Zamperini answered "desperation with ingenuity, suffering with hope, and brutality with rebellion." Hillenbrand chose Zamperini as the topic for her bestseller for much the same reason that she chose the story of the horse Seabiscuit for her previous book: they exemplify exceptional performance and illustrate how courage can cause ordinary people to accomplish extraordinary things.

On November 16, 2010, President Barak Obama awarded Army Staff Sergeant Salvatore Giunta the Medal of Honor, making him the first living U.S. soldier since the Vietnam War to receive the honor.

The Medal of Honor, the highest military decoration presented by the United States government to a member of its armed forces, was created during the American Civil War. In order to qualify for this distinction, recipients must have distinguished themselves in three ways:

1. The deed must have involved risk of life.
2. The deed must be so conspicuous as to clearly distinguish the individual above his or her comrades. It must go above and beyond the call of duty, and had the service member not undertaken the action that led to the nomination, there would have been no criticism.
3. The deed must be witnessed by at least two people.

Obviously, one of the criteria for receiving the Medal of Honor does not apply to business leaders—no one expects you to put your life at risk. But the second and third criteria do.

Courage and heroism mean different things to different people, but most definitions share a common thread: being a hero involves taking a chance, gambling with uncertain outcomes, and going where uncertainty lies. It isn't for everyone, but those who display it usually also feel passion about what they want to accomplish.

Optimism and hope help the virtuoso paint credible pictures of possibilities. They know they can't control everything, but they have the fortitude to survive what they cannot change. They see desired outcomes as attainable and continue to exert efforts for engendering those outcomes, even when obstacles present themselves. They don't give up. They show us that *expecting* good actually causes it to occur.

Psychologist Martin Seligman introduced the term "learned helplessness," which impairs adaptation and coping. Learned helplessness refers to a generalized expectancy that events are independent of one's own responses. Consequently, individuals believe their coping behaviors futile. When this happens, people start to perceive that factors beyond their control will determine their destiny. Instead of searching for ways to overcome adversity, these people accept it. Because, in their minds, they are powerless to overcome the problem, they give up. This, of course, reinforces the idea that they were helpless in the first place, and the perceptions of helplessness and pessimism increase.[10]

Star performers attended a different school—the one that teaches learned optimism. They didn't fall victim to the misguided self-esteem movement, which started in California in the 1960s and persists to this day, either. From governing bodies to the classroom, millions of children have learned that feeling good about themselves is much more important than actually achieving. This movement has made "competition" a dirty word to many, but not to virtuosos. They figured out that achievement causes high self-esteem, not the other way around. They were smart enough to realize that not every kid in the league deserved a trophy, and not everyone person deserved the same grade. They found their strengths and leveraged them. That's what bolstered both their self-esteem and their optimism: "I can succeed if I realize what I'm good at and concentrate my efforts on being the best."

Understanding Stars

It all starts with a person's innermost thoughts and feelings, but it doesn't end there. A strong social support network allows faith, optimism, and hope to flourish. Most of the star performers I've known love their work, but they love their loved ones too. They don't always excel at work/life balance, but when they go home, someone lets them in. Many whom I've encountered, studied, or coached attract people who understand their passion—often other virtuosos of a different ilk. They create personal lives that sustain their work and professions that often pay handsomely, so they nourish their personal relationships with both their presence and the financial rewards that often accompany exceptional performance.

Top performers don't sail through life unscathed; on the contrary, many have overcome some significant adversity. This ability to bounce back proves to them that they can recover from whatever life throws at them, so they develop confidence. They see misfortunes as temporary setbacks and aberrations, not patterns. Overcoming adversity helps to foster a sense of achievement and ego strength. People who have never conquered, withstood, or overcome have reason to doubt they *could*. But those who have look adversity in the eye and dare it to "give it your best shot."

The aforementioned star performers correspond to my perceptions of excellence in a variety of venues. I offer these examples because they represent three things: the various ways in which people excel, the traits that unite them, and the traits that distinguish them. For instance, you'll find a competitive spirit common among many stars and absent in others. Certainly, if we were to include some of the sports figures and business icons that have graced the front pages of our newspapers for the past century, we'd find numerous examples of those who showed us their best work while under pressure and while experiencing stiff competition. On the other hand, if you were to list Mother Teresa, Martin Luther King, and Nelson Mandela, you might draw a different conclusion. I never met or assessed any of these three icons, yet I will hazard a guess that something other than "winning" spurred them in their excellence—perhaps because they defined "winning" differently. Sometimes we witness virtuosity simply because people want to produce excellence. They don't need to see someone else lose in order to win, and they don't need to think someone else inferior to be superior.

Understanding stars requires a journey through their lives and into their hearts. That requirement led me to interview a true virtuoso, internationally renowned operatic soprano Christine Brewer. When not gracing the stages of symphony halls and opera stages in the United States and around the world, Brewer lives in a sleepy little southern Illinois town called Lebanon, the home of her alma mater, McKendree University, and my childhood home.

Successful people of all stripes have a similar story. They have a God-given talent that they hone continuously and religiously, but seldom do they have enormous advantages in their lives. Brewer did not come from famous parents; her hometown didn't even have a McDonald's, much less a symphony. (I'll borrow a line from author Dan Pink to tell you that even during the 1960s, Lebanon was a hotbed of social *rest*.) However, after discovering her talent, she steadfastly committed to ongoing learning, and hired the best coaches and teachers to help her along the way. Brewer's story doesn't differ from the other stars I've researched. On the contrary, it offers a road map for those who want to stand out or be outstanding.

Brewer began her operatic career with the Opera Theatre of St. Louis in the much-sought-after role of tree-holder. Actually, the company hired her to sing in the chorus, but she realized she'd need to do more if she hoped to learn quickly from the best around. So, she volunteered for any and every job that let her be around the principal artists. Her debut literally involved standing on stage holding a tree.

Of course, the decision-makers in St. Louis saw something else—a rare talent. Although singled out early for the distinctive quality of her voice, Brewer did not start singing the very difficult Wagner pieces she's now famous for until she had passed her 40th birthday. She simply hadn't been ready, but she practiced and studied until she was.

In the previous chapter, I said that stars consistently deliver above-average performance. That's one of the prerequisites for others' considering a person a star, but Brewer and those like her do more. They distinguish themselves. They offer rare talent plus the "it" factor. They take risks, exude confidence, and force others both to remember them and to take them seriously.

For example, several years ago, after finishing lunch with a friend in St. Louis, Brewer received a frantic call from her agent that soprano Debbie Voigt could not sing the very difficult *Missa Solemnis* by Beethoven in Boston that night. They were sending a plane.

Brewer packed a bag, found her music, and started rehearsing on the plane. As the pilots called the tower for instructions, Brewer vocalized and spoke with James Levine, the conductor, asking whether they would perform in "Church Latin" or "German Latin." Five hours later, as Brewer stepped onto the stage in Boston in gown and makeup, she heard the strains of Beethoven's difficult music, a piece noted for its characteristic disregard for the performer. She regretted her hair that night, but no one in the audience seemed to focus on that particular detail when they heard

Brewer's distinctive voice filling the room. Could others have filled the famous Debbie Voigt's shoes that night? Perhaps a few, but cancelling the performance would have been a surer bet.

What equipped Brewer to rescue the Boston production? That takes us to the core of understanding the exceptional performers among us. In addition to embodying the traits I outlined in Chapter One, Brewer offered some other characteristics that personify stars. First, she had educated herself in her field, so learning the details of the Boston performance happened quickly. She knew the part, so she only had to find out the specifics for this production. Second, because she has a proven track record of delivering stellar performances over a period of time, she felt confident that she could do the same that night. Third, when it comes to music, Brewer thinks fast.[11]

Conclusion

We use words like "thought leader" or "expert" to describe some kinds of stars. But most don't think of themselves as "an" expert but rather as "the" expert. In tennis parlance, they "force" errors in the competition and don't make "unforced" errors themselves.

Stars often suffer general self-doubt or self-censorship, but it doesn't interfere with their realization that they can perform at a level that others can't. Often they hold themselves to unrealistic standards—expecting superhuman performance of themselves. But frequently these expectations exist with good reasons: they do what they do well and evaluate themselves on exceptional performance only in their areas of expertise. When composer extraordinaire Frederic Chopin was asked why he composed only for the piano, he answered, "That's what I'm good at. Why should I do anything else?" I should note that Walter Isaacson wrote three of the biographies I've cited in this chapter. Taking a note from Chopin, Isaacson has distinguished himself as a literary virtuoso who specializes in biographies—the thing he's good at.

A governor is a device used to measure and regulate the speed of a machine, such as an engine. Today, BMW, Audi, Volkswagen, and Mercedes-Benz limit their production cars to 155 mph. Stars have no such governors; they don't arbitrarily set limits for themselves, and they don't let others install such devices in their psyches.

Even though all the examples I've cited here represent famous people, don't confuse fame with virtuosity. How many Hollywood stars could we mention that have, for some unaccountable reasons, demanded top dollar at the box office? At one time, we would have put Mel Gibson on a list of stars along with the Baldwin family and Charlie Sheen, but they all seem to spontaneously combust periodically. Many of the famous would fail the ethics part of the virtuoso test, and we have observed how few notables have led truly happy lives, if multiple marriages and divorces give us any indication.

Organizational stars are a breed apart, but they share many of the characteristics of the avatars and exemplars I have cited here. When you know what to look for, you'll equip yourself to build the galaxy of shooting stars that your competition can't stop.

Chapter Seven

Falling Stars and Snakes in Suits

When exceptional people lack ethics, empathy, remorse, and loyalty to anyone but themselves, we start to think of them as tragic losses—stars that have fallen. Stars tend to over-achieve. Whatever they do, they do to the nth degree. When they fall, they plummet quickly and profoundly, and they often take the organization with them. These people often enter the organization as rising stars and corporate saviors, only to abuse the trust of colleagues and supervisors, leaving the workplace in shambles. Then we consider them snakes.

These people snake their way into an organization because initially they appear to be a dream come true—right up until they turn into nightmares. At times psychopathology explains why top performers fail—and why we start to think of them as snakes, but at other times, flawed judgment, insufficiently developed interpersonal skills, eccentricities, and a simple bad match for the job more clearly clarify the reasons for the stars' professional demise. Leaders can help some falling stars but not others, but only when they separate falling stars from the snakes in suits.

Beware Snakes in Suits

Calm under fire, psychopaths excel during times of chaos. They embrace change and the upheaval it brings. Unfortunately, the general state of confusion that change brings can also make psychopathic personality traits—the appearance of confidence, strength, and calm—look like the answer to your problems. Attracted to fast-paced, high-risk, high-profit environments, these snakes move quickly, often ignoring rules that cause impediments to the goals they want to achieve while adhering tenaciously to protocols that don't really matter. In short, they confuse people but simultaneously give them hope.

The ability of clever snakes to hide their true natures makes spotting them difficult. They creep into the organization and quickly burrow in undetected, often camouflaged by chaos. We admire many of their traits, taken in moderation. For instance, they have a talent for reading people and for sizing up situations quickly, abilities that help them excel in sales or negotiations.

Also, they frequently display advanced verbal agility. Con artists who can convert others with their rhetoric, they present elaborate schemes, complete with convincing arguments. They remain vigilant in the pursuit of a target, always alert to circumstances or enemies that could block their success. This tendency toward pomposity and suspicion forms the Achilles' heel of the narcissist.[1] As we remember from Greek mythology, the fortune-teller informed Thetis, Achilles' mother, that he would die in battle. To prevent his death, his mother took Achilles to the River Styx, which offered powers of invulnerability, and dipped the baby into the water as she held him by the foot. In adulthood Achilles survived many great battles, but one day an enemy shot a poisonous arrow into his heel, and he died shortly after.

The Achilles myth holds significant truths for pathological virtuosos. Often their exceptional ability in one arena causes them and others to perceive them as invulnerable in others. However, they run the greatest risk of isolating themselves at the moment of success. Because they constantly look out for enemies, sometimes degenerating into paranoia when they experience extreme stress, they have difficulty trusting others and eventually give those around them reason to question their trustworthiness.

Because they have mastered "impression management," social inhibitions don't restrain them, so they meet people easily and stand ready to jump into conversations. They exude confidence, which causes the listener to accept at face value both the message and the delivery method. Their insights into the psyche of others, combined with a convincing verbal fluency, allow them to change their personas as adeptly as their serpentine brethren molt their dead skin.[2]

Narcissism, the psychopathology you'll most often find in rising stars with personality disorders, describes the trait of excessive self-love, based on self-image or ego. The term comes from the Greek mythology of Narcissus, a hero renowned for his beauty and cruelty, a person who scorned those who loved him. The gods punished his excess by causing him to fall in love with his own reflection.

Modern-day narcissists consider themselves different—special. They manipulate, break rules, exercise power, and control others with displays of temper. A reasonable dose of healthy self-esteem and self-respect allow people to balance their needs in relation to those of others. It spurs them on to greatness because they expect it of themselves. Taken to a pathological extreme, however, it causes people to have a grandiose sense of self-importance and entitlement, a preoccupation with power, a need for excessive admiration, and a lack of empathy. Their tendency toward grandiosity and distrust creates their Achilles' heel, and often their demise.

Narcissists thrive in chaos, so they tend to create it. Considering themselves bullet-proof, they disregard caution and listen only for information they seek. They can also lose the ability to see cause/effect relationships in their personal decision-making. While they often excel in this ability when they play the role of dispassionate outside critic, when the decisions involve them personally, they can't see connections between their behavior and outcomes. Sensitive to criticism themselves, narcissistic leaders shun emotion and keep others at arm's length, refusing to trust or believe even the most well-intended caution from others. They don't care what others think and won't tolerate dissent.

Until recently, *The Diagnostic and Statistical Manual of Mental Disorders* classified narcissism as a personality disorder. The 2013 edition, however, eliminates it and several others form the list. One of the sharpest critics of the DSM committee is a Harvard psychiatrist, Dr. John Gunderson, an old lion in the field of personality disorders and the person who led the personality disorders committee for the current manual.

Asked what he thought about the elimination of narcissistic personality disorder, he said it showed how "unenlightened" the personality disorders committee is. "They have little appreciation for the damage they could be doing." He said the diagnosis is important in terms of organizing and planning treatment.[3]

The diagnosis does not hold particular relevance to this discussion, however. A narcissist called by any other name will still remain as destructive to good order and discipline, and the reader should realize that, even if diagnosed correctly, pathological narcissism does not respond to treatment.

History provides numerous examples of social and political leaders who created their own downfall because they allowed the hallmarks of narcissism—ego or a sense of importance—to cloud their judgment. Clinton's lies under oath, Nixon's Watergate cover-up, and Kennedy's infamous Bay of Pigs invasion showcase how a leader, sometimes one who has otherwise led impressively, can create his own permanent or temporary collapse. More recent examples of narcissists fashioning their own ruin—like New York Representative Anthony Weiner—grace the pages of *The Wall Street Journal* nearly every day.

Often pathological narcissism shows up early in a career, but from my experience, it frequently surfaces later, sometimes in someone who has been fabulously successful for decades. Clever and calculating, narcissists know how to con the system, so when they lack power, they don't attempt to exercise it. Instead, they wait for the promotion or status change to wreak havoc at a crucial juncture.

In leadership positions, these venomous top performers allow the perks of power to override their moral sense. Many of them experience a weakened moral sense of "right" in the face of excessive temptation and easy access to authority. Others among them feel justified in reaping rewards, arguing that their extravagances seem excessive only to those who have little hope of enjoying such gains. Still others embrace the self-serving mantra that "greed is good" and that success at any cost to others is justifiable. This group, snakes in suits, displays pathology rooted in lying, manipulation, deceit, egocentricity, and callousness.

What can you do personally and professionally to avoid these destructive reptiles who masquerade as exceptional people? First, be aware of their existence. They try to rush relationships because they can't sustain the "act" too long. A trusting personal or professional relationship takes time to build and doesn't have as its foundation inappropriate disclosure, lies, or manipulation. If a person seems too good to be true, that's probably the case. Snakes don't form relationships; they take hostages.

Second, look for patterns of unresponsive behavior. Snakes can pretend to listen and show empathy when they don't have a vested interest in the outcome of a conflict, but in the long run, they choose the self-serving action, ignoring the feelings of others.

Finally, stay away from creatures you suspect might be snakes. When I see a legless reptile slither across my path in the garden, I don't stop to do an identification. With alacrity I take myself someplace that the snake isn't. That advice applies to the two-legged kind, too. You can't reform a snake. You can get away from it, or it can bite you. On rare occasions, however, you might need to defang it.

Defanging the Snake

As previously stated, when dealing with a snake, you have two alternatives: get away from it or get bitten. I stand by that recommendation. However, in the organization, sometimes these options don't exist. The snake happens to share DNA, family associations, or leadership positions. Sometimes you don't want a snake bite, but escape doesn't seem realistic either.

Narcissists, the snakes we most often encounter in the workplace, both appeal and appall. You fall prey to them when you cross the threshold of their natural habitat, the corporation, and fail to recognize them. Your second mistake involves your entering the fray unarmed and unprepared. You'll cope more readily if you spot snake traits early in the relationship and adjust your behavior accordingly. Here's what to look for:

1. Lack of Empathy

Narcissists simply don't feel empathy, nor do they care how they affect you. Therefore, you can only hope that understanding the concrete consequences of their behavior might influence them.

Years ago my dad worked for Sam, a narcissist business owner. Sam had quite a temper and a tendency to take out his rage on anyone in his line of sight. He screamed and swore, behaviors that my father found unprofessional and demeaning. He tried to explain this to Sam, to no avail. Finally, Dad just quit. (I should add that as the CFO, Dad had identified millions of dollars of cost savings and revenue streams his first year with the company. Sam couldn't afford to let this virtuoso leave.)

Sam begged him to come back, but Dad said he needed a $10,000 raise. Sam gave it to him, and things remained calm until Sam had his next temper tantrum. Dad quit again, and Sam rehired him at the same sign-on bonus. This happened five times! Fifty thousand dollars poorer (in the 1970s when that was a lot of money) and finally insightful about consequences, Sam learned to control his temper, at least with my father.

2. Demeaning Behavior

Because they lack even a basic understanding of what others feel, narcissists don't hesitate to demean. Sam tried this tactic but didn't succeed because my father had power in the relationship. Sometimes you will, and sometimes you won't. In either case, you can refuse to take the debasing feedback by holding up a mirror.

When I received this kind of feedback from my former narcissistic boss, I simply said, "Tom, you just accused me of intellectual laziness. I'm not lazy in any form, so let's look for another explanation. I didn't write the report the way you wanted for two reasons. One, I didn't know your expectations, and two, I've had no experience with this kind of report writing." I then suggested ways to prevent this from happening again. Tom backed down, as bullies often will.

Remember: insecure to their very cores, narcissists have to tear down others to build themselves up. In their minds, your talent, contributions, and very nature have to be less laudable than theirs at all times, so they keep a keen eye for anything negative that they can say to or about you to help them feel better about themselves.

3. Self-Absorption

"Give-and-take" does not exist with narcissists. They don't want to hear about your success, see a picture of your new baby, or talk about your vacation. However, they love to give advice and opinions. You can't rely on them for support and encouragement, but narcissists will readily share ideas that make them look smart and insightful.

4. Superiority

Using objective criteria, in organizations you'll often find the narcissist is the smartest, most talented person in the room. Otherwise, why would people have put up with him for so long? Frequently, in specific arenas, these people offer what others can't. However, they don't limit their superiority needs to the narrow niche in which they perform their best. They want to shine in every galaxy they enter. Also, they tend to exaggerate their achievements and to minimize those of others. You can control the narcissist's reactions if you simply don't challenge their number-one position. Let them pretend to be the smartest person in the room.

5. Rigidity

The expression "my way or the highway" exists because of narcissists. Once they make up their minds, don't try to change them. You can, however, get there first—before rigor mortis sets in.

Narcissists aren't open-minded, but they like to think they are. Often, if you approach them with a specific, transparent request, you can put an idea on the table before they squash it: "Jane, would you give me five minutes to convince you to ___?" You'll spin up Jane's receptivity if you make her think she's doing the right thing to listen to you. The next to the last thing you should say to a narcissist is "I don't agree." The *very* last thing you should say? "You're wrong."

6. Lack of Remorse

Often in the wrong but never in doubt, narcissists don't admit mistakes. They seldom feel remorse, so they don't express it. You'll never hear the words "I'm sorry" or "I was wrong." If you expect an apology or an admission of guilt, you'll be disappointed. You need to hold steadfastly to the goal of not becoming the scapegoat, however.

7. Non-Compliant Behavior

Narcissists believe two things about rules: "They are really important for others, but they don't apply to me." Expedient and self-indulgent, narcissists feel no obligation to follow the standards and protocols that pertain to lesser humans. They feel entitled to special treatment and can't be bothered with procedures or codes of conduct. Therefore, explaining the rules to them won't work, but clearly describing the consequences will: "Carl, the industry regulations clearly indicate ___. If you violate this, I won't be able to protect you."

8. Suspicion

Mark Twain once said that a man never looks behind a door unless he's hidden behind some himself. Narcissists have much to hide. Skeptical and distrustful, they question things that others accept at face value. They eagerly lie, cheat, and steal, so they assume others do too, and they don't want to become the victim of an unscrupulous person. So, give them answers before they ask the questions. They won't necessarily respond favorably to your transparency, but at least you'll avoid the frustration of yet another "third degree" interrogation.

9. Unrealistic Demands

You can't make a snake happy; don't try. It will frustrate you and annoy the snake. Also, don't try to understand snakes. Trying to comprehend their behavior is a little like trying to smell the color nine. It can't be done.

When we work for or with snakes, we often develop the enabling mantra of "If I could just ____, he would be happy." This sort of wrong-minded thinking will get you nowhere. No matter how high you jump, the narcissist can set the bar higher. Manipulative by their very nature, narcissists read both people and situations accurately. They know how to control and exploit your desire to accomplish goals, build relationships, and achieve success. They will use all knowledge against you.

Instead of jumping higher, communicate reality: "Joe, I'd like to reach that goal too, but the facts tell a different story. We've never increased sales by that much in a six-month period. What I can do is ____." Narcissists feel entitled to the best of everything. If you can convince them that, while not perfect, you're the best available, you can take steps in the defanging process.

We hesitate to offer this much candor to a narcissist because the conversation quickly goes in an unpleasant direction. Somehow we cling to the hope that bad news will get better with age. It won't. When you eventually have to tell the narcissist the bad news, he'll be angry about two things: the bad news itself and the unpleasant surprise. Better to take the smaller hit earlier.

10. Need to Be Liked

Counter-intuitive as it may seem, most snakes want to be liked, especially by those whose opinion they value. That may or may not be you. In general, they divide the world into two groups: those for me and those against me. If they typically see you as "for me," you'll get further because they demonize those against them. Therefore, every chance you get, play to the ego. Compliment them and call attention to their superiority. Warning: You'll hate this, and you'll enable more unproductive behavior. But it doesn't matter. Enabling or disabling, their behavior won't change.

As you review this list of "symptoms," realize that identifying narcissists is not a yes/no situation. Rather, narcissism exists on a continuum.

Under pressure or facing a deadline, a hard-charging go-getter can appear un-empathic, demanding, and rigid. But this same person, in ordinary circumstances, will impress you with his warmth and responsiveness. He, therefore, doesn't qualify for membership. Pathology exists when the narcissist's behavior exists across the board in most situations. Generally speaking, a true narcissist will routinely display eight of the 10 aforementioned behaviors. You can assume that a person who displays some of the above once in a while may simply be overusing a strength to the point that it becomes a weakness—the improvement opportunity I most often identify in the top-performing people I coach.

For example, Jack personified a task-oriented, focused, achievement-driven top performer. The firm's top rainmaker, Jack consistently exceeded expectations, but he annoyed people. He interrupted, failed to listen, and disregarded opinions that didn't match his own. In all fairness, Jack's ideas usually were better than those of others. He's just that smart. To his peers, however, Jack seemed self-absorbed, rigid, superior, and entitled; yet I maintain he isn't pathologically narcissistic.

Why? His tendency to seek approval caused him to want to change. Narcissists want approval, but true narcissists want *you* to change and learn to like them the way they are.

When I presented Jack with irrefutable data that others did not respond favorably to his tendency to talk his point of view to death while failing to draw out the opinions of others, he expressed his willingness to learn new skills. His peers reported immediate and profound improvement. Two years later, I still think Jack talks too much, but he wouldn't qualify for a star who had fallen—much less a snake in a suit. No one accused Jack of demeaning behavior, and even though he didn't consider himself wrong too often, he did admit guilt and apologize, when appropriate.

To defang a snake, you have to put your hands in its mouth and put yourself at risk of a bite. That's why I echo my original advice. Given a choice, run from snakes. You cannot change them, and they won't change themselves. But you can improve your skills for identifying them before you have a chance to run.

The Snake Marking Guide

We'd like to think that if we met someone who didn't have a conscience, we would size up the situation quickly and accurately. If we were to encounter the corporate equivalent to the fictitious Hannibal Lecter, the evil psychiatrist Anthony Hopkins made famous in *Silence of the Lambs,* we believe that, like FBI agent Clarice Starling, we would not only assess him accurately, we would know what to do to overpower him. And we'd be wrong. Snakes in the organization don't look creepy; they're often handsome. They don't wear identifying markers or T-shirts that let you know to stay away; they wear designer clothes. They aren't creepy; they're suave and often powerful. These traits make snake identification difficult but not impossible. You just have to know what to look for—and how to distinguish a snake from a fallen star.

Flawed Judgment

Recklessness and the headstrong desire for the gratification that it brings have caused many leaders to strike a Faustian bargain that led them in a diabolical direction. Recklessness, an identifiable behavior among pathological narcissists, explains how and why leaders can fall prey to stunningly poor lapses in judgment. Add power to the mix, and you have a formula for a once highly respected star to end up in the jailhouse, the doghouse, or the poor house.

Narcissistic-driven judgment has contributed to the ruin of religious leaders such as Jimmy Baker and Jerry Falwell, and corporate titans like WorldCom's Bernard Ebbers and Enron's Kenneth Lay. Like the mythical Icarus, who disregarded his father's advice and soared too close to the sun, these once-admired leaders offer tragic examples of hubris and failed ambition. But how do you attempt to soar above competitors without melting the wax on your wings? Smart risk-takers define the playing field for everyone else by taking calculated risks and anticipating the future, not by idiocy and folly. Smart risk-takers seek the advice of others, accepting criticism of their ideas and learning from their mistakes.

In 2011, New York City Congressman Anthony Weiner stated he would rather not bring the FBI or U.S. Capitol Police into the investigation of the bizarre Twitter post of a lewd photo of a man's groin that went to 45,000 of his followers. When asked whether the picture was of him, Weiner responded, "I have photographs. I don't know what photographs are out there in the world of me." Couldn't that response jump-start an eye roll? Really? You don't know if you own pictures of yourself in your drawers and whether they are on your phone for easy access? By 2013, another scandal had surfaced, and Weiner resigned, but not without dragging himself and his wife through the mud.

Two weeks prior to the 2011 Weiner episode, we learned of Arnold Schwarzenegger's love child, and a week later news of France's Dominique Strauss-Kahn's alleged rape of a hotel maid dominated the headlines. Two weeks after Weiner's second unfortunate foray in the media, San Diego Mayor Bob Filner resigned amid allegations of 17 inappropriate sexual encounters. (But he did check himself into a rehab facility for two full weeks, a typical snake thing to do—pretend remorse and reform.)

You shouldn't assume that all flawed judgment signifies a snake, however. For example, on September 16, 2008, when General David Petraeus formally turned over his command in Iraq, then Secretary of Defense Gates stated that Petraeus "played a historic role" and created the "translation of a great strategy into a great success in very difficult circumstances." Gates also told Petraeus he believed "history will regard you as one of our nation's greatest battle captains" and bestowed Petraeus with the Defense Distinguished Service Medal. Two years later, after Stanley McChrystal made inappropriate comments in an interview with *Rolling Stone* magazine, President Obama announced that Petraeus would succeed General McChrystal as the commander of U.S. forces in Afghanistan

Petraeus relinquished command of U.S. and NATO forces in Afghanistan on July 18. He received the Defense Distinguished Service Medal and the NATO Meritorious Service Medal for his service. By all objective measures, Petraeus should have graced historical archives as one of the bravest and strongest leaders of the 20th and 21st centuries. That all changed.

In 2011, President Barack Obama nominated and the Senate confirmed Petraeus as the new director of the Central Intelligence Agency. His tenure in the position would prove short-lived when he joined the ranks of falling stars after his affair with Paula Broadwell was discovered.

Why do these men in power—men whom we elected to office or lauded as great—behave badly? In the cases of Generals Petraeus and McChrystal, I see no evidence of a pattern of narcissism, but clearly we can agree they showed a lapse in judgment, even though each general had a commendable track record for making stellar decisions until he did. Unfortunately, we often remember people for their lapses in judgment, not their previous exemplary record for it.

Sometimes you'll be shocked by a star's bad decision because it will serve as an outlier, as it did for the generals. At other times, you will wonder how someone could have turned a blind eye to the pattern of bad decisions and ask yourself, "How can people who show so little judgment and so little honor rise to such heights in politics, business, sports, and entertainment?" Here are my observations:

- Often powerful men gain dominance because they take risks when others won't. These same men can become powerfully reckless. When they stand at the brink of their grandest achievements, they feel the rush of adrenaline from the uncertain outcome they face and forge ahead. They take more risks, but they assess risk differently, too—enjoying the excitement of the adventure while minimizing the dangers. Sometimes their daring causes a breakthrough solution or cutting-edge product that saves the day, which further emboldens their risk-taking tendencies.

- Deviation from traditional approaches often explains success. When evidence indicates a man has the ability to walk the path less taken, he can develop a narcissistic attitude that "the rules don't apply to me."

- Prominent people tend to be persuasive and competitive. Once they identify an objective, they overcome obstacles to attaining it, even if that means hard work for long hours. They woo investors, enchant employees, and captivate the media. These abilities and this same focus and determination can work against them when they pursue objectives that involve lapses in professional judgment and personal conduct.

- Power draws enablers and sycophants—people who will tell these people of power what they want to hear—but they don't suffer naysayers, detractors, or contradictory information. In fact, often the enablers will take over and shield the person in power from critics and disbelievers. In my work with CEOs, I often caution them not to believe all they hear and never to assume their jokes are as funny as the laughter in the room would imply.

- Supremacy in any arena brings opportunity. Tiger Woods, JFK, Elvis Presley, and John Edwards—all had chances for sexual liaisons simply because of their fame. These kinds of men simply have more occasion to behave recklessly in other ways, too, and when they don't have the self-control to offset the opportunities, they find themselves in trouble.

- As self-absorption and self-importance intensify, empathy wanes. Anticipating consequences of behavior takes a back seat to the hedonistic pleasure of the moment. No concern about how an act will affect the innocents in the equation ever shows up on the internal radar of this kind of person—not until he stands before a nation crying and asking forgiveness.

Too often public figures destroy *themselves* when competitors or distracters couldn't. I often wonder if these once-great men have subconsciously set up an internal competition to bring down the victor. Low self-esteem stands at the root of much of the imprudence. In fact, low self-esteem probably explains why most people don't succeed. They fear both failure and success—the two imposters.

On the heels of the original Anthony Weiner story, the local Fox affiliate asked me to join the anchors to discuss why men in power behave badly. They flashed pictures of John Edwards, Arnold Schwarzenegger, and former Congressman Weiner. Initially the questions centered around things like "What were they thinking?" but eventually progressed to "How do women in power behave badly?" If you're trying to recall a sex scandal involving a powerful woman, you've probably already given up. They just don't occur.

As I said in the interview, women in power behave badly in other ways. Sarah Palin embarrassed herself in her interview with Katie Couric.

Ms. Palin hadn't prepared, so she reacted defensively to the question "What do you read?" Later she failed to fulfill her obligations as governor of Alaska and resigned before her tenure had expired.

CIA documents indicate agency members gave a total of 40 briefings for lawmakers over a period of several years on the question of waterboarding. House Speaker Nancy Pelosi's name appears once, as having attended a session on September 4, 2002, but she bluntly accused the CIA of misleading her. Either she forgot or she lied—neither would stand up to a virtuoso litmus test.

Leona Helmsley, a billionaire New York City hotel operator and real estate investor, had a reputation for tyrannical behavior that earned her the nickname "Queen of Mean." In 1989, she was convicted of federal income tax evasion and other crimes. Martha Stewart went to prison for insider trading, and Hillary Clinton engendered disfavor among many when she attempted health reform as the First Lady.

It all makes for dull copy. No nude photos, no love children, nothing we'll flip the channel to see. The lessons remain universal, however. In each of these cases—male or female—the person in question designed his or her fate. Whether you operate in the political or organizational arena, the same rules apply: the rules apply. You can't break the law, appear ignorant, fail to uphold your obligations, overstep boundaries, or break the law. If you do, the court of public opinion will find you guilty.

On the other hand, we realize that few saints dwell among us. Sarah Palin still makes the news on occasion; Nancy Pelosi has retained power in the Democratic Party well into her 70s; Hillary Clinton has held positions of high esteem, including the role of Secretary of State; and Martha Stewart continues to make us all look bad in the kitchen.

In a never-ending attempt to bring about improvement, thought leaders consistently and constantly challenge traditional approaches and conventional wisdom. They experiment, theorize, press for new solutions, and pioneer innovation. Yet, they never lose sight of the value of principles and custom, even while pushing for change. They realize that winning demands a balance between taking risks and playing it safe.

Underdeveloped Interpersonal Skills

More widespread than psychopathology or flawed judgment, weak communication skills often explain why an otherwise exceptional person doesn't progress. It all starts with empathy—or the lack of it. A lack of empathy, another hallmark of narcissism, explains why many executives fall and fail. Pathological narcissists lack empathy, and by definition so do sociopaths and psychopaths. But not all those who are un-empathic have personality disorders. Some simply lack insight. Others just don't care.

Empathy builds on self-awareness, because the more people are open to their own emotions, the more adept they will be at reading those of others. However, when people are confused about their own feelings, others' emotions absolutely bewilder them. During interactions, they lose the nuances of conversation—the notes and chords that weave through the exchange and often communicate far more than the actual words themselves.

In my work with executives, I have found people often demonstrate one or both of two kinds of empathy. The first kind I call "no dog in the fight" empathy, which occurs when a person has no vested interest in the outcome. This emotional reaction requires no true understanding or compassion, but it causes people to express appropriate reactions to someone's bad news, dutifully show up at funerals, send flowers to congratulate, and generally display social astuteness to match the occasion. People who possess *only* this kind of empathy don't lack sensitivity in all circumstances, just ones that involve someone contradicting them.

The second kind of empathy, which I call "invested empathy," causes people to identify closely with others and their problems. People who feel this kind of empathy truly feel concern for others and misfortunes, value close emotional ties, and celebrate others' triumphs. From a business standpoint, people who demonstrate this kind of empathy tend to be able to put themselves in another's shoes, even during conflict, and to imagine what that person might feel or fear in any interaction.

The inability to show empathy, probably the most rampant derailer among star performers at the executive level (aside from limited cognitive abilities), manifests itself in a variety of destructive ways. Often it shows up as a complete inability to listen to, much less consider, an alternative point of view. At other times, the un-empathic merely seem emotionally aloof. They do not allow feelings to intrude on their decision-making and prefer impersonal relationships to close ones. Generally unresponsive to those around them, they show little compassion for other people's problems, especially when the problems create a threat to a leader's goals or repute. Executives who cannot or will not express empathy regularly put their relationships at risk, causing those around them to question whether they want to maintain an association.

Successful leaders—those who consistently retain top talent and build trusting business relationships—take the time to understand the issues, their people, and the underlying emotions. They invest the time to probe for understanding and then patiently work through solutions that help both the quality of the decision and the development of the direct report. Executives who are too busy to do either often find themselves acting as talent repellents instead of talent magnets.

Lack of Self-Awareness

Often underdeveloped interpersonal skills have their foundation in weak intrapersonal abilities: people simply don't know themselves. Of course, the evidence of poor self-awareness manifests itself through interaction, so we become aware of people's deficiencies when they communicate—or fail to communicate—emotions, or they do not succeed in responding to the emotions of others. Empathy builds on self-awareness. The more we are open to and aware of our own emotions, the more capable we become in reading the feelings of others.

We often describe this set of circumstances as a lack of empathy, but often something more plays a role. Sometimes *alexithymia* explains emotional flatness. Harvard psychiatrist Dr. Peter Sifneos, who first identified and named this personality construct in 1972, coined the term from the Greek words to mean "lack of" (*lexi*) and "emotion" (*thymia*). These people simply have no words for emotions because they don't understand them. The core characteristic of alexithymia is marked dysfunction in emotional awareness, social attachment, and interpersonal relating.[4]

Stars frequently demonstrate advanced degrees of dispassionate thinking—the very trait that distinguishes their decision-making abilities and equips them to look at information rationally, see patterns, and get to the core of unfamiliar, complicated problems. Overused, however, this dispassion can prove disabling. They simply overlook emotional reactions or considerations as irrelevant or unimportant.

When I coach stars, I often encounter this phenomenon. The vast majority of these exceptional people, of course, don't display a pathological dose of alexithymia any more than they do other problems. It simply interferes with the advancement of some people at some level. Self-awareness exists in us much as blood pressure does. We all have a blood pressure—sometimes in the normal range, sometimes in the too high or too low range. (Unlike blood pressure, however, I've never met anyone who was too self-aware, just too self-absorbed).

Business leaders become particularly frustrated when they encounter an exceptional performer who doesn't seem to self-regulate well. Consider Don, the executive I introduced in Chapter One. A large company called me to coach Don because he showed such great potential, and some decision-makers thought he represented the future leadership of the company. Highly talented and motivated, this virtuoso had clearly established himself in the succession-planning pipeline, except for one fly in the ointment. The same leaders who hoped Don could someday run the company also informed me that if I couldn't "fix" Don, they would fire him.

Don had grown up in China, coming to the United States to attend graduate school. He had known very little English before coming to the United States but learned quickly. He also learned the industry in which he took his first job and the requisite skills to advance quickly to a top management role.

Don fundamentally lacked self-awareness—knowledge of his own emotions. He could say whether something felt "good" or "bad," but he lacked nuances in language to go much further. Perhaps language and cultural differences could explain much—but not all—of the trouble.

After Don completed the cognitive and personality assessments, I had all the proof I needed that the decision-makers had called this one accurately. As I mentioned previously, in my first conversation with Don I asked, "Do you want to run this company or get fired? Because both are likely scenarios." Don didn't seem particularly surprised, but then, as an exceptionally smart guy, he had probably dispassionately examined all possible outcomes. He committed to me that he would do whatever I advised because he wanted to run the company—and sooner rather than later.

Don stands as one of my all-time success stories. His bosses reported the quickest turnaround in behavior they had ever witnessed. Within six months, Don had received two promotions and had set his sights on the executive chair.

In our work together, Don had to do two things. First, he needed to become aware of his own feelings—both the positive and the negative. Then, he had to imagine what the feelings of others would be in a given exchange. Further, he needed to realize how his behavior influenced the reactions of others so that he could moderate and monitor his message sending. Similarly, he had to listen more attentively to the messages he received. In short, Don improved his interpersonal communication patterns only after working diligently to discover his own feelings—no easy accomplishment, and one people can seldom do without a coach or therapist. But Don had one thing going for him: he *really* wanted to succeed and had no fear of it.

Fear of Success and Failure: Falling Star Derailers

Sometimes star performers fail because they were really snakes in suits all along. At other times stars fall for other reasons. Sometimes they tumble because they fear success, and sometimes they plummet because they fear failure. Two sides of the same coin, both find their roots in low self-esteem, not serpentine identity.

Counterintuitive though it may seem, many otherwise exceptional people harbor feelings of insecurity. While they excel in one arena of their lives, and enjoy the feelings of confidence that come from those achievements, general self-regard and self-respect may wane. My research indicates that the engine of self-doubt drives the *behaviors* that cause the problems for the virtuosos. Often others don't understand the emotions behind the behaviors, because all objective measures indicate the top performer should feel confident and secure. But observable evidence will contradict this conclusion. When I coach stars who indicate these emotions might be the source of their problems, I look for the root cause but then give them feedback related to how the emotions manifest themselves in day-to-day functioning and leading. For instance, often overly cautious, insecure stars never put themselves at risk to fail.

People who win over the long haul embrace success, but they also don't fear failure. Take Harry Statham, for example. In 2010, Harry Statham, member of the National Association of Intercollegiate Athletics Basketball Hall of Fame, enjoyed his 1,000th win after 44 seasons at McKendree University. At the time of his 1,000th win, he was unmatched by any other men's basketball coach at a four-year college or university in the United States.

Statham and his players know the value of the foul. The best players, the ones who started and ran up the scoreboard, also fouled in every single game. The best didn't foul out and leave their teammates short-handed, but they knew how to nuzzle the line between success and failure.

Many of my business clients can't get this balance. They fear failure so dramatically that they won't take a chance or risk. They stay in their comfortable, safe area, not rocking the boat, not fouling, but not driving up the score either. Similarly, they don't try new things, like more education or an expanded base of knowledge. Sure, they want the raises and the perks, but they won't risk anything to get them.

Fear of failure probably explains why most people never reach their potential. Immobilized by irrational thoughts that somehow they won't be successful if they make a bad call or attempt the unknown, they won't venture into unchartered seas. Because I don't work with police officers, who absolutely could get killed for a mistake, I can say categorically that my clients' mistakes won't have life-or-death consequences.

I'm not talking about recklessness. I'm suggesting you push yourself to the point of discomfort—and then take two more steps. My mantra: "If you aren't fouling, you aren't playing hard enough." The current economy causes us to worry even more. But I suggest we would never remember Harry Statham and those of his ilk for their uniqueness if they hadn't been willing to put fear of failure aside and foul once in a while. It all comes down to good judgment and appropriate risk-taking. Get these wrong, and the number of stars on your bench won't matter. Exceptional talent will leave or fail to play a big enough game.

Challenge the status quo, but don't crush it for the sake of doing something different or a desire for excitement. Every basketball player realizes that if you never foul, you aren't playing hard enough; however, five fouls will land you on the bench. Your organization deserves better than a leader who fouls out or fails to deliver.

Snake or a Bad Match?

Sometimes stars who excel in one role or company simply don't match the altered conditions of different surroundings or roles. Carly Fiorina offers a perfect example. Fiorina, an exceptional performer from the start, joined

AT&T in 1980 as a management trainee and quickly rose through the ranks at AT&T and Lucent, eventually becoming the CEO of Hewlett-Packard.

In 1998, *Fortune* magazine named her the "most powerful woman in business" in its inaugural listing, and she remained in that magazine's listing throughout her tenure at Hewlett-Packard. In July 1999, HP named Fiorina chief executive officer, making her the first woman to lead a Fortune 20 company. In 2004, *Time* magazine included her in the *Time* 100, an annual list of the editors' choices for the 100 most influential people in the world. *Forbes* listed her 10th on its list of the World's 100 Most Powerful Women for 2004. One year later, just six years after she took the helm, the board of directors for Hewlett-Packard forced Fiorina to resign as chief executive officer and chairman following differences with the board of directors about how to execute HP's strategy.

What led to her demise? Perhaps the skills that explained her success until the CEO position simply proved inadequate for the bigger game HP demanded she play. Maybe other factors also contributed to her not being a good match.

The company's controversial deal to buy Compaq in the spring of 2002—after a bruising proxy fight led by one of the Hewlett family heirs—did not produce the shareholder returns or profits she had promised. Fiorina either failed to anticipate the implications of and obstacles to her decision to buy Compaq, or she simply didn't pursue feedback that may have revealed errors in her judgment or resistance to her plan. Had she explored multiple perspectives, particularly those of the Hewlett family, she may have been able to identify probable consequences and to avert the temporary plummet in HP stock, widespread job losses, and her own downfall. Both HP and Fiorina paid when this once highly regarded virtuoso failed to match the requirements at her new job.[5]

John Sculley offers another example of a virtuoso—a top-paid executive with an impressive track record—who ultimately failed because of a bad match. He served as vice president and then president of PepsiCo from 1970 to 1983, and in 1977 he was named Pepsi's youngest-ever president. He will probably be best remembered for the "Pepsi Challenge," an advertising campaign that used heavily advertised blind taste tests to compete against Coca Cola to gain market share. The results, Sculley claimed, proved Pepsi-Cola tasted better than Coca Cola because participants consistently chose Pepsi's soft drink as the preferred product. Of course, critics criticized the tests, as critics do, but that didn't detract from the marketing genius of the ads, from Sculley himself, or from the fact that Pepsi gained market share from Coke.

In 1983, Steve Jobs lured Sculley away from Pepsi with his legendary pitch: "Do you want to sell sugared water for the rest of your life? Or do you want to come with me and change the world?" The timing seemed perfect because Apple's president, Mike Markkula, wanted to retire and feared that Jobs lacked the discipline and temperament needed to run the company. Sculley offered traditional business acumen, a proven track record, recent success, and stability—some leadership characteristics that Jobs lacked

It worked. Sales at Apple increased from $800 million to $8 billion under Sculley's management, and he was credited with helping the industry push the personal computer beyond office desktops and into the homes and onto the laps of America. "His contribution to the field was significant," said Nicholas Negroponte, the director of the media laboratory at the Massachusetts Institute of Technology. "He can almost single-handedly be credited with America's re-entry into consumer electronics."[6]

The match didn't continue in a heavenly fashion, however. Apple forced Sculley out in 1993, amid eroding margins, diminished sales, and declining stock prices, but the problems began long before that. Although their initial relationship was warm and cordial, eventually a power struggle developed between Jobs and Sculley. Sculley tried to "contain" Jobs and limit his ability to launch expensive forays into untested products, but that didn't work. Rather than submit to Sculley's direction, Jobs attempted to oust him from his leadership role at Apple. Sculley discovered that Jobs had been attempting to organize a putsch and called a board meeting at which Apple's board of directors sided with Sculley and removed Jobs from his managerial duties. The directors eventually decided Sculley couldn't manage Apple's product line and forced him out too. Of course, Jobs eventually returned to Apple and led the company to greatness before his premature demise.

This story, perhaps more than any other, highlights the crucial role "match" plays in a star's success. Sculley had been enormously successful at Pepsi, and Jobs had been successful both before and after Sculley. But the two didn't mix well. They hadn't figured out their respective roles and responsibilities, and kept stepping on each other's toes. In later interviews, Sculley wondered aloud whether the board should have named Jobs as the

CEO and the reporting relationship had been different. We'll never know. We'll also never know what would have happened if Sculley had asked Jobs to come back during his tenure. We do know that these two exceptional people couldn't occupy the same space at a given time, and all involved suffered because of that. With 20-20 hindsight, we can agree that this was a case of a bad match, but in the throes of the situation, how can you tell if you're herding snakes or trying to rescue falling stars? And what should you do to ameliorate the situation?

Can Coaching Help?

If you suspect pathological narcissism of someone in your organization, absolutely do not offer this person coaching. Two things will happen. First, coaching has not and will not ever save someone who has a personality disorder. Second, by their very nature, narcissists excel at self-serving behavior. While they don't welcome coaching or mentoring, the smart ones that we would have considered virtuosos in the first place realize that the offer of coaching may also communicate conditions for continued employment or advancement. In other words, they may not want the coaching, but they will pretend to accept it in order to manage their impressions. Also, they may learn just enough to mask the problematic behavior without ever attempting to eradicate it. The troublesome behavior will seemingly disappear, only to return later—often with no notice.

Taking psychopathology out of the picture, you'll want to consider whether the person is valuable enough to warrant the investment of your time and perhaps the dollars required to hire an external coach. Before accepting a coaching assignment from my clients, I encourage them to take the updated self-scoring assessment at *www.henmanperformancegroup.com*.

Here are behaviors that respond well to coaching and mentoring:

- Coaching skills. Often virtuosos have learned skills so quickly that they don't really understand how they acquired them. Similarly, they don't know how to teach somebody else to do what they do. Therefore, exceptional performers frequently need guidance about how to serve as internal coaches to their direct reports and others in their chain of command. Once they understand the specific benefits of their involvement, they usually embrace coaching and excel at it.

- Delegation skills. Teaching delegation skills can offer more challenges. Usually top performers want to do the job themselves—that's why they pursued a particular line of work or specialty in the first place. Asking them to coach someone else to accomplish this work, and then to further suggesting that they turn over control of the outcome, can rankle the best. They will fear the loss of control that delegation demands, and they will mourn the loss of the work they loved. If exceptional performers can't or won't respond to observations that they should delegate, carefully re-evaluate whether that person is cut out for leadership. Perhaps she or he should remain a high-contributing solo performer.

- Communication skills. Most virtuosos excel at message sending. However, empathically and patiently listening to others may try them. Their tendency will be to jump in and fix things, even when they should uncomplainingly allow peers and direct reports to draw their own conclusions in their own time.

- Giving feedback. Although they frequently excel at message sending, even articulate, verbally agile virtuosos can struggle with how and when to give developmental feedback to their direct reports. Many exceptional people have grown up in a pleasant environment—filled with admiration, adulation, and compliments. They simply lack the skills to turn negative feedback into a constructive exchange that benefits the listener and leaves the boss feeling useful and productive.

- Interpersonal skills. Many of the virtuosos I have coached have introverted, shy personalities. They don't meet people particularly easily, and they aren't comfortable in many social settings—at least until they have time to acclimate. They need help in establishing rapport more quickly and simply making small talk more adeptly.

- Teambuilding skills. By their very nature, virtuosos tend to start life as solo performers, often out-performing those around them. They don't naturally gravitate to group settings, so sometimes they don't understand how to build cohesion and establish accountability for a team of their direct reports.

There are other behaviors that resist change. Normally a list of things that I define as "uncoachable" skills would include the cognitive abilities related to learning potential, strategic thinking, decision-making, quantitative facility, problem-solving, and critical thinking. However, by my definition, virtuosos demonstrate these cognitive skills. Similarly, they would have made their motivation, achievement drive, and integrity evident. They may lack creativity or detail orientation too, but because these are less important to overall performance, the fact that they resist coaching won't prove problematic.

Recently another consultant asked my advice about how to set metrics for a client she intended to coach. In the laundry list that comprised his "get well" program, she listed unethical behavior, bad judgment, and weak interpersonal skills. I pointed out that the weak interpersonal skills would respond to coaching, but nothing else on the list would.

Then I asked a question that she didn't want to answer: "Why in the world would you want to equip an unethical person with bad judgment with the interpersonal skills that would enable him to more adeptly influence others and quickly move his bad, unethical ideas to action?"

I don't ever coach a candidate who has displayed either lack of integrity or bad judgment. Neither responds to feedback, no matter how gifted the coach, and neither will improve in the long run. Fire for ethical violations; don't mentor to reduce them. Poor performance will eventually ruin your organization, but unethical behavior can cause an immediate and profound ruination.

You can't fix a top performer's deep psychological problems, nor should you try. Your ultimate concern should be with their actions and results—and the effect these people and these actions have on others. Some people don't really want to change; others have damaged their reputations too much within your organization to remain salvageable. But, by their nature, stars have given you reason to believe in them, their contributions, and their talent. If they have one serious shortcoming that consistently limits their effectiveness, but it is not a fatal flaw, why not hire an external coach to help? The cost will be minimal compared to the price of trying to replace one of these exceptional people.

Conclusion

Most of us have encountered a snake in the wilds of an organization. Some, like cobras, strike their victims suddenly and kill them instantly. Others, like boa constructors, slowly crush their victims over a period of time. Not all snakes have the same markings, and not all thrive in the same kind of environment. Therefore, we literally don't know where to look for them, but we should understand what to look for.

Often a typical pre-employment interview won't spot them. I've assessed several men for C-suite positions who had passed the scrutiny of an executive recruiter, a VP of HR, and their future peers. In each case, the candidate hid his true nature. But on several occasions, I noticed the candidate's surly response to a receptionist or administrative assistant who had to report that the taxi back to the airport would be delayed. Because I do in-depth assessments of C-suite candidates, I have the advantage of mountains of data to help me identify snakes before my clients hire them. But so often, after I call attention to behaviors, the client realizes the signs were there all along. If a person can't behave courteously to a receptionist at the time of a job interview, what are the chances he'll uphold the rules of civility once he's hired?

Usually snakes will camouflage their behavior until they find themselves comfortably ensconced within the doors of the prey organization—complete with golden parachutes and generous severance agreements. If there's one thing snakes understand, it's how to protect themselves.

We shouldn't confuse any snake with a falling star, however. Who among us would forgo the chance to hire someone like the three generals I mentioned? These men dedicated themselves to the service of their country. They and their families made tremendous personal sacrifices for them to realize the results they achieved. Yet, all tripped at the finish line of their careers. When we can identify snakes and distinguish them from falling stars—or better yet, stars who are about to fall—we take significant steps in improving our organizations and giving everyone concerned a fair outcome.

Part Three

The Leader

Chapter Eight

Aligning the Stars

In astronomical terms, we know that the nearest star to Earth is the sun, which serves as the constant source of most of the energy on our planet. We also know that novas are stars that draw attention because they brighten very significantly very rapidly. More dramatic even than the nova, the extremely luminous supernovae can cause a burst of radiation that often briefly outshines an entire galaxy before it fades over weeks or months, sometimes causing the star itself to destruct. Although rare in number, during its short role on the celestial stage, a supernova can radiate as much energy as the sun will emit over its entire life span, often causing the creation of new stars.

Like their celestial counterparts, human stars create energy in the organization, often causing explosions of ideas that send shock waves throughout the industry. The human supernovae also influence the formation of other luminaries. To position your company for growth in a global economy and to create the agility to respond to future unforeseen turbulence, you need to create the atmospheric conditions that will allow the unvarying sun to shine, the novae to influence, and the supernovae to explode. But traditional approaches won't work. Instead, you'll need a new way of thinking about how to draw the best from these brightest, which will require your thinking of your legacy in new ways—ways that will foster trust, evoke excellence, and drive the business.

Why Traditional Approaches Won't Work

Conventional views of leadership are somewhat superficial—a list of expectations, characteristics, traits, and values that sets us up for disappointment and proves unrealistic. We too often expect our leaders to provide a bigger-than-life parental figure who rescues us from our messy selves, a hero who can set things right when we can't. Stars don't have these fantasies and wouldn't welcome this sort of leadership, even if it were humanly possible. Stars want exemplary leaders, ones who inspire, guide, and encourage; but they neither want nor demand the human equivalent of a Border Collie because they don't consider themselves sheep-like.

In years past, young men entered the same profession as their fathers, and they remained there until retirement. People developed a sense of community and identity with their peers and coworkers. The company's leader acted as a kind of mayor as much as he did the sheep dog. Words like "visionary" and "innovator" didn't usually apply. The word "leader" had more to do with status and power than responsibility or accountability. Times have changed, but our needs haven't.

A New Need for Community

Research tells us that the needs for inclusion, affection, and control shape us throughout our lives. Traditionally, the combined contributions of the family, the church, the community, and the organization satisfied our needs. Now, with dispersed teams, virtual workplaces, divided families, and decreased church attendance, satisfaction of basic human needs falls overmuch to the organization. Additionally, when people work long hours—as stars tend to do—they have fewer hours for leisure and life balance. Consequently, they rely more on those at work to fulfill their basic needs. That's one of the reasons organizational culture has become more significant.

Among other things, culture defines a coherent value system for those in the organization. As author and leadership theorist John Gardner put it, "The community teaches. If it is healthy and coherent, the community imparts a coherent value system. If it is fragmented or sterile or degenerate, lessons are taught anyway—but not lessons that heal and strengthen. It is community and culture that hold the individual in a framework of values; when the framework disintegrates, individual value systems disintegrate."[1]

When culture fades, individuals often experience a loss of meaning, a sense of powerlessness. They lose the conviction that they can influence the events of their lives or community. Too often, highly accomplished people, left without moorings by the disintegration of group norms and torn from any context of shared obligations, have gotten drunk on self—or they have left to find a community of people who will augment and elevate their best work.

Last spring I visited a restaurant in a location that attracts young people during spring break. Each table boasted different sweatshirts with different university logos, but each table had at least one person wearing a shirt with writing on it. The TV in the bar flashed both live March Madness games and updates from games not showing. Virtually everyone in that establishment wanted to feel connected to the excitement of basketball games or to a university he or she attended or hoped to attend. It's what we do. We crave connectedness.

Those who aspire to lead stars recognize that even though they won't usually wear a company logo on their shirts, stars want others to identify them as a member of something important. Groucho Marx once said, "I don't want to belong to any club that would have me as one of its members." Stars have a different mantra. They want to boast about their membership in an organization, and they respect the person that recognizes their talents and manages the culture in which it can thrive.

Stars require a new paradigm, one that sees leadership as a *process*, not a title—something that confers responsibility, not just privilege and power. This process involves the leader shining the light into the darkness, inducing others to pursue organizational objectives, and influencing outcomes—exceptional outcomes. They inspire because they model the way through exemplary behavior and stellar decision-making. In Chapter Three, I outlined the constructs of a stellar organization: excellence, talent, culture, and strategy. As the leader, you have three main responsibilities related to creating this kind of organization: make decisions, develop the bench, and drive the business. When you tie these three to the requisite aspects of the stellar organization, you'll take huge strides in developing a new and different approach to leadership. Decades ago Einstein said, "Perfection of means and confusion of ends seems to characterize our age." The age to which he referred has long passed, but the syndrome of which he speaks has not.

The time has come for something better; history holds the key to what that something should be.

Sometimes It's the Boss's Fault

At the end of the Vietnam War, a considerable strain of skepticism aimed at national and Air Force leadership ran through the fighter force. Some pilots concluded that the leadership did not care about them. Less than five years after the war ended, an exodus of pilots, displeased with the Air Force, voted with their feet as they walked into commercial airline jobs. Then-captain Ron Keys expressed their collective feelings eloquently in a paper that has since become famous as the "Dear Boss" letter.

Keys and others in the Tactical Air Command had received orders to write down their concerns so they could be forwarded to General Creech. Keys had no intention of putting in his papers to get out of the Air Force and hadn't even planned to write anything, except that his boss said it was both mandatory and urgent that he do so.

In September 2012, I had the privilege of hearing retired General Ron Keys address the Air Force Association conference when he recalled the circumstances of the now-famous "Dear Boss" letter.[2]

I have summarized the letter:

Dear Boss,

Well, I quit. I've finally run out of drive or devotion or rationalizations or whatever it was that kept me in the Air Force this long. Why leave flying fighters and a promising career? I'm resigning because I'm tired. Ten years and 2,000 hours in a great fighter, and all the time I've been doing more with less—and I'm tired of it.

I thought I could do it just like all the rest thought they could... and we did it for a while...but now it's not the job. I can do it. I did it. I can still do it—but I won't. I'm too tired. Tired of the extremely poor leadership of our senior commanders—people who can't even pronounce esprit de corps. And let me clue you—in the fighter business when you're out of esprit, you're out of corps—to the tune of 22,000 in the next five years.

Why hang around in an organization that rewards excellence with no punishment? I've worked hard. I've established myself; I can do the job better than anyone else—does that make a difference?

It's the organization itself. A system that allows people that lack the aptitude or the ability to do the job. Once they're in, you can't get them out. So now we have lower quality people with motivation problems, and the commander won't allow anyone to jettison them. If you haven't noticed, that leaves us with a lot of people in fighters, but very few fighter pilots.

And the clincher—integrity. Hide as much as you can...particularly from the higher headquarters that could help you if only they knew. They never will though—staff will see to that: "Don't say that to the general!" Ah well, put if off until it becomes a crisis—maybe it will be overcome by events. Maybe if we ignore it, it won't be a problem.

And that's why I'm resigning...long hours with little support, entitlements eroded, integrity a mockery, zero visible career progression, and senior commanders evidently totally missing the point (and everyone afraid or forbidden to inform them).

I've been to the mountain and looked over and I've seen the big picture—and it wasn't of the Air Force.[3]

After writing the letter, Ron Keys went on to serve 27 more years in the Air Force, retiring at its highest rank. A virtuoso by any measure, he held responsibilities at the highest level of the Air Force, accumulated more than 4,000 flying hours (including more than 300 hours of combat time), and commanded several squadrons and wings, the Fighter Weapons School, and organizations reporting directly to major commands.

The Dear Boss letter stands as a legend because it captures the frustrations exceptional performers have always felt and outlines what those who lead them should do differently. Top performers want access to their bosses, resources, other motivated people to work with, career progression, and integrity. Most of all they want bosses who listen to them—to what they say and don't say—in other words, a new way of leading.

A New Model of Leadership

Though stellar organizations require the qualities traditionally associated with leadership, such as intelligence, toughness, determination, and vision for success, the list doesn't offer a complete picture of what leadership requires. Leading others to accomplish results also requires self-awareness, self-regulation, motivation, empathy, and social skills. Common sense suggests, and my personal observations confirm, that without a responsive, fair orientation, people can have the best training, an analytical mind, and an endless supply of great ideas, but they still won't be the kinds of leaders that will attract and retain the stars.

What explains the differences between leaders who rise steadily through the ranks and derailed executives whose careers mysteriously jump the track short of them reaching their potential? When people quickly find the fast track, show they can get the job done, and offer enough intellectual acumen to succeed and *still* don't lead effectively, we have to suspect that flawed leadership *style* is the culprit. Even those leaders who have studied management theories find themselves wondering what they should actually do to improve.

The F^2 Leadership Model explains the *behaviors*—not skills, talents, attitudes, or preferences—executives need to display to be effective. F^2 leaders indicate a balanced concern for both task accomplishment and people issues. They are firm but fair leaders whom others trust, leaders who commit themselves to both relationship behavior and impressive results.

The F^2 Leadership Model shows the tension that exists between the opposing forces of firmness and fairness and challenges us to ask ourselves how to have both a clear task orientation and an appreciation for the people who achieve the results.

Both *prescriptive* and *descriptive*, the four-quadrant model allows leaders to understand their own behavior *relative* to their direct reports, but by its nature, it implies a preferred way of behaving. The model explains what leaders *should* do to be effective instead of merely describing what they tend to do or prefer to do. Keep in mind, the model represents an ideal, so no person fits into one quadrant all the time. Leaders who want to be more effective strive for F^2 behavior, but they occasionally drift into one of the other quadrants. When this happens, problems occur.

More receiver-oriented than leader-driven, the model keeps the leader's focus on those who count—the stars in the organization who will define success. It helps leaders figure out whether they are losing balance—tending to act too much like either Genghis Khan or Mr. Rogers.

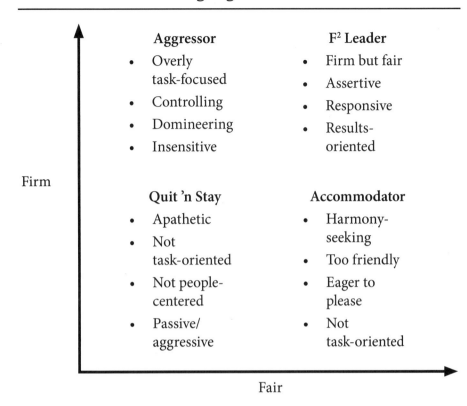

Firm

Aggressor	F² Leader
• Overly task-focused	• Firm but fair
• Controlling	• Assertive
• Domineering	• Responsive
• Insensitive	• Results-oriented

Quit 'n Stay	Accommodator
• Apathetic	• Harmony-seeking
• Not task-oriented	• Too friendly
• Not people-centered	• Eager to please
• Passive/aggressive	• Not task-oriented

Fair

The Aggressor

The upper-left quadrant represents a traditional approach to leadership—too forceful and aggressive. The person whose behavior fits into this quadrant displays too much dominance and control and general insensitivity to others. Often aggressors justify their behavior because, in the short run, it gets results, but in the long run, the stars in the organization can't and won't flourish with this style. Though many of these leaders acknowledge their autocratic style of leadership, they see no reason to change—until the stars take their talent elsewhere.

The Quit 'N Stay

The lower-left quadrant represents people who commit neither to task accomplishment nor to building relationships. Cautious, unassertive, secretive, or submissive, people who display Quit 'n stay behavior too much or too often usually don't make it to the level of executive in organizations.

These leaders don't even qualify for "ordinary" status. Stars don't respect the quit 'n stays who tend to drag their feet on decisions, take forever to accomplish a task, and avoid changes that will cause upheaval in their lives. Consequently, behavior in this quadrant represents the surest and fastest way to fail—and to lose exceptional performers who have no patience for anyone who would settle for average or below average performance.

The Accommodator

The lower-right quadrant describes the accommodator, the highly sociable, overly optimistic, talkative, and eager-to-please person. These leaders tend to gloss over conflicts, ignore troubling facts, give in for the sake of harmony, or spend inappropriate amounts of time socializing at work. Leaders who can't make tough decisions or who won't give negative feedback fit into the accommodator quadrant. Though friendly and pleasant to work for, when the stars start to tally results, accommodators come up short.

The F^2 Leader

The upper-right quadrant describes successful, magnetic executives—leaders who tend to demonstrate a collaborative and democratic leadership style. Although highly skilled in task accomplishment, they don't sacrifice the rules of civility in the process.

Visionary and strategic, F^2 leaders consistently strive to influence others, shape ideas, and impact outcomes through persuasion and logic, no coercion. Direct reports, peers, and other leaders value F^2 leaders because they not only get things done, they do so in a manner that motivates the people around them. Their balanced leadership style brings out the best performance in others, and accounts, in large part, for their success. F^2 leaders challenge others to deliver their best; they stay focused; and they demand excellence. They allow the situation, not their own mood or tendencies, to determine the degree of forcefulness they use. They don't shy away from the tough calls, but those in their chain of command don't find them domineering or controlling.

Trust: The Glue That Makes Stars Stick Around

"Trust" has become a conversational shuttlecock that people bat around—assuming everyone defines the word in the same ways and values it to the same degree. Everybody seems to agree that trust is a good thing. They just don't all agree on exactly why.

Trust has four main constructs. The first and most obvious involves faith in people, that they won't lie, cheat, or steal—a sort of "honor code" genus of trust. A client or direct report wants to think, "I can rely on this person to do what's right simply because it's the right thing to do. This person has always conducted himself/herself with honor and integrity, so I have no reason to worry about continuing with this relationship."

The second part addresses my belief in your competence. I have to trust that you have the ability or skills to deliver on your promises. I trust my daughter to keep my books and invoice my clients, but I wouldn't trust her to take out my appendix—even on a good day.

The third aspect of trust relates to reliability or consistency of performance over time. I may trust your integrity and value your product, but if you can't consistently deliver above-average performance, I ultimately won't trust you. You have to offer a proven track record.

The fourth characteristic of trust involves my feeling that you have my best interest at heart. I trust that you want me to succeed or benefit, independently of other factors. I trust you when I think you will look out for me.

What price do leaders pay when trust wanes? The most dramatic price usually entails loss of valued customers. When you deliver world-class products or services, clients develop loyalty to you. But if you can't distribute them in some reliable fashion, even the most devoted of your fans won't stick around. Or, if you give customers any reason to question your ethics, they're gone.

The second price includes loss of key talent. Top performers simply won't tolerate situational integrity, incompetence, or substandard performance. Like the pilots described in the "Dear Boss" letter, they will leave. Stars take pride in their work, and if you won't let them do their best work at your place of business, they will take their talent to your competitor.

A third price involves the contagious nature of low trust. When senior leaders cheat on their expenses, overcharge customers, sell inferior products, or offer second-rate service, some employees eagerly pick up the unprincipled gauntlet. They start expensing meals they didn't eat, billing for services not rendered, and doing the wrong thing for a perceived "right" reason like helping the company. Eventually leaders spend all their time looking behind doors—ones they've hidden behind too often.

There's a simple solution. Trust and offer trustworthiness, and do both consistently. Not only ethically desirable, steadiness, dependability and predictability are also practical. When leaders don't behave in expected ways, they cause nerve-wracking insecurity for those who rely on them. Inconsistency, the enemy of trust, is one of its fastest-moving destroyers. Conversely, predictability defines the heart of trust, and stars expect it. They want consistent messages and standards. Even when they benefit from favoritism, stars resent inconsistency because it engenders cynicism in the rest of the organization.

Therefore, keep policies and standards consistent. When leaders play favorites, allow a few pet performers to bend the rules, or tolerate malcontents, others notice. If you establish a rule, everyone should be required to uphold it. If you don't consider an issue important enough to have a company policy about, don't bother with it. In other words, don't have a policy about something unless you will fire your most valuable employee for violating it.

Expect competence, high-quality performance, and civilized behavior from everyone. Although the same standards of behavior should apply to the genius, technical expert, top salesperson, rainmaker, or company curmudgeon, often they don't. Instead, leaders tend to overlook people who operate at one end of the continuum or the other. Too often top performers and the profoundly unpleasant or under-performing employees get away with aberrant behavior simply because the leader chooses to avoid confrontation.

Look decisions, especially the tough ones, squarely in the eye, and make the call. Even when you get the decision wrong, others will react to your decisiveness more favorably than they would waffling. Give honest feedback, address rumors, and communicate candidly. Then do these:

- Admit mistakes.
- Apologize.
- Put yourself in the emotional shoes of others.
- Control your temper.

- Ask and listen.
- Change your mind when new information indicates you should.
- Follow the rules—all the rules—even the ones you don't agree with.
- Be realistic in your expectations.

Stars expect much of their leaders. Gardner also wrote that stars want leaders who "create the conditions and climate of challenge, expectation, and opportunity. They can remove the obstacles, unearth the buried gifts, and release the world-renewing energies."[4] To lift them and move them, leaders have to believe in their people and give them reason to believe in return. History teaches us that sometimes circumstances create situations that cause leaders to flounder or to flourish.

For instance, October 28, 2012, marked the 50th anniversary of the Cuban Missile Crisis—the central crisis of Kennedy's presidency—and perhaps of the entire Cold War. In an attempt to establish a Soviet nuclear presence just 90 miles off the coast of Florida, Khrushchev sent Russian ships carrying nuclear warheads to Cuba. Emboldened by Kennedy's failure at the Bay of Pigs, Khrushchev stated that Kennedy would do anything to prevent nuclear war: "Kennedy doesn't have a strong background, nor generally speaking, does he have the courage to stand up to a serious challenge." He assured Cuba's Che Guevara that "You don't have to worry. There will be no big reaction from the US side."

The Soviets and Cubans underestimated Kennedy. Following an October 14 reconnaissance trip over Cuba, for the first time in history the Strategic Air Command advanced its alert posture to DEFCON 2, one step short of nuclear war.

Kennedy resisted calls for direct engagement and ordered, instead, a naval blockade of Cuba. The move prevented the Soviet ships from gaining entry to the island and bought time for cooler heads to prevail. On October 22, Kennedy declared that any missile launched from Cuba would warrant a full-scale retaliatory attack by the United States against the Soviet Union. On October 24, Russian ships carrying missiles to Cuba turned back, and when Khrushchev agreed on October 28 to withdraw the missiles and dismantle the missile sites, the crisis ended as suddenly as it had begun.

More than a year earlier, however, Kennedy's leadership during the Bay of Pigs invasion had not turned out so well. In fact, historians often blame Kennedy's failed leadership during the Bay of Pigs crisis for the ultimate boldness that caused the missile crisis.

The purpose of the Bay of Pigs invasion had been to touch off a nationwide uprising to against Castro, which members of the Eisenhower administration had put into place at the end of their tenure. When Kennedy took office, he abolished Eisenhower's Planning and Operation Coordinating Board, thereby eliminating the checks and balances inherent in Eisenhower's council.

By financing and directing anti-Castro Cuban exiles, the United States hoped to overthrow Castro. It didn't work. On April 17, 1961, the landing of 1,453 Cuban exiles on the southwestern coast of Cuba turned, within 72 hours, into a complete disaster, resulting in the capture of 1,179 invaders and the deaths of the remaining 274.

Not only did the offensive fail, it also aggravated already-hostile relations between the United States and Cuba, intensified international Cold War tensions, and inspired the Soviet Union to install missiles with nuclear warheads in Cuba the following year.

Most historians agree that Kennedy and the participants who planned the invasion made some fundamental errors in judgment that they didn't repeat during the missile crisis:

- Perhaps naiveté, hubris, or inexperience caused Kennedy to disregard Eisenhower's plans and the input of dissenting voices during the planning of the Bay of Pigs invasion. No such overconfidence guided his judgment during the missile crisis.

- Kennedy made the decision to invade Cuba based on the *theory* that the incursion would start a large-scale uprising, a miscalculation that proved later to be erroneous and costly. He more successfully based his conclusions on definitive information during the missile crisis.

- In general, the United States created an impression of irresolution in the invasion when it did not show enough aggression in its support of Cuban rebels. Kennedy specifically compromised the U.S. commitment when he refused the air support needed to protect the exiles. Conversely, Kennedy's firmness in his negotiations with Khrushchev during the missile crisis showed the Russian leader that he had been mistaken in his assumptions that Kennedy would not have the courage to stand up to a serious challenge.

- During the Bay of Pigs invasion planning sessions, a high degree of cohesion and pressure to conform existed among CIA members. They hesitated to challenge one another and intentionally kept dissenting opinions, when someone had the nerve to express them, from the President. They sidestepped methodical research, planning, and checks and balances, focusing instead on the Machiavellian approach that overthrowing Castro justified any means to that end. Kennedy did not question or uncover their subterfuge and shoddy research until it was too late.

- Kennedy allowed members of the invasion planning group to think affiliation with him and top CIA and military leaders rendered them invulnerable. They shared the illusion that they were insulated because of the secrecy and presidential involvement, so they invented justification for their actions. Kennedy tolerated no such illusions during the missile crisis.

- During the initial discussions of the invasion, Kennedy voiced his opinion before he heard from his experts. He needed dispassionate data, but he heard echoes instead, thereby dooming any chance for robust examination of all angles and possibilities.

Kennedy's leadership during his short tenure in the White House offers some of the most profound leadership lessons of modern time. First, the same man led in both situations—one a complete fiasco, the other a disaster averted. He shows us that leaders can learn from mistakes, as long as they show a willingness to examine what went wrong and commit to a different course of action.

Second, he illustrates that a failure—even one as large as the Bay of Pigs invasion—need not define a leader's tenure. Historians now laud Kennedy for his pressure under fire, his willingness to compromise with Khrushchev, his resolve, his diplomacy, and his courage. He drew a metaphorical line in the Atlantic and warned of dire consequences if Khrushchev dared cross it, but he also negotiated a peaceful resolution that avoided nuclear war and gave Americans reason to trust his leadership. He had star performers advising him in both situations, but his leadership drew the best from the brightest when he changed his leadership approach.[5]

Instead of Paying Top Dollar for Talent, Get Top Talent for the Dollars You Pay

In the 1960s, Laurence Peter began to notice incompetence. He observed that whereas some people function competently, others rise above their level of competence and habitually bungle their jobs, frustrate their coworkers, and erode efficiency. He concluded that for every job that exists in the world, there is someone, somewhere, who cannot do it. Given sufficient time and enough promotions, however, that person would get the job. Peter searched for the underlying principle that would explain why so many important positions were occupied by persons incompetent to fulfill the duties of their offices.

He developed "The Peter Principle," a belief that posits that when organizations promote based on achievement, success, and merit, employees will eventually be promoted beyond their level of ability and rise to their level of incompetence. If people don't advance solely based on their track records, what else remains? *Potential.*

The principle holds that in a hierarchy, people will receive promotions so long as they work competently. Eventually they will be promoted to a position at which they are no longer competent—their level of incompetence. Too often, there they remain, unable to earn further promotions, but also clogging the pipeline for those who can still move up. Often virtuosos fill the roles of those who wait impatiently.

Frequently a person's cognitive skills have proven adequate at one level but will prove insufficient when the problems become more complex, the surprises more frequent, and the priorities less stable. Sometimes individuals with exceptional tactical abilities excel at getting the work finished and the product out the door. Similarly, some people can handle a budget but don't understand how to function in a role that has profit/loss responsibilities. They simply lack the quantitative reasoning to play in the tougher league.

The employee's incompetence, however, is not necessarily a result of the higher-ranking position being more difficult. It may be that the new position requires different work skills which the employee does not possess. For example, an engineer with great technical skill might get promoted to project manager, only to discover he lacks the interpersonal skills required to lead a team.

Peter offered advice for those who lead virtuosos—those he called "super-competent." As he noted, competent managers will promote a super-competent for the betterment of the organization. Incompetent managers, however, will feel intimidated and threatened by those who excel too much.[6]

As you examine your hiring and promotion systems, consider the following for avoiding the Peter Principle:

- Develop an "up or out" policy that requires termination of an employee who fails to advance, either through promotion or skill development. Those who remain in positions for which they have shown incompetence compromise general morale and cause resentment from those beneath them in the organization who perceive they are being kept from advancement by an incompetent.

- Create solo contributor tracks. Too many organizations with the "up or out" framework fail to recognize that not every virtuoso will make a good leader. Find a way to let them do their best work without having the additional duties related to leading others.

- Promote slowly and methodically only those who have demonstrated the skills and cognitive abilities to perform at the next level.

- Identify virtuosos at every level in the organization, and don't lose sight of them as they progress through the pipeline. Star performers, by their nature, disrupt the perceived natural order of most organization. Sometimes incompetent managers resent them and withhold mentoring. If you find these stars working for an incompetent manager who resists developing or promoting them, as the senior leader, step in.

- Don't promote for effort. Though laudable, effort alone doesn't drive the business. Results do. Promote when you see results that exceed your expectations.

- Avoid developing an egalitarian organization. Senior leaders don't have to start in the mail room. Virtuosos can frequently jump into advanced roles, even when they are new to the company. (Exception: In family-owned businesses, I encourage the owners to have their children literally start on the lowest rung of the ladder, often as summer workers while they are still in high school. When you stand to inherit the family company, knowing every level of the business makes sense.)

- Train people for new positions. *Before* they take on the title or promotion, have them shadow the current person. Hire them a coach who specializes in preparing people for promotion, have them enroll in formal training, or find some other way for them to learn the requisite skills.

- Use consultants or contractors for short-term, specialized projects. Training internal people for these kinds of situations wastes time and sets the person up for failure.

- Evaluate evaluators. Bosses promote or recommend their direct reports for promotion. Look at the boss' track record. How many promotions have worked out? Some bosses who lack gold standards themselves simply can't recognize gold when they see it. Stellar performers sometimes project. They think others figure things out as quickly as they do, even when no evidence exists to support the notion.

Hire for Talent; You Can Buy Experience by the Pound

A few years ago, I saw *Moneyball*, the blockbuster movie based on Michael Lewis's best-seller *Moneyball: The Art of Winning an Unfair Game*. The movie has been successful for some obvious reasons, like America's love of baseball and Brad Pitt. But I liked it for an imperceptible one. It illustrated the advice I've been giving clients for years: hire for talent; you can buy experience by the pound.

Brad Pitt plays Billy Beane, a one-time phenomenon who flamed out in the big leagues and who later went to work as the general manager for the Oakland Athletics. As the movie opens, the franchise faces the loss of their three best players. Because the team doesn't enjoy the financial position of perennial favorites like the Yankees and the Red Sox, Beane realizes he needs to radically change how he evaluates what players can bring to the squad. Then he meets Peter Brand, the first and best talent decision Beane made during his journey to success.

Brand was a 25-year-old recent Yale economics graduate who specialized in sabermetrics, a scientific approach that uses objective, empirical baseball statistics that measure in-game activity.

Beane realizes Brand understands how to subvert the system of assessing players that's been in place for nearly a century. However, as the duo begin to acquire less-than-first-round choices, they face stiff resistance from both the As' longtime scouts and the team's manager, Art Howe. They experience a bumpy start, but ultimately, Beane and Brand prevail.

Let's look at the lessons for leaders:

- Like business leaders today, Beane faced severe economic restraints—chains that did not hinder his competitors. In 2002, The Athletics paid approximately $41 million in salary while competitors like the New York Yankees spent more than $125 million in payroll that same season. The team's smaller revenues forced Oakland to find players undervalued by the market. Clearly, the economic playing field wasn't level, so Beane needed new ideas. If he had embraced the traditional approach of hiring for experience, Oakland could never have maintained a competitive edge.

- Beane did not possess the talent to analyze players, so he hired Brand for his expertise. Most importantly, he took the advice he received from Brand.

- The current economic situation will not allow you to do what you've always done and get the same payoff. You, too, need a new approach to hiring the talent that will allow you to outplay your competition. Often you won't have the budget for the most experienced player, but if you objectively analyze the talent you can afford, you too can win.

Teams that value sabermetrics are often said to be playing "moneyball." Baseball traditionalists, in particular some scouts and media members, decry the sabermetric revolution and have disparaged *Moneyball* for emphasizing sabermetrics over more traditional methods of player evaluation. Nevertheless, the front offices of major league teams like the St. Louis

Cardinals, the New York Mets, the Yankees, the San Diego Padres, the Boston Red Sox, the Washington Nationals, the Arizona Diamondbacks, and others have hired full-time sabermetric analysts. The general managers of these teams understand what I tell all my clients: *Instead of paying top dollar for talent, get top talent for the dollars you pay.* Ironically, virtuosos don't work for pay, but the pay allows them to practice their passion. The paycheck is a scorecard and requisite part of the deal, not the deal.

Why the CEO and Not HR?

Until and unless you reach virtuoso status in your organization—meaning you have a critical number of virtuosos—you should expect that the B and C players will block the hiring and promotion of those they find threatening. Eventually the stars can overwhelm the mediocrity of C players in the succession process, but until then, CEOs, not HR, must stay actively engaged in the selection process.

It all starts with recruitment. The CEO must take over decision-making as it relates to policies, processes, and best practices. This will involve setting specific hiring goals and the requirement that only virtuosos—or those who show the potential to become virtuosos in the near future—can join the company in key positions. But it also involves putting recruitment squarely in the laps of the hiring managers. Encourage them to build their networks and to stay in touch with the exceptional performers in your industry. You all know who they are, and chances are, one of your people knows each of them by two degrees of separation. With the advent of LinkedIn and other social networks, keeping track of the best and brightest has never been easier. Then, require more accountability from your people. If you hold hiring managers responsible for the caliber of talent they bring in and tie their performance ratings and bonuses to these responsibilities, you'll see instant improvement.

HR Won't Hire the Talking Dog

A man shopping at a garage sale spies a sign above a dog: "Talking dog. $10."

The man asks the dog, "Can you really talk?"

"Sure," answers the dog.

"That's amazing. What's your story? Why are you being sold?"

"Well," says the dog. "I recently returned from Afghanistan where I worked for the U.S. Army. Because I'm a dog, I was able to spy behind enemy lines. I'd then return to the base and debrief with the generals. Before that, I was in Iraq working for the State Department, reporting directly to Hillary Clinton. The Iraqi leaders didn't notice when I'd slip into secret meetings, so I'd listen and then fly back to the Pentagon to debrief Secretary Clinton and the president. Then, I met my master, and he wanted me to retire and come live with him here. And now he's selling me. I don't know why."

"Wow," said the man. "Hang on, I'll be back."

The man returns to the dog's owner, "I can't believe you have a talking dog! That's amazing!"

"Yup, it's a talking dog all right," answers the man, in a bored tone.

"Well, I'll take him," he says, handing the man 10 dollars. "But, I gotta ask. Why are you selling a talking dog?"

The man looks at him impatiently and replies, "Cause he's a liar. He never even met Hillary Clinton."

When I work with clients to improve selection or succession planning, I often encounter an inability to spot exceptional talent and a general unwillingness to hire those who embody it—usually because it doesn't come tidily packaged. Instead of a decision-maker saying, "Wow! This is a talking dog! What else matters?" people start to examine the talent rubrics they created in some off-site meeting and evaluate the candidate according to the measures. My experience has taught me that there are four reasons for this behavior, reasons people don't hire the best and brightest:

1. They simply don't know what gold looks like, but they do know how to evaluate a person against the pre-set metrics. They wouldn't spot a talking dog if it bit them before it spoke.

2. They feel threatened by the idea of hiring someone who might outshine them.

3. Status quo talent practices make them feel secure, replete with all the random metrics.

4. Star performers can be high maintenance—challenging traditional approaches, insisting on innovation and improvement, killing sacred cows, and generally making a nuisance of themselves. Average people are easier to manage.

I don't advocate hiring liars, but I do challenge clients to avoid establishing arbitrary criteria in their hiring and promoting plans. Too often decision-makers focus on the wrong things, like subjective standards, experience, or conditions for a given job. These observations forced me to question whether most companies would have hired their industry's equivalent to Steve Jobs.

As I mentioned in Chapter Six, Steve Jobs was not a model boss or human being, tidily packaged for emulation. According to biographer Walter Isaacson and most accounts, Jobs was neither typical nor particularly likable, but he did display talking-dog characteristics. A college dropout, Steve Jobs launched a startup in his parents' garage that he built into the world's most valuable company. Not always nice and occasionally not very smart, he was a genius—his imaginative leaps instinctive, unexpected, and magical.[7] His insights came out of the blue, wherever that is. We will remember him as the greatest business executive of our era, and history will place him in the virtuoso hall of fame, but would your company have hired him?

Continuing to hire average performers won't position you for a competitive advantage, much less an exceptional advantage. You'll need to do more. If you want a Steve Jobs or a talking dog, you have to create an environment in which they can do their best work. Or, you can let your competition hire them. Your choice.

The Final Two Steps

Once the CEO starts taking more responsibility for the selection and succession-planning processes, the next step involves what I call "Culling the Cs." That means you ask, and require your managers to ask, the "Two-Question Two-Step":

1. Would you hire this person again?
2. Would you be sorry to see this person leave?

If the answer to either is "no," you probably need to start the culling process. If the answer to both is "no," you should start the process for replacing the person. Jack Welch, who in the annals of business remains the gold standard for identifying top talent, estimated he devoted one-third of his time to improving talent. I don't know too many other CEOs who could make the same claim. But then, Jack Welch left a legacy unlike that of most others.

Conclusion

On January 19, 2013, St. Louis lost an icon, one of the greatest hitters in baseball, Stan "The Man" Musial. In 22 major-league seasons, all of them in St. Louis, Mr. Musial led the Cardinals to three world championships, won seven batting titles, and earned the National League's most valuable player designation three times. He built a career, a brand, and a legacy—one that will live on in St. Louis, Cardinal, and baseball history.

Throughout the world of baseball, fans knew Musial for his unorthodox corkscrew-style batting stance. In St. Louis, we knew him as the premier ambassador of the game—our own favorite son. He lacked the flamboyance of some of his contemporaries, let alone the baseball greats of today. But he offered much more—a role model for leaders who want to leave a legacy.

Mr. Musial wasn't flashy, big, particularly fast, or conventional in his batting. But he was the best Stan Musial we've ever had. He didn't raise the bar; he set it. He showed us that legacy-making takes talent and the ability to consistently deliver exceptional performance. Even injured, he played the game full out, explaining, "There may be someone there who's never seen me play before."

And he was a nice guy. Always ready to sign autographs for the kids or to greet fans with his low-keyed "Whattayasay, whattayasay," Musial carved his own place in St. Louis history during a time when we were known for shoes and beer.

Musial walked to the plate with one thing in mind: do the job. I have shelves lining the walls of my office, each definitively defining the salient traits of leaders. Mr. Musial offers a simpler explanation. Consistently deliver superior performance, and be a person people respect. Deliver superior performance for the clients that already support you, but even when you're injured, play your biggest game in case a new client has never seen you play before.

We understand legacies when we're discussing baseball, but we have a harder time articulating what we mean when it comes to business. People like Jack Welch knew what he had to do to align his stars, to position his company for growth, and to create the atmospheric conditions that allowed his stars to shine. He didn't set out to become a star himself; he fashioned a company that set a gold standard for the industry. That's the kind of legacy that will draw the best from your brightest.

Chapter Nine

Don't Recruit a Star; Create a Constellation

For centuries we have understood that a galaxy is a massive, gravitation-ally bound system consisting of individual stars that naturally attract one another. Scientifically we understand the naturally occurring phenom-enon of gravity and the role it plays in keeping celestial stars in orbit with one another, but we haven't used this knowledge to understand how human stars can create their own gravity with one another to create a professional galaxy of top performers.

A galaxy starts with individual stars, just as exceptional organizations and sports teams start with the success of key individuals. Pele, David Beckham, Magic Johnson—just to name a few—carried a disproportionate share of the credit and responsibility for their teams' successes. Steve Jobs put Apple on the map and created a company that has both survived his demise and thrived in his absence. Like their celestial counterparts, these supernovae consistently caused a burst of energy that outshone the entire team—their respective galaxies. Unlike their celestial counterparts, these luminaries did not fade from view almost immediately. Instead, they led their teams to athletic or corporate victory over an extended period of time.

When you recruit a star, you've taken an important first step in build-ing a galaxy—but only a first step. If you stop there, you won't enjoy much more success than if you'd saved the money and hired ordinary people in the first place. Similarly, if you recruit a collection of stars and fail to help them develop some degree of cohesion, you doom yourself to the track re-cord of leaders who thought assembling some top performers would suffice. Just as a world-class orchestra needs sections of string, brass, woodwind, and percussion instruments, and a conductor who can help them make beautiful music together, organizations need exceptional, diverse talent in key positions that their leader can orchestrate to create something bigger and better. Top performers don't make this easy, however.

Research offers overwhelming evidence that groups of extremely bright and talented individuals often appreciably underperform when compared to groups comprised of average or above-average talent. Too often, leaders think they've done their jobs by collecting the individual stars. Then they and everyone else retreat to a safe distance to watch the innovative fireworks. Frequently, however, instead of engendering "oohs and ahhs," the group—which never formed into a team—causes a hugely expensive dud.

Measuring Team Members

In my work with executive teams, I have noticed the links between input (the team members) and output (the team's decisions, actions, and results). Only those teams that start with exceptional people can expect extraordinary results. Seldom have I found ordinary people uniting to create something great—even though these kinds of teams can often build synergy and fashion something that surpasses the sum of their collective talents.

Usually before I work with an executive team collectively, I have assessed each member individually, using a battery of tests that measure decision-making, problem-solving, knowledge of leadership, and relevant personality characteristics. Often I have also engaged in a 360 interview process to identify behaviors that help or hinder top performance, and I have examined performance reviews. The aggregate of these data gives me a clear picture of the individuals on the team and forms the foundation for the strategy or change management work that lies ahead.

Drawing from my general framework of looking at people from a variety of perspectives, leaders can use the following model to assess the individuals they want to assign to a team.

Talent Assessment Model

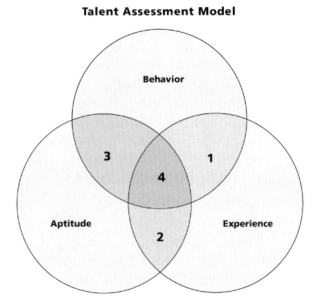

1. Behavior + Experience

People that you consider a One would not make good virtuoso team members because they lack the aptitude to keep up with the others. Unless they offer a specialized skill related to their experience, don't consider them candidates.

2. Experience + Aptitude

You'll often find situations when you'll want to include Twos on a team because they have the intellectual firepower and experience to figure out what has to happen. They will excel at decision-making, but because they don't have the requisite behaviors, they may fail to influence others. Or, they may consciously or unconsciously sabotage the best thinking and efforts of their teammates. Depending on the problem behaviors that stand in their way, the leader can often coach these individuals to success.

3. Aptitude + Behavior

People that you would consider Threes often make excellent virtuoso team members because other members of the team can compensate for the experience that an individual person doesn't have. Collectively, therefore, they can shore up the team's efforts.

4. Behavior + Experience + Aptitude

Fours are the ideal candidates for team membership—and everything else. When you put a team of them together, you can expect amazing results. But you can also expect incredible problems—especially if you assume that they'll automatically gel with a collection of other Fours. They won't. They will need your help and insight to guide them through the predictable and inevitable turbulent waters of virtuoso team membership. Anticipating both the problems and opportunities associated with the formation of a virtuoso team starts with an understanding of eight factors.

The Eight Functions of Virtuoso Teams

Building a team of exceptional people involves appreciating how individual members' characteristics and personalities unite to form the unique culture of a virtuoso team. Satisfaction, performance, productivity, effectiveness, and turnover depend, to a large degree, on the socio-emotional makeup of the team. But one thing remains constant. Stars commonly think they lose their ability to shine when in a galaxy—their distinctive quality diminishing as others shine beside them. Consistently teams underperform, despite all the extra resources—problems with coordination, motivation, and fear of losing control chipping away at the benefits of collaboration.

Leaders who aspire to assemble a team of top performers will face daunting obstacles if they don't structure and build the team at the onset. Without structure, a team of stars will flounder unproductively, often concluding that the team's efforts are a waste of time. Pessimism will pervade. Conversely, when leaders define expectations, impose constraints, and help members clarify norms, roles, and responsibilities, the team can spend its time carrying out the task.

Leaders find themselves most motivated to spend time involved with the team when it faces a roadblock, but often that will be too late. A more proactive approach would be to do the building of the team when it's actually forming or when things are going well. The following eight functions will help you with this structuring and position you to create a galaxy of stars, not a collection of egos:

No two teams, not even two teams of stars, will look alike. However, when they understand the universal dynamics that contribute to successful interactions among exceptional people, leaders can adapt and adjust their communication to the situation and make choices that will benefit the team and the organization. It all starts with trust.

Trust

As I mentioned in Chapter Eight, trust has four main constructs: integrity, competence, predictability, and the belief that you are cared about. In order for star performers to trust their leaders, they must satisfy all four aspects of trust. Star performers who form teams carry these same expectations into the team setting and apply them to their team members, but things become more complicated with more moving parts.

People realize they're vulnerable to their bosses by dint of the boss/employee relationship. They accept this structure. But allowing themselves to become vulnerable to peers in a team situation introduces another level of complexity. Using the four constructs, then, each member must "trust" each other member to act with integrity. In a team situation, members often describe the nuances of integrity when they report that they find a member credible—that they can not only feel confident about the content of comments but also have faith that the member offered them in a spirit of mutual respect.

The leader will see evidence of trust among team members when they begin to admit mistakes to one another, and to offer and accept apologies. They do this only when they feel comfortable enough that neither the boss nor any other team member will use the information in any harmful way. The immediate and long-term payoff is that candor will remain high, whether the news is good or bad. Similarly, members will give each other dispassionate, accurate feedback about both ideas (content) and behaviors (process). Don't count on balanced feedback, however. Stars tend not to compliment themselves or others nearly enough. They spot flaws and report inconsistencies; they don't usually praise.

When trust builds during a period of time, members start to believe that teammates will behave in predictable ways, even when those ways aren't necessarily positive. For example, one member, perhaps the lead finance person, might seem fixated on the fiscal implications of every decision, whereas the compliance officer can't discuss options that threaten regulatory restrictions. Fair enough. Those members have the fiduciary responsibility to oversee a part of the organization, so their concerns will carry over to their team roles. Others can predict that they will raise the red flags in discussion, even when they seem to act as business prevention units.

The willingness to be vulnerable—to link one's own success to another's—starts with the fundamental belief that you are cared about. Not necessarily that you are protected or nurtured, but that you won't be sacrificed on the corporate altar if things go awry. Stars repeat an internal mantra: "If I sink or swim as a result of your efforts, you'd better be a good swimmer yourself and someone who will throw me a lifeline if I need it." When that caliber and quantity of trust pervade the team's interactions, productivity will follow.

Accountability

When members literally don't understand what their teammates expect of them, how can they reach their potential and avoid the pitfalls along the way? Problems surface when members haven't established clear lines of responsibility. They don't communicate, they haven't clarified publicly what each person needs to do—tasks to be completed and decisions to be made, and members haven't discussed openly their expectations about appropriate behavior. Ambiguity reigns and establishes itself as the enemy of accountability, which compromises commitment. This lack of understanding creates barriers among team members that significantly impede efficient and effective teamwork.

The world of aviation gives us grist for this particular mill. During the Cold War, the Air Force's Strategic Air Command (SAC), the major command that would have dropped nuclear bombs, had that become necessary, determined that teams performed better as "hard crews." These men trained together as a crew, flew as a crew, and were evaluated as a crew. The men knew what to expect of one another; trust remained high; and performance improved.

The commander of SAC then transferred to the Material Airlift Command (MAC) and imposed hard crew protocols on the pilots in that command. In addition to encountering significant resistance, few found the approach effective. MAC prided itself in standardization. In other words, no matter what pilot or co-pilot sat in the seat, others could expect him to perform in a standard, orthodox way. Leaders didn't attempt to identify star aviators; they wanted predictability, precision, and safety.

The airlines operate on a model closer to that of MAC. Crews change regularly, sometimes several times in the same day. Once again, no one attempts to distinguish one pilot from another in terms of performance and skill. The FAA, the airlines, and the passengers agree on one thing: they all want safety.

In any of these crews, accountability is key. As the pilots go through the checklist, they listen for pre-ordained phrases and standardized responses. For instance, when they hear "Down the gear" instead of "Gear down," the standard command, more often than not, the listener will hear "Say again."

The accountabilities on these crews are so well-honed and practiced that the pilots train themselves to hear what they expect to hear. When they don't, progress stalls.

Leaders who aspire to build a team of stars can learn lessons from all these groups but should not infer universal best practices that will transfer to exceptional business teams. In SAC, decision-makers saw the value of familiarity and linked it to accountability. In the other Air Force commands and in the airlines, leaders seek standardized practices and procedures and don't want creative deviations from the norm. You'll want accountability and minimum competency levels, but you're going to need more.

In your world, you want reliability coupled with entrepreneurial thinking and creativity that goes beyond minimum competence. You want the value that comes from standardization without the regimentation. You need a degree of safety and predictability but also the ability to agilely out-maneuver your competition. You want your stars to take calculated risks but not reckless ones. It's a tricky balance, but teams achieve it when they continuously clarify objectives, roles, and decision-making authority.

Having candid discussions about areas of accountability and each of the aforementioned issues can help the team overcome the discord so members can get back on track. When I work with executive teams, I encourage them to use an accountability charting format similar to the traditional RACI approach—responsible, accountable, consulted, informed. (See the Appendix.)

Accountability charting helps team members operate more effectively by clarifying each team member's responsibilities and expectations. Charting helps everyone understand who should participate in which decisions and identifies the right people for work assignments, projects, meetings, and task forces. It also helps people learn how not to step on each other's toes and how not to assume someone else will take care of a particular task.

As the leader, once you have created a culture of accountability and commitment, your role changes. At that point, you should leave the policing of behavior to the team. Peer pressure goes a long way on virtuoso teams. Each individual realizes he or she is playing in the big league and doesn't want to disappoint the other players. This fear alone will cause people to behave in functional ways—or it won't. Either way, the team will need to work things out. Usually tolerance of sub-standard performance or violation of team norms vanishes on this kind of team. You may be called upon to act as the external arbiter, but when you do meet to discuss issues, reward and punish the team as a whole—not as individuals. And keep the spotlight on the *decisions* the team makes, not just on tasks accomplished.

Decision-Making

Conventional approaches to understanding teams usually address the *work* the team performs—the tasks they accomplish by functioning collectively rather than individually. When you create a galaxy of stars, however, the emphasis shifts. You assemble stars when you need bold decisions and stellar analytical reasoning—not all hands on deck.

In *Landing in the Executive Chair*, I used the team aboard *Apollo 13* to demonstrate how exceptional people working together can achieve unprecedented success, even during a time of crisis. We recall that on April 11, 1970, James Lovell commanded the third *Apollo* mission that was intended to land on the moon. *Apollo 13* launched successfully, but the crew had to abort the moon landing after an oxygen tank ruptured, severely damaging the spacecraft's electrical system. Despite great hardship caused by limited power, loss of cabin heat, shortage of water, illness, and the critical need to reengineer the carbon dioxide removal system, the crew returned safely to Earth on April 17. Even though the crew did not accomplish its mission of landing on the moon, the operation was termed a "successful failure" because the astronauts returned safely. It also remains a case study in exceptional teamwork.

Author and researcher Meredith Belbin began using the term "Apollo Syndrome" for a different reason. After assembling teams of people who had sharp, analytical minds and high mental ability, he discovered that they don't always or even usually achieve the success that Lovell and his crew enjoyed. In fact, Belbin discovered that when these kinds of teams developed a "failure is not an option" mentality, often they committed collusion in their own failure.

The failures seemed to be due to certain flaws in the way the team operated. That is, they attempted to function as a team of average or above-average performers, yet they were stars. They spent excessive time in abortive or destructive debate, trying to persuade other team members to adopt their own views, demonstrating a flair for spotting weaknesses in others' arguments. This led to the equivalent of the "deadly embrace."

In computer terms, "deadly embrace" signifies a problem when two computer programs vie for control, a phenomenon that occurs when each program waits and prevents the other from making progress. A similar situation can occur in team discussions when people try to influence others to concede the flaws in their arguments, without conceding the flaws in their own. Instead of looking for points of agreement, everyone stays rooted in the orientation and value of spotting inconsistencies.[1]

My own research of virtuoso teams reflects Belbin's findings. If leaders don't recognize and embrace the differences between virtuoso teams and ordinary teams, these problems become likely:

- Team members tend to make decisions that reflect their own best interest.

- Members spend more time debating than analyzing, so they waste time.

- When you assemble a group of dominant thinkers who have grown accustomed to being right, members abandon the give-and-take required for effective solutions.

- Members spot problems early, oppose and propose, and the group abandons viable solutions too early. Brainstorming ceases.

- When rivalry sets in, members lose focus.

Only a strong leader can shepherd the talents, skills, and egos of star performers to help them realize their greatest accomplishments through collaboration. Athletic coaches do it every day, but other leaders haven't been quite so successful. Abraham Lincoln provides the exception to the rule.

On May 18, 1860, William Seward, Salmon Chase, and Edward Bates, all rivals for the presidential nomination, waited to hear the results from the Republican National Convention. When Lincoln emerged the victor, his opponents felt dismayed and angry, but Lincoln himself put the former contention aside. Displaying his signature statesmanship, Lincoln knew he had to assemble a cabinet that represented the best talent available, regardless of previous differences. Lincoln also included Montgomery Blair, Gideon Welles, and Norman Judd, all former Democrats, and William Dayton, a former Whig. Lincoln could have made more predictable choices in establishing his cabinet, but he didn't. Instead, realizing the challenges ahead for healing a warring nation, he created his galaxy of stars—one characterized by diversity of thought and ideology.

Lincoln understood his rivals and respected them, even when he disagreed with their ideas. Those feelings led him to bring his disgruntled opponents together to create the most unusual cabinet in history. By marshalling the talents of these men, Lincoln preserved the Union and won the war. But each day brought new conflicts and decisions.

The cabinet consisted of strong men—all stars in their own right—but Lincoln taught us something else. Because this prairie lawyer from Illinois understood that extraordinary times demanded that he abandon ordinary solutions, through courage and prescience Lincoln guided his team of rivals to make unprecedented decisions that would shape the nation and the world. Here's what he did:

- Lincoln faced reality. He never lost sight, and didn't allow others to lose sight, of the complex task he faced in building a cabinet that would preserve the integrity of the Republican Party in the North while providing the fairest possible representation from the South.
- He put a premium on collaboration, but he didn't hesitate to encourage confrontation to achieve it. The members of his cabinet clashed violently and continuously, but together they emerged victorious.
- Lincoln led with logic and didn't let his personal feelings for these men or his past experiences during the campaign cloud his judgment. Instead, he sought and obtained the best thinking available.[2]

Few leaders invite conflict, even when it can result in the best outcome, but not many of us would consider anything about Lincoln or the times in which he led our country typical or representative. Lincoln put aside his own emotions and required his team to do the same. They may not have liked each other, and certainly they didn't share common opinions, but together they shaped history.

Conflict Resolution

As Lincoln's team of rivals taught us, not all virtuoso teams form seamlessly or easily. Some have to navigate turbulent, unrelenting waters before they reach shore. But the steering of the vessel remains paramount to success in all scenarios, as it did with Lincoln's team—and the team that discovered insulin.

Before the discovery of insulin, diabetes led to death. Doctors knew that sugar worsened the condition of diabetic patients and that the most effective treatment demanded putting the patients on very strict diets with sugar intake, and food in general, kept to a minimum. Doctors and researchers developed the mantra: "The less food, the more life." At best, this treatment caused patients to live a few extra years, but it never saved them. In some cases, the harsh diets even caused patients to die of starvation.

Dr. Frederick Banting, a Canadian physician, developed a deep interest in diabetes after reading an article in a medical paper on the pancreas. The work of other scientists had indicated that the lack of a protein hormone secreted in the pancreas, which they named insulin, caused diabetes.

Determined to investigate the possibility of extracting insulin from the pancreas, Banting discussed possibilities with various people, including Professor John Macleod at the University of Toronto, a leading figure in the study of diabetes in Canada. Macleod didn't think much of Banting's theories, but Banting managed to convince him that his idea merited further research. In 1921, Macleod gave Banting a laboratory with a minimum of equipment, 10 dogs, and a research assistant named Charles Best.

Hardly the gleaming vision that he had imagined, Banting found the lab shrouded in veils of dust and cobwebs, resembling the lab in a *Frankenstein* movie. But greatness would not suffer obstacles. One of the most significant advances in medical science began, therefore, in a sub-standard lab with bleach, a bucket, sponges, mops, and the sweat and labor of two great scientists.

Substandard lab conditions presented only one of many obstacles. After Banting and Best discovered insulin and proved that it could save the lives, they encountered trouble finding ways to purify and extract it. Macleod assigned chemist James Collip to the group to help with the purification. Collip solved the problem by removing harmful impurities from insulin while retaining its life-saving qualities.

Harmony did not reign among these great scientists, however. As the reality of a human trial became more plausible, Banting and Best raced with Collip to develop next steps. Macleod decided that Collip, as the best biochemist, would supply the purified extract. Because neither Macleod nor Collip was a practicing clinician, Dr. Walter Campbell oversaw the clinical administration of the trial, under the direction of Professor Duncan Graham.

When Banting learned of the plan, he was furious. He assumed *he* would be the one to administer the first clinical test. Macleod argued that when human life hung in the balance, precedence became irrelevant. Succumbing to pressure, however, Graham reluctantly agreed to use Banting and Best's extract, despite its being less pure than Collip's. Amid this high drama and posturing, doctors admitted Leonard Thompson , a 14-year-old diabetic boy, to Toronto General Hospital on December 2, 1921. The boy received "Macleod's serum," which rendered inconclusive results.

When Collip heard of the reversal of the plan, he considered it a personal betrayal. Banting told everyone the trial had failed because the quantity had been insufficient, voicing his tale of injustice and tribulation loudly and indiscriminately. Graham encouraged Macleod to dismiss Banting, which Macleod found impossible to do because of Banting's supporters. At one point, Macleod commented to his wife that he should start taking a chair and whip to work to tame the lions on his team. (Considering Banting eventually resorted to fisticuffs in his attempts to communicate his displeasure with Collip, Macleod's lion-taming solution might have proved useful!)

During all this tumult, the science continued on two tracks: research and clinical. On January 23, Campbell began injecting Thompson with Collip's extract. As the boy had been near death, those involved saw his recovery as nothing short of miraculous.

Banting and Best published the first paper on their discovery a month later, in February 1922. Although Macleod had left the laboratory and did not participate in the work, in 1923 the Nobel Prize was awarded jointly to Banting and Macleod "for the discovery of insulin." Once again infuriated, Banting thought Best, not Macleod, should have received a share of the award. Banting finally agreed to accept the prize but gave half his share of the money to Best. Macleod, in turn, gave his share to Collip.

Very soon after the discovery of insulin, the medical firm Eli Lilly, and American global pharmaceutical company started large-scale production of the extract. As soon as 1923, the company began producing enough insulin to supply the entire North American continent, which positioned Lilly as one of the major pharmaceutical manufacturers in the world.

The story of this miraculous discovery, which began with a team of Canadian virtuosos who fought each other both literally and figuratively, has a happy ending; but few involved would have characterized the experience as pleasant, much less happy. People seldom find conflict resolution enjoyable. The rewards came from the keen dedication of the team members to accomplish the daunting goal of controlling the then-killer disease of diabetes. Two things allowed the research to become a reality: the exceptional talent of the scientists and the dedicated leadership of Dr. Macleod. Had either been absent, countless lives would have been wasted until a strong leader could have surfaced to orchestrate the efforts and conflicts of this team of virtuosos.[3]

Communication

During game six of the 2011 World Series, Cardinals player Matt Holliday made an error that would have embarrassed a high school player—he dropped an easy fly ball to left field. As he and Rafael Furcal collided, the game looked more like a *Three Stooges* episode than a competition involving world-class athletes. Why? Two words: "It's mine." Holliday didn't say them.

The same thing happens in organizations every day. So called "teams," which really resemble committees, fail to determine areas of accountability among their players. Metaphorically, they too drop the ball because no one steps up, yells "Mine!" and makes things happen. Instead, members of the group plod along, neglect defining roles, overlook common goals, and don't hold themselves and each other accountable. This sort of behavior, typical though it may be, frustrates nearly everyone, but it de-motivates top performers who want to play a bigger game—one where people don't drop the balls.

What's a leader to do? During the game in question, then-Cardinals coach Tony La Russa looked down and shook his head. My baseball expert adviser son-in-law, Pat, tells me he probably also cussed. Neither strategy will help your team.

As I mentioned in Chapter Two, history has shown us repeatedly that although conflict can impede a team's progress, overly harmonious communication does not hold the key to success, either, when it results in groupthink—a communication phenomenon that helps explain why the infamous Bay of Pigs invasion failed.

Banting and Best illustrate the problems teams face when they don't learn to address conflict effectively; decision-makers on Kennedy's team show us that too much harmony creates its own impediment. Open, honest, responsive communication supplies the missing link—that connection that allows stars to go beyond ordinary solutions and results.

A building full of virtuoso talent who won't communicate with each other won't help you any more than average talent would. If you truly need and want a team, reward them as a group. Hold them accountable to team results, not just individual contributions. Tie their bonuses and compensation to their work as a team. One player can't go to the World Series, and neither can one of your team members carry the others.

Clear Objectives

When exceptional individuals join together in the pursuit of a common goal, miraculous things can happen. Sometimes an exceptional leader can recast the ordinary into the extraordinary, as George Washington did at Valley Forge, but more often marvels occur when leaders have stellar talent to start with. That happened at the Winter Olympics in 1980.

The U.S. victory over the long-dominant and heavily favored Soviets quickly earned the title the "Miracle on Ice," the event many consider the greatest sports moment of the past century and what *Sports Illustrated* called "the single most indelible moment in all of U.S. sports history."

What made it miraculous? To begin with, the U.S. hockey team entered the games seeded *seventh* out of 12 teams that qualified for the games. Second, composed of collegiate and amateur athletes, the U.S. team faced a formidable opponent in the well-developed, legendary Soviet players who had won the gold in the previous four Olympics.

Even though the U.S. team faced overwhelming odds, it did not put less-than-stellar players on the ice. The romantic notion that a bunch of college scrubs felled the world's greatest team through sheer nerve and determination is both misguided and inaccurate. The United States started with star performers—even though these stars had not garnered fame or press up until the Olympic Games.

The team also had a determined coach in Herb Brooks who had spent the 1970s as head coach at the University of Minnesota, leading that team to three NCAA titles. Brooks spent a year and a half nurturing the Olympic team, holding numerous tryout camps before selecting a roster from *several hundred* prospects. The team then spent four months playing a grinding schedule of exhibition games across Europe and North America.

Brooks emphasized speed, conditioning, unusual tactics, and discipline, but not popularity. Known for his prickly personality and fanatical preparation, Brooks united the previous rival players—often against himself. The team shared a common enemy in the locker room as well as on the ice.

The Americans entered the games as the underdogs, but they formed a team of competitive canines. From the hundreds of hopefuls, Brooks selected the 20 players who would go on to represent the United States in the miracle. Of the 20 players, 13 eventually played in the NHL. Five of them went on to play more than 500 NHL games, and three played more than 1,000 NHL games.[4]

Scrubs? Underdogs? Second best? No, the U.S. team was nothing short of a team of virtuosos. Brooks, a talented coach and former player, united the team and produced a synergistic, miraculous effect. But before we notify the Vatican of this miracle, let's keep in mind that Brooks started with impressive raw talent.

Business leaders do well when they learn lessons from sports greats. Athletic coaches never attempt to "save" players who can't produce. They cut them. These coaches know they can't win unless they put the best available players in the game. They patiently wade through hundreds of applicants to find the select few who can deliver miracles. Then, they steadfastly commit to developing the talent. It doesn't happen every time—just every four years, when the best in the world compete with other virtuosos of their ilk. Maybe we should make it happen more often in our businesses.

It doesn't happen because of unclear objectives. Members of an athletic team may have personal agendas (I want to score the most baskets; I hope to gain the attention of a scout, etc.). But winning teams don't let these goals stand at cross purposes with the team's objective: win the game. In business, unless the leader articulates a clear direction for the team, there is a real risk that different members will pursue their own agendas. The top scorers on the team may be the stars that shine the most brightly, but they and everyone else know they need the assists and defensive maneuvers of their teammates. Only through collaboration can stars win a team sport.

Collaboration

When tackling a major initiative, like a merger or acquisition, leaders realize they need to assemble a diverse team of highly successful individuals—and then force them to work together. A team composed of dissimilar, highly educated specialists often holds the keys to the success of the challenging initiatives. Paradoxically, the qualities required for success are the same factors that will undermine success, as the aforementioned examples indicate. Complicated projects demand different skills, but we tend to trust most those who share the most in common with us. Similarly, complex endeavors require highly skilled participants, but they tend to fight with one another, as we learned from the team that discovered insulin. When success hinges on cohesive efforts, leaders need to uncover ways for specialists to work together, under high pressure, in a "no retake" environment.

What levers can executives pull to improve team performance and collaboration? In their study of 55 teams that demonstrated high levels of collaborative behavior, despite their complexity, researchers Gratton and Erickson uncovered eight things leaders can do to build collaboration:

1. Invest in facilities and methodologies that foster communication.
2. Model collaborative behavior.
3. Mentor and coach to help people build networks they need for success.
4. Teach communication skills.
5. Support a strong sense of community.
6. Assign team leaders that are both task- and relationship-oriented.
7. Put a few people who know each other together.
8. Clarify roles and tasks.[5]

Strengthening an organization's capacity for collaboration requires a combination of long-term investments in building relationships and trust, and in developing a culture in which leaders model cooperation. It won't happen automatically, but through careful attention to the eight functions of a virtuoso team and the eight things that build collaboration, leaders can solve complex business problems without inducing the destructive behaviors that can accompany the collaborative efforts of stars.

Leadership

Formation of a top performing team relies on two kinds of leadership: the external leader and the shared leadership that exists among the team members. Think of the external leader as the coach of the athletic team. The coach's most important responsibilities involve selecting the team, training them, and then guiding them during the game. At the start of the game, the team huddles around the coach for final words of motivation, but once the buzzer sounds, the players take the field to perform—dependent on each other but independently of the coach. That's when the shared leadership kicks in. Sometimes the balance doesn't occur, however, and a team relies too heavily on the external coach.

That's what happened at Milan High School in 1954 when a small-town Indiana basketball team won the state championship, a victory made famous by the 1986 film *Hoosiers*. In most states, high school athletic teams are divided into different classes, usually based on the number of students in the school, with separate state championship tournaments held for each classification.

In 1954, Indiana conducted a single state basketball championship for all of its high schools, which challenged Milan High School, with its enrollment of only 161, to play in competitions they'd never enter in today's world. Milan was the smallest school ever to win a single-class state basketball title in Indiana, and it hasn't happened since—in this case, providing an exception to the rule: an alchemy of external leadership and talent must occur consistently and continuously to ensure top performance over the long haul. Teams that rely too heavily on the external coach, and not enough on the talent of the members, can't and won't win over time. Similarly, top talent with no external leadership can't hope to succeed either.

Milan High School hired Coach Marvin Wood two years prior to the famous victory, and with him came a new coaching style. He closed practice to outsiders, an act that angered many and removed one of the major forms of entertainment for the town's basketball-crazed population. The coach had above-average talent, especially for a small town, and he expressed his amazement at the unusual scope of size and talent available among the many boys trying out for the team, talent forged by a strong junior-high program.[6] The team won the 1954 nail-biter championship by two points, but neither the players nor the coach enjoyed much distinction after that. The story provided the backdrop for a feel-good, tear-jerking movie, but teams in organizations have to do better. They have to win the game repeatedly, and preferably by more than two points.

Remember that, unlike a sports team, in an organization a team of stars doesn't *work* together as much as it *thinks* together. Traditionally people have focused on a division of labor in work groups; however, top-performing teams require a shift in paradigms—a movement toward and focus on a division of *knowledge.* The knowledge that each member offers forms the foundation of that person's contribution and reputation. The collective resources, therefore, of the team combine to explain its resourcefulness.

Teams of stars initially respond favorably to the external leader's direction—and then they don't. They proceed unfettered until they hit an obstacle, the time when leadership among the members becomes most important. These obstacles can be related to content, procedures, interpersonal interactions, or ethics. When they occur, leadership related to *influence* rather than *dominance,* along with effective communication skills, provides the path around or over the obstacle.

In my work with teams of stars, I have found these obstacles most often related to fuzzy accountability. Either the team never took the time to outline decision-making responsibilities, or a member attempted to stray away from the agreed-upon protocol. When I encourage them to invent, reinvent, or revisit the accountability discussion, usually the problem fades. But not always. That's when the external leader needs to jump in.

Mountains of research exist to explain why and how leaders emerge in groups. If you have assembled a team of stars, however, disregard all of this. Stars form teams differently for many of the aforementioned reasons, and they share leadership differently, too.

During the initial stages, stars vie for "smartest person in the room" status. Dominant and forceful, stars have grown accustomed to acting as the go-to person in their departments. Others have learned to rely on their expertise; their self-reliance and independence have explained most of their success. Just as they don't readily join teams in the first place, stars don't gladly abdicate power and position. Yet they don't want to collaborate with "B" players either.

Leading the Luminaries

When it comes to accepting direction, star performers show caution and restraint. They offer raw talent, expertise, discipline, and excellence, so they want to see the same qualities in those who lead and teach them. Members of the St. Louis Cardinals see these traits in their hitting coach, John Mabry.

Mabry, a former Major League Baseball player, had 898 career hits in 3,409 at-bats, for a batting average of .263. That included 96 home runs and 446 RBI. During his 14-year MLB career, Mabry played for eight teams, including three different stints with the Cardinals. In December 2011, he joined the Cardinals as assistant hitting coach and, in 2013, took the position of hitting coach. In his first year as hitting coach, the Cardinals made it to the World Series, and the team set a new baseball record for hitting efficiency with runners in scoring position.

Like the highly trained instructor pilots of TOPGUN, to whom I referred in Chapter Four, when they seek a coach, professional sports teams rely on stars who have proven track records of success. Because these exceptional performers know what it takes to succeed, they can impart their wisdom to those who come after them. But how? How do these legends in all professional sports pass on their knowledge and talent to the next generation? And why do they succeed so admirably in sporting venues when so many fail to reach the same level of stellar coaching in corporate settings? I asked John Mabry.

Baseball legend Yogi Berra once said, "Ninety percent of the game is half mental." Mabry agrees. By the time a major league player asks John Mabry for help, the player has established his talent. Every star player on the field has talent—copious amounts of it—or no one would have given him a chance to be there in the first place. But, according to Mabry, that doesn't separate the stars from the "also rans."

When the coaching staff looks at a young recruit, nods in agreement, and states, "He gets it," they mean he understands how to work within the parameters and demands the game will require. He will have to handle success and failure, manage his time wisely, draw on inner motivation, and, most importantly, self-regulate. These players understand that once the season starts, they will usually have one day off a month, and if the team goes into post-season play, even that day can disappear.

Professional ball players have to do the same things every other star performer has to do: balance work and family, perform when they're tired or don't feel good, work long hours with people (whether or not they like them)—but professional athletes have do it all with the cameras rolling. They have to have the confidence to walk out on the field and deliver consistently above-average performance—as compared to other star athletes who make that average pretty high—and do it all without developing the arrogance that they have nothing left to learn.

Those who "get it" understand that they will have some of the world's best coaches to help them but that the discipline and humility to ask for that help has to come from within. According to Mabry, for coaching to be effective at this level, it must be 100-percent player-focused. The coach must wait for the right time to give feedback. (When a player returns to the dugout after striking out, he doesn't want to hear insights about what the pitcher is throwing, for example.)

Mabry doesn't have a "one size fits all" approach to coaching. Rather, he studies each player for dozens of hours to learn what to say to whom. Each hitter needs a slightly different approach, and each individual person often needs a different style, depending on what else is going on in his life. Overall, however, Mabry does believe in the power of positive reinforcement and accentuating the player's strengths.

As Mabry pointed out, above all, the player must trust the coach. The kind of trust Mabry described harkens back to the four constructs of trust I offered previously. The player will ask himself, "Do you have the integrity to keep my confidences, the expertise to teach me, the predictability of your performance and responsiveness, and a sincere belief that you care about my success?" Answers to all questions must be "yes."

Mabry offered the following advice to those in business who would like to improve their own coaching:

- Coach with empathy. Think about what a person is going through and meet him there.
- Move your company in the right direction, not just the direction you want it to go.
- Communicate to others your vision and desire to do what's right for everyone, not just yourself or a chosen few.
- Think of coaching as serving others.[7]

When I coach executives for promotion, one of the objectives we almost always address involves their need to give more coaching and feedback to their direct reports. Most of the executives have played sports, so intellectually they understand the importance of receiving constructive feedback. No Little Leaguer would ever meet John Mabry or those like him if it weren't for dedicated coaches who took the time to watch the swings, give correction, and pat a back. They all know this *intellectually* but fail to translate their experiences to the corporation. When the stakes are the highest, and the person has the most to lose, the coaching and support vanish.

Leaders who aspire to lead exceptional organizations know they have to do better. They understand that they can observe gold standards of coaching all around them by turning on the television during virtually any season and witnessing the hard work these professional coaches put into the development of others. Leaders who find themselves fortunate to have stars in their organizations know they can't rely on hands-off, laissez-faire leadership. The stars won't shine without the leader's help or each other's. Top performers want to win the World Series of your industry, and ordinary leadership won't allow that to happen.

Conclusion

Creating your galaxy begins with a constellation of stars—people whose performance distinguishes them from the ordinary and whose gravitational pull allows your organization to serve as a magnet to other stars in the solar system. It all starts with the individual but quickly becomes more about the stars orbiting one another in a way that builds cohesive, collaborative efforts.

Building a team of exceptional people involves appreciating how individual members' characteristics and personalities unite to form the unique culture of a top-performing team, but research repeatedly tells us that stars tend to be strong solo contributors who would prefer to work alone. Yet no one person can win the World Series nor can one person create a symphony, so these exceptional people soon learn that only through collaboration can they achieve their greatness. Successful business leaders understand that they must build cohesion among disparate personalities and functions. Only then can the organization achieve the success that will guarantee that the virtuoso stays and performs well.

Chapter Ten

Failsafe Steps for Extraordinary M&A Growth

When companies merge or acquire, stakeholders usually expect that the whole will be greater than the sum of its parts. Unfortunately, the facts tell a different story. One plus one does not equal three; too often it moves shareholder returns to the wrong side of zero. A once-exceptional organization can quickly take a turn toward mediocrity or, worse, demise if leaders don't plan meticulously, acquire intelligently, evaluate assiduously, and integrate attentively.

Study after study puts the failure rate of mergers and acquisitions between 70 and 90 percent. Many researchers have tried to explain those abysmal statistics, usually by analyzing the characteristics of deals that worked and those that didn't. That's a start, but that only informs decision-makers about the *features* of the deals that caused them to fail or prevented them it. It doesn't truly get to the core of the cause/effect relationships among planning, evaluating, and integrating.

Traditionally leaders have lacked a more comprehensive approach, a way to determine how to merge for an exceptional advantage—a robust examination of the causes of both successes and failures. It all starts with a strategic purpose for the transaction and a commitment to distinguish between deals that might improve current operations and those that could dramatically transform the company's growth prospects. A clear strategic advantage for the acquisition should lead the way.

Formulate a Solid Business Strategy

Both organic and acquisitive growth strategies often exist for a limited period, but sometimes an organization identifies expansion as a long-term objective and considers both forms of growth as part of their evolving strategy. Among all other influences, the desire to grow has one of the most dramatic, often hazardous effects on strategy. Limits and tradeoffs take a back seat to the desire to escalate, increase, or expand. The low-hanging fruit of growth opportunity entices. Therefore, perceived opportunities for growth tempt leaders to go in new directions—paths that can blur uniqueness, trigger compromises, and undermine competitive advantage. Adding new products, features, services, or markets is both alluring and appealing, but doing so without screening these opportunities or adapting them to the company's existing strategy also invites trouble. Organic growth encourages its own kind of mischief, but acquisitive growth goes beyond, to an arena where true damage can occur. Caution should prevail.

Businesses make the decision to acquire for a number of reasons. On the one hand, companies will decide to acquire when they want to boost their current performance, to hold on to a premium position, or to cut costs. This kind of acquisition delivers bottom-line results but almost never changes the company's trajectory. The improvements stop the leaking of assets but don't truly put significant numbers of them in the coffers. For this kind of deal, CEOs often have unrealistic expectations about how much of a boost to assume; they pay too much; and they don't understand how to integrate after the fact. Many of these deals fail to delight, even when they don't truly fail.

Business leaders also make decisions to pursue acquisitions either to augment their organic growth efforts or to replace them when they have been exhausted, both decisions designed for top-line growth. Another, less familiar reason to acquire a company is to reinvent the business model and fundamentally redirect the company. Almost nobody understands how to identify the best targets to achieve this goal, how much to pay for them, and how or whether to integrate them. Yet they are the ones most likely to confound investors and pay off spectacularly—when they work. Even more caution required in this scenario.

Whatever the reason for considering an acquisition, senior leaders and board members face the challenge of offering and demanding a disciplined approach—an intellectual framework to guide decisions and serve as a counterweight to the quick and easy fix of unfettered growth. This requires an examination of which industry changes and customer needs the organization will respond to and which ones it will reject. Penetrating existing markets and reinforcing the company's position help to maintain distinctiveness and competitive advantage, but a goal to squelch their enemies (competitors) usually provides only distraction and ill-advised compromise. Of course, major changes in the industry may require an organization to change its strategy, but taking a new position must be driven by the ability to find new tradeoffs and leverage a new system of complementary activities.

When executives feel motivated to pursue a new strategy that includes an acquisition, almost always they want to acquire new resources and capabilities. Sometimes that means a true strategic direction change; at other times it involves changes to the tactics. At no time should the decision to acquire compromise the strategic principle and strategic advantage I explained in Chapter Two—at least not without a conscious awareness that you're gambling with the mortgage if you do so.

In any strategic initiative, the company should not concede its strategic principle—the power that exists at the intersection of distinction, passion, and profitability. This strategic principle explains why customers choose your products or service, why you make money at what you do, and why people want to work for your organization. It forms the foundation of your competitive advantage, the area that exerts the greatest influence on your business. Therefore, any deal that threatens your strategic principle is one you want to walk away from. But which deals should you walk toward?

It all starts with a well-thought-out strategic objective for growth, a decision that is rational and data-driven. It should *not* start with a directive from the board or a mandate from the owner or CEO to "double in five years." When I hear that sort of goal, the professional hairs on the back of my neck stand up—and for good reason. The day-to-day decisions that drive that sort of growth objective often serve as the sniper's bullets that take the company down. Leaders start making window-dressing hiring decisions they never have made before, they negotiate short-term pricing deals that can't sustain them, and they opt for the quick fix instead of steadfastly positioning themselves for future rewards.

Instead, decision-makers should carefully craft the criteria for an acquisition—the "must haves" of the deal. They should also list and prioritize the "wants" of the deal but carefully and astutely distinguish these from the "must haves." These criteria should have specific measures attached to them—ways by which everyone will agree success will be measured. Finally, everyone should evaluate the value each decisive factor will have. Borrowing from my mentor, Alan Weiss, I encourage clients to adopt an OMV (objectives, measures, values) orientation to these discussions:

- What are we trying to do?
- How will we agree we've done that?
- What good will it do?

The value of the deal merits the most discussion because that quite literally is where the money is. Beyond growing for the sake of growing, what good will this do in terms of actual dollars? What will the tangible payoffs be? Don't confuse value with opportunism.

Does the acquiring company wish to buy a business simply because it is available? That's what International Telephone and Telegraph did. From 1960 to 1977 ITT acquired more than 350 companies—at one time at the rate of one acquisition per week. They included well-known businesses such as Sheraton hotels, Avis Rent-a-Car, Hartford Insurance, and Continental Baking, the maker of Wonder Bread. During these 17 years, ITT grew from a medium-sized business with $760 million in sales to a global corporation with $17 billion in sales.

In the 10 years between the 1980s and 1990s, ITT continued on its buying spree, creating a broad group with interests ranging from hotels to pumps. In 1995, the company embarked on a continuous course of restructuring through strategic divestitures and acquisitions, which culminated in 1995 when ITT split into three separate, independent companies.[1] Ten years later the company was sold, and by 2011, it had separated into three stand-alone, publicly traded, independent companies, but not before earning the dubious distinction of being the first major defense contractor convicted of criminal violations. In reality, the serial acquiring frenzy did not create value; the group became unwieldy; and stakeholders paid the price for the company's lack of acquisition rationale and solid strategy formulation.

Start With a Comprehensive Understanding of Likely Futures

Once you have reached the conclusion that you should acquire, set the criteria for a successful deal *before* any mention of a particular company. On the other hand, you can generate this list of criteria as part of your strategy formulation, before you've even reached such a conclusion. In fact, my best clients create this list and then augment or edit it at each juncture as the economic and industry landscapes change.

For instance, one of the large companies I worked with found itself mired in one labor dispute after another. They had started sending work to China because the cost of shipping the materials there, having the work done there, and then shipping the finished product back was far less than having their workers do the job at their own plant. They didn't make this information public, nor did they telegraph their decision to pursue acquisitions that would allow them to bring non-union companies under their umbrella.

They set their labor-related criteria years before they started searching seriously for an actual target. When opportunity presented itself by way of a comparably sized company that did similar work, they were ready to close the deal almost overnight. They now operate the two companies separately, with different leadership in different states, and everyone involved considers this a successful deal—well, everyone except the union representatives. The parent company doubled in size. The target stayed in business and retained its culture and talent, and more money ended up in the coffers.

A more conventional approach would be for the parent company to start with a list of criteria and then begin the arduous process of evaluating potential targets vis-à-vis the list. Sometimes this "dating" stage takes years before the "marriage" can take place, particularly with small, family-owned businesses that have strong emotional commitments to their employees and family members who want to retain their positions. Leaders in these kinds of companies want to make sure they are making an ethical, moral, socially responsible business decision before they hand you the keys to their parents' or grandparents' legacies. Their need for handholding and reassurances sometimes unrealistically goes beyond the needs of a typical publicly traded or even a large privately held enterprise.

Be Realistic About Possible Synergies

People considering an acquisition use the word "synergy" as though it represents one of the acquisition sacred cows. But too often the word characterizes a far-off nirvana, not a likely scenario.

When you consider synergy, can you justify, in detail, what you hope it will achieve? What confirmation will you need to see? And what evidence exists to suggest the synergy will occur? You can measure and quantify things like cost reduction, but sales growth synergies will be much harder to calculate and achieve. Repeated research has taught us the general business lesson that companies cannot cut their way to success. Top line growth, more revenue, and more profit create the formula for strategic success, whether or not an acquisition takes place.

Identify the Trap Doors

Companies that have successfully acquired in the past have learned that effective due diligence holds the key to success. Just about everyone agrees that you must engage in financial and legal due diligence; others suggest assiduousness with regard to other kinds of evaluations that I'll address later.

During the strategy formulation stage, however, you'll want to engage in what is known as commercial due diligence. That is, you'll want to know how market or competitive uncertainty will impact the value of a company, the feasibility of realizing profits and revenues in the near future, and the validity of assumptions about revenue projections that are based on the success of new products, customers, or markets.

Deloitte, a company that specializes in helping clients with M&As, suggests these kinds of commercial due diligence analyses:

- Evaluate future market trends, competitive strength of the business, and underlying drivers of these trends.
- Analyze customers and their key purchase criteria.
- Estimate the achievability of forecasted assumptions, in light of market and company analysis.
- Hire an M&A specialist/M&A strategy team to analyze the buy-side and sell-side of the deal.[2]

Sometimes internal officers of the parent company attempt to do most of the due diligence themselves, but I discourage this approach for two reasons. First, unless your team has been involved in a number of acquisitions, they lack expertise in this arena. Second, your functional leads probably already have enough to do without adding the extra work of examining another company. Taking eyes off the parent company during an acquisition accounts for too many disappointments in the archives of failed M&A work.

In 1987, Ferranti overlooked another kind of trap door when it purchased International Signal and Control (ISC), a U.S. defense contractor based in Pennsylvania. Unknown to senior leaders at Ferranti, ISC's business primarily consisted of illegal arms sales started at the behest of various U.S. clandestine organizations. On paper, the company looked extremely profitable on sales of high-priced "above board" items, but in fact, these profits did not exist. With the sale to Ferranti, all illegal sales ended immediately, leaving the company with no obvious cash flow.

In 1989, the UK's Serious Fraud Office started a criminal investigation of alleged massive fraud at ISC. In December 1991, James Guerin, founder of ISC and co-chairman of the merged company, pleaded guilty to fraud committed both in the United States and United Kingdom. The U.S. trial encompassed all offences which would have formed part of any UK prosecution, so no UK trial ensued. But the resulting financial and legal difficulties forced Ferranti into bankruptcy in December 1993.[3]

Ferranti would not have bankrupted itself by buying ISC had it conducted commercial due diligence (CDD) and spoken to a few (nonexistent) customers instead of just relying on accountancy firm KPMG's audit. KPMG had given Ferranti International Signal clean bill of health weeks before the discovery of frauds totaling 215 million pounds. The auditors at KPMG didn't anticipate fraud, so they didn't expect to see it; however, if decision-makers had engaged in or hired a specialist to conduct more commercial due diligence, they would have realized neither the customers nor the key purchase criteria existed. After the fact, analysts admitted that the fraud was designed and executed with extraordinary care and skill. Two fictitious contracts—one for the United Arab Emirates and the other for Pakistan—had been created to deceive the accountants into accepting a certain level of profit—one that didn't exist.

But due diligence is not just about finding problems. In particular, good CDD identifies and quantifies the synergies, helps the acquirer to value the business through clear assumptions, and provides useful information for negotiation. Very importantly, CDD should identify both trap doors and key integration actions.

Facilitate the Deal

To keep from hampering the deal, much of the requisite evaluation must start in the strategy formulation stage. Begin by asking whether all the necessary internal and external processes and relationships are in place. If fever and passion grip the organization at some point, as they often do, an acquisition, however poor, quickly turns into a runaway train. Don't let the train leave the station too soon, but equally important, don't block the tracks with internal approvals that aren't in place, processes that have bogged down, or regulatory approvals that haven't shown up. Above all, avoid annoying the seller and allowing a competitor to slip in and woo your frustrated target away from you. Poorly briefed sellers can lose their patience and confidence over run-of-the-mill terms with which they are unfamiliar; similarly, if relationships break down during the critical final days of the deal, an unforeseen trap door will open in the earth, and all the players and their good intentions and due diligence will fall through it. As Enterprise pats itself on the back, Dollar rues the day it let the Vanguard deal slip through their fingers—and it all happened so quickly.

Tie Implementation to Strategy

When researchers survey business leaders on their opinions about why an M&A initiative has failed, often they flag implementation as the primary cause of problems. Blaming implementation rather than looking at the acquisition strategy, however, looks at effect, not cause. The reasons for failure may show up during the implementation stage, and people will eagerly jump on the "incompatible cultures" bandwagon, when, in reality, leaders hadn't thoroughly or effectively evaluated exactly what they intended to purchase.

If decision-makers have given the green light to the acquisition, a holistic approach to the deal should begin. Human resources, IT, legal, and finance should work closely with business units to define specific roles and responsibilities required for the entire M&A process, but it doesn't stop there. Functional and business leaders must have a clear understanding of how their roles will change not only during the acquisition process but also of how their worlds will change forever after. It all starts with a clear understanding of the new business.

All tangible benefits don't come in dollars, however. Sometimes the company will enjoy tangible benefits related to the ability to attract better talent, decreased turnover, key customers, etc. And sometimes the value will relate to intangible benefits to the CEO, the CEO's direct reports, or to the company itself. For example, the company may enjoy improved repute in the industry or better customer satisfaction. Sometimes senior leaders find themselves in a game they never intended to play in the first place, as the leaders of ITT did. At other times, parents receive unexpected rewards when they position themselves to play a bigger, more rewarding game. That's what Enterprise did.

In 2007, Enterprise Rent-A-Car marked their 50th anniversary and had much to celebrate. With more than $9 billion in global revenue, they were the largest car rental company in the world and one of the largest family-owned and -operated companies in the United States. That all changed when Enterprise owners learned in February of 2007 of the proposed merger of their two biggest airport rivals, Vanguard (which owned National and Alamo) and Dollar Thrifty Automotive Group. This transaction, had it come to fruition, would not only have compromised Enterprise's growth strategy, it would also have placed an almost insurmountable barrier to Enterprise's goal to expand airport business.

Enterprise had a strong growth strategy and realized that to continue to grow at the rate they desired, they needed to increase their share of airport rentals, so they immediately recognized the threat of standing by idly as four rival brands combined into one competitor—a monolith that would have endangered their best efforts. That didn't happen. Instead, Andy Taylor signed the papers to buy Vanguard on August 1, less than six months after he read the article in the *New York Times* that his rivals intended to merge.[4] The deal paid for itself in less than three years, and total revenues for all three brands now surpass $16 billion—pretty healthy growth during a six-year period when many other companies shuttered their doors or wish they had.

Enterprise's success holds no mystery, secret sauce, or unavailable formula. They did most things right—and quickly. They had a clear growth strategy in place, one that remained open to acquisitions. Second, Enterprise has little bureaucracy at the top, so senior leaders can respond to industry trends (the proposed merger of Vanguard and Dollar) in unprecedented time frames, and senior leaders recognized that after formulation, evaluation, and integration had to follow.

Evaluate

Although this section is devoted to an in-depth discussion of the role of *evaluation* in an M&A process, appraisal, valuations, and assessment of the target company should happen at each turn—before, during, and after the decision to acquire has been made. Evaluation has neither a "start" nor a "start date." Rather, it involves a circular, continuous process of reevaluating new information as it becomes available and reassessment of existing data as new events shape reality. At all times, the parent company's strategic objective must serve as a lighthouse for all the ships at sea, a beacon that will show the way to success.

Any discussion of strategy should include an examination of the company's strategic forces, the power that drives the business's strategy and governs its tactics. Tregoe and Zimmerman described this strength as a company's driving force—"the primary determiner of the scope of future products and markets." This driving force helps you understand why you are in the business you're in and not another, why you make the products you make and not others, and why you serve the markets you serve and not others. It also helps you evaluate whether your own company's driving force will match or complement the driving force of a target company you're considering. The "driving force" concept holds the key to strategically managing major product and market choices that your organization must resolve, and it serves as the touchstone for making the strategic decisions you will face as you consider a merger or acquisition.[5]

When senior leaders in the parent company have made strategic decisions, either consciously or unconsciously, they have reached agreement about the driving forces. Often leaders use the organization's driving force as a litmus test for generating and evaluating future alternatives because it provides a mechanism for developing, specifying, and understanding the different available alternatives. For example, McDonald's driving force is method of distribution. People go to the fast-food restaurant not for fine dining, gourmet fare, or ambiance. They want inexpensive food fast, available without leaving the car. So, when decision-makers at McDonald's consider alternative futures, they usually stay within the framework that has worked.

When senior leaders consider an acquisition, they need to make the implied obvious and the discussion concrete, not abstract. They should first examine their own driving forces and speculate about how they might profit from adding to or complementing them. But they will also want to examine any driving forces–related threats that might lurk post-acquisition, an often-overlooked aspect of due diligence. Like physicians who embrace the Hippocratic Oath, acquisition decision-makers must first do no harm. They can't *infer* benefits post acquisition just because at first blush the companies' strategies seem aligned and their driving forces compatible. They must dig for evidence to support their hopes. Therefore, in addition to weighing the general benefits they hope to gain, senior leaders would do well personally and professionally to examine the following driving forces and strategic factors to determine how their lives and the lives among those in their chain of command will change with an acquisition.

Markets Served

A market is a group of current or potential buyers who share common needs. An organization whose driving force is market needs will provide a range of products to fill current and emerging demands of customers in that market. These companies will constantly search for alternative ways to respond to these customers.

With that in mind, to understand whether a target company serves a given market as part of its strategy, begin by asking, "To whom do they sell?" What drives profits up or down, and what is happening within the company to do that? Enterprise had answers; Hewlett-Packard didn't.

As Enterprise considered acquiring Vanguard, they spotted the obvious market share attractions: Both National and Alamo had already established themselves across the country. Further, neither Alamo nor National was a major contender in non-airport rentals, which meant they had virtually no overlap with Enterprise's facilities, technology, or personnel.

Working out why the business is really for sale helps too; the seller may have spotted an unapparent problem looming in the market. That's what seems to have happened when dot-com investors and traditional businesses acquired new economy start-ups and misjudged the market dramatically. People often overestimate the impact of new technologies and other market shifts in the short term, but underestimate them in the long term.

Enterprise's acquisition of Vanguard brought more than market share: it brought the key customers—very different customers—under the Enterprise umbrella. National attracted the business travelers, sometimes called the "rental experts" because they want to get in and out of their vehicles as fast as possible, without stopping to fill out forms or stand in line. And these customers are willing to pay a premium for those benefits—the Emerald Club serving as a major driver of reservations and repeat business. Alamo, on the other hand, appealed to vacationers, often from outside the United States. who headed to places like Las Vegas and Disney World. Its customers generally looked for bargains on the internet. Each brand had significant value and offered its customers what was most important to them.

Products Offered

Companies that use products and services as their driving force ask themselves continuously, "*What* will we sell?" These senior leaders of these organizations realize that products or services play a key role in the future of the company. Therefore, the most profitable strategy for this kind of company is to continue to deliver products similar to those it has, and leaders look for novel ways to improve these products. For example, Coca-Cola has had the number-one or -two position in the soft drink industry since its inception more than 125 years ago. Originally developed for medicinal purposes, it quickly seized the soft drink market and became the most recognizable brand in the world.

Decision-makers at Coke have added new products to their portfolio, including variations on Coke, sports drinks, and juices. They have even introduced recipes on their Website that include Coke as an ingredient. They improve next year's model by responding to trends, like adding vanilla or cherry to the recipe, but they haven't deviated too far from their success formula: develop soft drinks and similar products that people use for entertainment.

When companies aspire to merge with a company that offers similar—but not exactly the same—products and services, the vast sea of the unknown takes on scary proportions. That's what happened when eBay bought an internet telephone upstart called Skype in 2005 for $2.6 billion, hoping online buyers would prefer video calls to e-mail.

Senior decision-makers *inferred* that online buyers and sellers would want to talk to each other. They learned a tough and expensive lesson. After four unfulfilling years, eBay sold 65 percent of Skype at a loss to private investors. eBay eventually saved most of the day and recovered some of its losses, which makes the series of transactions less than desirable but not totally dismal.[6]

In addition to evaluating a company's products, consider, too, its production capability. Production capability includes the manufacturing know-how, processes, systems, and equipment required to make specific products and the capability to improve those processes. The target company's products can differ from the acquirer's while still offering the utilization of existing production systems and equipment.

Methods for Sales and Distribution

In addition to evaluating their target's key customers, Enterprise executives examined Vanguard's methods for selling their services. Not surprisingly, Vanguard had a much deeper understanding of airport operations. At Orlando, Los Angeles, and other big airports, National and Alamo mangers presided over thousands of rental transactions every day. Their systems and processes operated on a much bigger scale than Enterprise's did. After thorough evaluation, the senior leaders at Enterprise eventually adopted Vanguard's programs because they determined they were better than Enterprise's existing ones for airport rental.

The *way* products reach the customer, and the systems and equipment to support the method, drive this kind of company. Sometimes this driving force can combine with another to form something greater than the individual entities, as it did with Enterprise. But sometimes it won't. Would people buy Girl Scout cookies off the shelf at the supermarket, even if they knew the profit to the Girl Scouts would remain the same? Doubtful. The driving force behind the success of Girl Scout cookies has everything to do with little girls selling to their neighbors and nothing to do with the actual product or any other driving force.

Acquiring companies that have ignored the importance of methods of distribution have paid greatly, as Quaker Oats did. In 1997, ending what some analysts have called the worst acquisition in memory, the Quaker Oats Company sold Snapple to the Triarc Companies for $1.4 billion less than Quaker paid for the drink company in 1994.

Quaker bought Snapple, which had been a successful pioneer in the market of fruit and tea drinks, just as sales growth in "new age beverages," was slowing. From the outset, critics said that Quaker had paid at least $1 billion more than Snapple was worth.

Senior leaders at Quaker dove head-first into a new marketing campaign and set out to introduce Snapple to every grocery store and chain restaurant they could. But they sabotaged their own efforts by damaging relationships with Snapple's independent distributors. Quaker soon discovered that its highly regarded skills in distribution to supermarkets and grocery store chains mattered little in a business that had previously relied on sales to convenience stores, gasoline stations, and similar outlets.

Their efforts failed miserably as the domino effect of the acquisition became apparent. Snapple had built its success on sales to small, independent stores; the brand just couldn't hold its own in large grocery stores. Further, with Snapple's woes overshadowing the rest of Quaker's operations, including Gatorade and the strong performance of the company's cereals and packaged foods, Quaker's stock stagnated while the overall stock market doubled. After just 27 months, Quaker Oats sold Snapple for $300 million—a loss of $1.6 million for each day that the company owned Snapple. Numerous executives lost their jobs, including CEO William Smithsburg, whose reputation suffered.[7]

New Technology Options

When technology drives an organization, the company offers only products and services that originate from or capitalize on its technological capability. In such an organization, technology determines the scope of products offered and markets served, rather than the products and markets determining the technology. The technology-driven organization seeks a variety of applications for its technology. It does this through the products or services it develops from this technology, or from selling the output of its technology to those who would develop further products or services.

Even though the company does not always initiate the technological breakthroughs, many technology-driven organizations focus on converting breakthroughs made elsewhere to a variety of applications. For instance, the U.S. Center for Disease Control does not engage in all the cutting-edge research and development to fight disease. Rather, it serves as the conduit for these breakthroughs to protect the health of Americans.

In 2005, Sprint paid a whopping $36 billion for a majority stake in fellow telecom company Nextel to boost its use base, and revenues and to create a wireless powerhouse. The "merger of equals" never came together as Sprint and Nextel planned.

Both companies thought they would be able to quickly merge customers and catch up to Verizon and AT&T. But Nextel's network ran on a different technology than Sprint's, making it difficult for the combined company to optimize its wireless infrastructure assets. Sprint had to put its radios on all of Nextel's towers, and vice versa. Nextel's push-to-talk technology grew less popular over the years, and customers began fleeing the network in droves, as did Nextel executives.

Sprint finally shut down the Nextel network in July 2013, with the final blow coming in the form of a software code. Sprint had planned for years to close Nextel's inefficient second-generation technology so the airwaves could be used for more profitable, newer data services. The shutdown also removed the encumbrance of maintaining multiple network technologies in the competitive wireless industry. Many blame "cultural differences" for the failure of the acquisition, but that offers a generic explanation for a specific cause related to a failure to evaluate how the driving force of technology differed in the two companies.[8]

Financial Synergy

Sometimes an acquiring company will evaluate a target and determine that the products, services, or markets served align closely enough to take the plunge—a push that they hope will help them create more profit—only to discover that they have plummeted into the abyss. For example, in 2008, Nelson Peltz, the owner of Arby's roast beef sandwich restaurants, acquired Wendy's, the fast-food chain famous for its made-to-order "square hamburgers" and chocolate desserts, for approximately $2 billion. The deal transpired after two chaotic years during which Wendy's sold or spun off operations, reduced its corporate staff, and suffered a tarnishing blow to its wholesome image when a woman falsely claimed she found part of a finger in her chili.

The combined company not only failed to attain financial synergy, in the midst of the Great Recession, it lost money in seven of its 10 quarters. Three years later, in 2011, the marriage of square burgers and roast beef sandwiches ended, but not without more financial trouble and role reversal. Arby's started as the suitor in the relationship, and ended the jilted lover.[9]

Bank of America learned, too, that it had been better off without Countrywide, even though their approaches to products, markets, and sales had been similar at one time. Once the nation's largest mortgage lender, Countrywide pioneered lending programs that aggressively reached into minority and low-income neighborhoods. But by early 2008, as the mortgage bubble was bursting, the firm was hobbled by soured loans and it needed a buyer. Kenneth D. Lewis, then Bank of America's chief, saw an opportunity to seize the company for a bargain price, the first of many expenses that led to a flood of red ink.

In January 2008, Bank of America agreed to pay $4 billion for Countrywide—a bargain. That bargain quickly turned bitter two years later when the penalties began. In 2010, Countrywide incurred a $110 million penalty for overcharging "cash-strapped borrowers." Two months after that, Countrywide agreed to pay $600 million to settle a lawsuit with its shareholders. And two months after that Bank of America paid $20 million to cover former Countrywide CEO Angelo Mozilo's $67.5 million civil fraud settlement with the Securities and Exchange Commission.

Three months later, in January 2011, the company paid more than $2.5 billion to buy back problematic mortgages and resolve claims from Fannie and Freddie. Throughout 2012 Bank of America paid more than $22 billion in settlements and fines.[10]

Would more robust financial due diligence have saved Bank of America from this fate? It's easy to speculate and play Monday-morning quarterback. But one thing remains clear: even when the strategy for acquiring a target is related to streamlining resources, consolidating costs, or aligning products, acquiring companies do well to look beyond what's in the books and examine what's in the *culture* of the target.

Financial performance—with a clear focus on revenue growth more than cost control—is the single most important grade in evaluating acquisitive success because even small changes in revenue can outweigh major changes in planned cost savings. But a dropoff in sales immediately after the acquisition will also be one of the worst things you can experience. Unfortunately, leaders find these kinds of dips in revenue, profits, and sales all too common, given confusion among the newly merged team and the customer base. Too often, you can never make up these losses.

Therefore, immediately and inexorably tie sales momentum—especially with key customers—to both implementation of the strategy and revenue growth. Make this the number-one priority. The new owners, not just the sales force, should get out in front of customers, tell them what's going on, and reassure them. It's amazing how rarely that happens. But if you don't control the message and make it the message customers want to hear, rumors and negative assumptions will fill the void. This step forms the natural link between evaluation and integration.

Integrate

Does the integration plan cater to customers in detail? Acquirers fall easily into the trap of focusing so heavily on internal reorganization that they ignore customers at the most critical time. Has the parent considered integration benefits? If so, senior leaders should have a plan prepared as a part of the valuation exercise and position themselves to take rapid action. This is often not the case automatically, however. In the heat of finalizing the deal, integration is often left until the last minute or ignored entirely.

Evaluation of the parent company's strategy and strategic forces sets the stage for examination of the target's strategy. Only after senior leaders have aggregated the data from a thorough assessment of both companies can the integration process begin—a process that will circle back to more strategic questions that will showcase cultural differences, the parts of the companies that should be integrated, and the parts that should remain separate. Not all acquisitions require integration, however. Sometimes the parent company will decide to run the newly acquired company as a separate entity with no future plans to join anything. More often some integration needs to occur.

Teams of experts typically work with functional leads to integrate IT systems, HR systems, and financial reporting protocols. Just as often, however, these same companies overlook one of the most significant causes of M&A failure: an inadequate understanding of cultural differences.

As I explained in Chapter Three, corporate culture involves the pattern of shared assumptions that a company has adopted and adapted over a period of time as they solved their problems and adjusted to the world around them. During a merger, the goal is to join two companies that might have adopted and adapted to the world in very different ways. When this happens, problems occur.

People talk about cultural differences compromising the success of M&A deals as though everyone defined culture the same way. To further muddy the water, many view *culture* as some sort of complicated, abstract, nebulous force that may or may not be with you as you begin the trek of fusing the ways companies do business. Although all aspects of culture play a role in any major transaction, the cultural differences that derail M&A deals have more to do with beliefs about the ways the companies make money, and less to do with customs and interactions.

Some authors refer to "incompatible business models" undermining a deal, but what does that really suggest? It means that when companies make money in vastly different ways, doing extremely different things, and no one recognizes or addresses these differences, the merged company risks destabilization. Though decision-makers should consider the mission, vision, and values of a target company, more importantly, they should ask these questions about a target company the "Critical Five Factors":

- How do they make money?
- Who are their best customers?
- What value do they provide them?
- How do they do that?
- What threats and opportunities might alter these in the future?

I find that too often the leaders of the company trying to make a decision about whether to acquire can't answer these questions for their own company, so certainly they don't think to ask them about another company's Critical Five Factors. No hope springs eternal, therefore, that the answers from both companies will guide a seamless integration. Here are some ways to ask the questions that will determine what kinds of important cultural differences you're likely to face.

How Do They Make Money?

Senior leaders should begin asking this question in the strategy formulation stage, continue asking it through evaluation, and never abandon it as integration decisions begin to surface. "Do we really understand how this business makes money?" Different companies in the same market make money for different reasons. In retail, Wal-Mart focuses on low prices, Nordstrom's on customer service, and Neiman Marcus on exceptional quality. Each company has been successful in the same industry for vastly different reasons. To determine whether a target will augment or complement your business model, you'll need to make time to understand how the target operates—how it makes its money and where it could be losing out. From this analysis, the acquirer must make a comprehensive assessment of if or how the parent and target will be integrated into the new joint operation—where the operational and business development gains are to be achieved.

Companies make money in a variety of ways, and thousands of business books can show you the various formulas for determining the role revenue, cost savings, cash flow, and returns on investments and assets should play. When the deal moves to the due diligence phase, the finance people will have myriad lenses to look through to examine the financial fit of the organization. But you'll also have to consider how these financial decisions affect the behaviors of all employees, from the senior leadership team down through the chain of command.

Can each employee at each level tell you the company's mission statement? When I asked this question to an audience of 200 people from different companies, three of the 200 hands proudly shot up to proclaim that the executive of that company could remember the mission statement, but the other 197 sat stoically. Yet, when I asked these same people to tell me what's on a Big Mac, the entire audience recited in unison, "Two all beef patties, special sauce...." In other words, a commercial that has not been on TV for more than 20 years stayed in their memories more prominently than their own mission statements! If you resemble the majority of that audience, you're missing a basic element of your strategic direction. If the leaders of your target company don't know theirs either, what chance do you have of landing on the same page?

In addition to defining the organization's identity, the mission guides its development through time. Although it should be resistant to capriciousness, as the external landscape changes, leaders must tweak the mission statement as they recognize how to translate purpose into practice. In other words, the mission statement helps you know who you are. Successful organizations have a clear sense of purpose that defines long-term directions so that they don't let shortsightedness jeopardize their best efforts.

You'll also want to know whether they have a clear strategy for the future, a plan for *what* they have to do to make money. You should also detect widespread agreement about goals and have an indication that the leadership team has gone on record about the objectives they aspire to reach. Ideally, you should discern that other organizations change the way they compete in the industry with your target company, but if the company is for sale that may prove unrealistic. Whatever answers you receive to your questions, one conclusion should remain clear: We can work with this company to align our mission, vision, and strategy so that we can start making money fast.

Who Are Their Best Customers?

For obvious reasons, an existing customer base makes a company attractive from a strategic standpoint, but from a cultural viewpoint, decision-makers need to look beyond who the customers are to understand how the target company interacts with them. You'll want to know whether or not senior leaders of the target company listen to their customers and whether or not customer input directly influences decisions to change. You'll need evidence that the executives of the company understand what their customers want, what they expect, their perceptions of playing a role in influencing decisions, and which customers would miss them if they went away.

This goes beyond understanding their value proposition, although that's a significant first step. You'll want to know that the company's leaders have listened to the voice of the customer and actually let that voice direct their direction—that they understand their customers, satisfy them, and anticipate their needs. This information will help you better understand the value they have provided in the past and are likely to provide in the future.

What Value Do They Provide Those Customers?

When I work with other consultants to help them decide on their value propositions, I encourage them to start with the generic one: "I improve the client condition." That helps them stay focused on meeting the client's needs, not on selling their processes or systems—no matter how good those may be. As the consultants evolve, they often choose something more specific to their skills set and interest. For example, a sales expert might say that she helps organizations increase their market share. An executive coach may state that she works with executives who want to improve their performance. In each case, the consultant clearly articulates how she improves the client's condition.

So, too, should your target organization communicate how their customers are better off because they use the products or services of the company. Sometimes the company will sell a commodity, so you'll want to understand why *that* product or service and not their competitors'.

But you don't hire a brain surgeon or buy a Bentley that way. If you were to find yourself in need of a brain surgeon, you would want the best surgeon you could get, and cost would not play much of a role, provided you had the means to pay for the best. You would want to know about the doctor's repute, experience, and success rate. If you were in the market for a luxury car, you would consider things other than a basic mode of transportation.

As you examine your target company's brand and repute, what do you find? Do they respond well to competitors and other changes in the business or industry environments? What about their record for taking prudent risks and reaping the benefits? What evidence do you see that they continue to learn and grow? Once again, if the company is for sale, the news might not all be good. So you'll want to evaluate their willingness to improve their processes and protocols as you simultaneously determine what those are. That willingness to adapt will contribute to or detract from your efforts to integrate the cultures.

How Do They Provide That Value?

In addition to finding out what they do to create value for their customers, you'll want to know whether their tactics for meeting their strategic goals match or could match yours. What resources, like advanced research and development or thought leaders, do they have that they use wisely and that you might tap into? How do they empower employees and involve them in reaching objectives? What key talent must you retain to keep things on track? What patents and other intellectual property do they own? What processes and procedures have served them well? The answers to these questions will do two things. First, you'll understand which among their sacred cows you'll spare, and second, you might discover ways to improve your own ways of doing business.

Do different functions and units of the organization work together well? Do departmental or group boundaries interfere with cooperation? What about their team orientation versus value for solo contributions? Some companies have an "up or out" mentality, whereas others make room for the strong solo contributor who never wants management responsibility. Have they invested in the development of their top performers and kept them from taking their talents to the competition? You'll want to understand what key talent needs to stay, but you'll also benefit from knowledge about their promotion procedures as well as their succession planning.

One of the biggest impediments to integration involves change—the change itself, the fear it brings, and the speed with which it happens. Everyone on both sides of the deal will expect change; the fear will surface when people don't understand what those changes will be or when they will occur. During these critical times, indecision will be your enemy.

The tough calls about priorities should happen without delay. Otherwise, people develop a what-shoe-will-fall-next phobia that will interfere with both morale and productivity. So, remove uncertainty by making the top-priority, value-enhancing changes quickly.

You'll need a plan to communicate messages about the change, another step that too many companies neglect. During any M&A deal, stress remains high; people at all levels of the organization misinterpret messages; and rumors spread. Repeat key messages and avoid hype and empty promises.

What Will the Future Bring?

During a night in the hospital, nurses will routinely visit a patient's room to take vital signs, looking for indications that the patient's health has improved or deteriorated. If things have worsened, the nurse will immediately notify a doctor to develop a new course of action. Similarly, if the patient shows remarkable improvement, things will change too. Businesses could learn many lessons from this protocol: monitor at regular intervals and then make small, relevant adjustments as needed. If they did, they could spot both challenges and opportunities while they lurked on the horizon. But too often, senior leaders wait until these crucibles knock on the door.

If you had evaluated Blockbuster in 2002, while Netflix was in its infancy and the web still nascent technology, and you asked the first four critical questions, you would have given the company high marks as an acquisition target. But, if you had asked how well prepared they were to deal with emerging distribution systems, you would have felt less confident about their ability even to sustain their value. With some foresight, you might have predicted they were six years from irrelevancy and nine years from bankruptcy. The same test would apply to companies in the music and publishing industries over the last five to seven years.

Sophisticated Due Diligence on People and Succession Planning

Most parent companies conscientiously concentrate on integration of business systems but ignore a more important part of the transaction: the assimilation of people. A year or two after close, senior leaders may realize they should have done things differently, but by that time much damage can accrue.

I have helped clients with people decisions at each juncture of the acquisition process—before, during, and after an acquisition. For instance, I was one of eight succession-planning experts who worked directly with John Tyson after his company's acquisition of International Beef Products in 2002. This is what John Tyson told *Harvard Business Review* journalists about our work:

> The CEO realized that his ad hoc approach to leadership development was not working. He formed a senior executive task force to look into the problem. The team included himself, his direct reports, and a small group of external succession-planning experts, who were there to ensure objectivity and high standards and to help facilitate buy in. The task force members took nothing for granted. They sat down with a blank sheet of paper and mapped out their ideal leadership development system for Tyson. The blueprint they came up with integrated succession planning and leadership development, made sure that promising leaders would be well versed in all aspects of the company's business, and put the accountability for succession planning and leadership development squarely on the shoulders of John Tyson's direct reports. "Leaders at all levels were either in or out," Tyson recalled. They couldn't waffle about contributing their time and effort to the new talent development system; they couldn't "protect" talent, hoard resources, or declare themselves immune from succession planning, he said.[11]

Our work with Tyson helped the combined companies position themselves for immediate success. Leaders realized they each had to take responsibility for driving the initiative and making the tough calls. No one expected overnight success or easy answers. But when billions of dollars stand in the balance, what reasonable person would expect simplicity?

Usually I enter the process earlier. Often I've worked with a company to make the decision to acquire; at other times executives call me in after they've made the decision to buy but before they close the deal. These clients realize they have to have immediate, accurate, objective data about key talent before they make the final decision to buy, the decision to retain or dismiss redundant talent, and the decisions regarding compensation packages. To this end, I have developed a Succession Planning Report that captures the following:

- Career history.
- Performance review data.
- Career aspirations.
- Success criteria (e.g., strategic thinking, learning speed, analytical reasoning, motivation, leadership potential, teamwork orientation, people skills, financial acumen).
- Cognitive assessment: learning speed, critical thinking, numerical reasoning.
- Leadership knowledge.
- Function work experience: HR, warehouse, finance, IT, sales, legal, manufacturing, administration.
- Primary strengths.
- Development imperatives.
- Leadership effectiveness.
- Promotion status.

Once decision-makers have this one-page report for each key person, they can begin the process of determining who will lead what. If you have two seemingly competent CFOs, for instance, how do you know which one to keep? The tendency will be for the acquiring company to keep its senior leaders in place, but this often spells disaster. Frequently I spot a star among the target's team, a star who will leave if not given a position and the compensation package that goes with it.

Like evaluation, integration continues from the minute the buyer signs on the dotted line, until everyone alive has forgotten that two separate companies ever existed—in other words, forever. Although commonality exists regarding best practices for making the integration go smoothly—embracing both the art and science of the amalgamation—differences and unique outliers surface too. Let nothing surprise you.

And have a clear plan for running your own business while you divert resources to the new initiative.

Conclusion

Recent history has taught some hard lessons about M&As—one of the most salient being that many, if not most, acquisitions should never have happened. The second lesson indicates that the first lesson might be moot if the parent had done more and better positioning for the acquisition. That doesn't mean more of the same due diligence all conscientious companies always would have done. That means a different formulation approach, starting with an in-depth understanding of the parent's strategy and culture. Only after senior leaders have aggregated these data should they begin the arduous journey of setting criteria, considering targets, evaluating these targets vis-à-vis the criteria, and negotiating deals. Then, they will be ready to apply the same robust examination of the target's Critical Five Factors.

Are you currently running the existing business well enough to sustain the strain of integrating another one? A company should start an acquisition from a position of strength and a firm foundation, as acquisition puts a substantial strain on the acquirer's resources. If a company faces difficulties on the home front, an acquisition is unlikely to solve them.

No matter what the facts tell you, don't assume the sanctity of all integration. Consider emotion too—yours, your employees', and your customers'. Who in Chicago will soon forget Macy's demanding the name change of Marshall Field's in 2006, compromising a brand name that has stood for excellence in Chicago since 1881? Too often the acquiring company insists on improving things, replacing things, and renaming things that didn't need to change in the first place. Marshall Field's could have retained its name, brand, and loyal customers were it not for the wrong-minded attempts at corporate Macy's.

The parent will have to make numerous unpopular integration decisions, but none has to be demoralizing. If you found the company worth buying in the first place, it's probably worth trusting, funding, and encouraging it to thrive without unnecessary interference.

Appendix

Accountability Chart

A = Authority to make decisions alone.

R = Responsibility for completing the task.

N = Notification: Person is notified of decision.

C = Consultation: This person must okay the decision before you proceed.

Major Decision/ Task	Name	Name	Name	Name

Notes

Chapter 1

1. Manyika, J., M. Chui, B. Brown, J. Bughlin, R. Dobbs, C. Roxburgh, and A. Byers, "Big Data: The Next Frontier for Innovation, Competition, and Productivity," *McKinsey Quarterly*, May 2011.

2. Charan, R., *Global Tilt: Leading Your Business Through the Great Economic Power Shift* (New York: Crown Business, 2013), pp. 15–17.

3. Collins, J., and M. Hansen, *Great by Choice* (Harper Business, 2011), pp. 9–10.

4. "Wal-Mart Grapples With Its Worst Sales Slump Ever," *The Wall Street Journal*, February 22, 2011.

5. Anderegg, C.R., *Sierra Hotel* (Washington D.C.: Air Force History and Museums Programs, 2001).

6. Rand, A., *Return of the Primitive: The Anti-Industrial Revolution* (New York: Penguin Books, 1999), p.130.

Chapter 2

1. Drucker, P., "What Executives Should Remember," *Harvard Business Review* February 2006, p. 147.

2. Drucker, p. 149.

3. *www.rand.org.*

4. Tregoe, B., and J. Zimmerman, *Top Management Strategy.* (New York: Simon & Schuster, 1980), p. 20.

5. Maister, D., *Strategy and the Fat Smoker* (Boston: The Spangle Press, 2008), pp. 4–6.

6. Kazanjian, K., *Exceeding Customer Expectations: What Enterprise, America's #1 Car Rental Company, Can Teach You About Creating Lifetime Customers* (Doubleday, 2007), p. xv.

7. Moorhead, F., and Neck, "Group Decision Fiascos Continue: Space Shuttle Challenger and a Groupthink Framework," *Human Relation* (Plenum Publishing Corporation, 1991), Vol. 44.

8. Verhovek, S., *Jet Age* (New York: Penguin Group, 2010), pp. 9–21.

Chapter 3

1. Schein, E., *Organizational Culture and Leadership* (San Francisco: Jossey-Bass, 1992), pp. 12–13.

2. Catton, B., *The Civil War* (New York: American Heritage Press, 1971), pp. 160–161.

3. Tellis, G., and P. Golder, *Will and Vision* (New York: McGraw-Hill, 2002), pp. 43, 46, 290–292.

4. Senge, P., *The Fifth Discipline* (New York: Doubleday Currency, 1990), pp. 127–135.

5. Wiseman, R. *www.laughlab.co.uk*

Chapter 4

1. Interview with Thomas Downing U.S. Navy, retired, and former commander of TOPGUN, August 2012.

2. Interview with C. R. Anderegg, USAF colonel, retired, and former Air Force Historian, May 2012.

3. *www.barbiemedia.com/barbie_facts_by-the-numbers.html.*

4. *http://corporate.mattel.com/about-us/history/mattel_history. pdf.*

5. Lee, Bill, *The Hidden Wealth of Customers* (Boston: Harvard Business Review Press, 2012), p. 3.

6. Diamond, J., *Guns, Germs, and Steel* (New York: W.W. Norton & Company, Inc., 1997), p. 15.

7. Diamond, p. 438.

8. Diamond, p. 435.

9. Interview with Amanda Setili, August, 2013.

Chapter 5

1. Shurkin, J., *Terman's Kids* (New York: Little, Brown, 1992), p. 10.

2. Jensen, A., *Bias in Mental Testing* (Free Press, 1980), p. 113.

3. Gladwell, M., *Outliers* (New York: Little Brown & Company, 2008), p. 35.

4. Seligman, M., *Learned Optimism* (New York: Free Press, 1990), p. 29.

Chapter 6

1. Spitz, Bob, *The Beatles: The Biography* (New York: Little, Brown, 2005), pp. 473–474.

2. Lewisohn, Mark, *The Complete Beatles Chronicle: The Definitive Day-By-Day Guide to the Beatles' Entire Career* (Chicago: Chicago Review Press, 2010), pp. 34–35.

3. Isaacson, W., *Benjamin Franklin: An American Life* (New York: Simon & Schuster, 2003), p. 484.

4. Isaacson, W., *Steve Jobs* (New York: Simon & Schuster, 2011), pp. 56, 180.

5. Gabler, N., *Walt Disney: The Triumph of the American Imagination* (New York: Random House, 2006), pp. xv, 563, 632.

6. Isaacson, W., *Einstein: His Life and Universe* (New York: Simon & Schuster, 2007), p. 545.

7. Isaacson, p. 551.

8. Interview with Richard Covey, September 28, 2011.

9. Hillendenbrand, L., *Unbroken* (New York: Random House, 2010), pp. 5, 119, 278.

10. Seligman, M., *Learned Optimism* (New York: Free Press, 1998), p. 15.

11. Interview with Christine Brewer, March 19, 2013.

Chapter 7

1. Maccoby, M., "Narcissistic Leaders: The Incredible Pros, the Inevitable Cons," *The Harvard Business Review* January–February 2000, p. 6.

2. Babiak, P., and R. Hare, *Snakes in Suits* (New York: Harper Collins, 2006), pp. 37–43.

3. Zanor, C., "A Fate That Narcissists Will Hate: Being Ignored," *The New York Times* November 29, 2010.

4. Sifneos, P., "Affect, Emotional Conflict, and Deficit: An Overview," *Psychotherapy and Psychosomatics* 56 (1991), pp. 116–122.

5. "Portfolio's Worst American CEOs of All Time: 19. Carly Fiorina," CNBC, *www.cnbc.com/id/30502091?slide=3*.

6. Markoff, J., "Company News—Visionary Apple Chairman Moves On," *The New York Times,* October 16, 1993.

Chapter 8

1. Gardner, J., *On Leadership* (New York: The Free Press, 1990), p. 113.

2. Anderegg, C., *Sierra Hotel: Flying Air Force Fighters in the Decade After Vietnam* (Washington, D.C.: Air Force History and Museums Program, 2001), Appendix.

3. Presentation by General Ronald Keys to the Air Force Association Conference, September 19, 2012.

4. Gardner, p. 161.

5. Updegrove, M., *Baptism by Fire: Eight Presidents Who Took Office in Times of Crisis* (New York: St. Martin's Press, 2008), p. 186.

6. Peter, L., and R. Hull, *The Peter Principle* (New York: William Morrow & Company, 1969).

7. Isaacson, W., *Steve Jobs* (New York: Simon & Schuster, 2011), pp. 56, 180.

Chapter 9

1. Belbin, R., *Management Teams: Why They Succeed or Fail, Third Edition* (Taylor & Francis, 2010), p. 14.

2. Goodwin, D., *Team of Rivals: The Political Genius of Abraham Lincoln* (New York: Simon & Schuster, 2005).

3. Cooper, T., and A. Ainsberg, *Breakthrough* (New York: St. Martin's Press, 2010), p. 86.

4. Coffey, W., *The Boys of Winter* (New York: Random House, 2005), p. viii.

5. Gratton, L., and T. Erickson, "Eight Ways to Build Collaborative Teams," *Harvard Business Review,* January 2010, p. 6.

6. Guffey, G. *The Greatest Basketball Story Ever Told: The Milan Miracle* (Bloomington, Ind.: Indiana University Press, 2003), pp. 104–110.

7. Interview with John Mabry, November 6, 2013.

Chapter 10

1. *www.itt.com/about/history.*

2. *www.deloitte.com.*

3. *www.mosi.org.uk/collections/explore-the-collections/ferranti-online/timeline.aspx.*

4. Taylor, A., "How I Did it: Enterprise's Leader on How Integrating an Acquisition Transformed His Business," *Harvard Business Review,* September 4, 2013.

5. Tregoe, B., and J. Zimmerman, *Top Management Strategy* (New York: Simon & Schuster, 1980), p. 40.

6. Kopykoff, V., "How eBay Fared in Latest Skype Deal," *New York Times*, May 10, 2011.

7. Feder, B., "Quaker to Sell Snapple for $300 Million," *New York Times*, March 28, 1997.

8. Grezta, T., "Spring's Nextel Network Is Finally No More," *Wall Street Journal*, July 1, 2013.

9. Rexrode, C., "Wendy's Sells Arby's to Equity Firm," *Huffington Post*, June 13, 2011.

10. Protess, B., "Tallying the Costs of Bank of America's Countrywide Nightmare," *New York Times*, October 25, 2012.

11. Cohn, J., R. Khurana, and L. Reeves, "Growing Talent as if Your Business Depended on It," *Harvard Business Review*, October 2005.

Bibliography

Anderegg, C.R. *Sierra Hotel.* Washington D.C.: Air Force History and Museums Programs, 2001.

Babiak, P., and R. Hare. *Snakes in Suits.* New York: HarperCollins, 2006.

Barbie Media. *www.barbiemedia.com/barbie_facts_by-the-numbers.html.*

Belbin, R. *Management Teams: Why They Succeed or Fail, Third Edition.* Taylor & Francis, 2010.

Catton, B. *The Civil War.* New York: American Heritage Press, 1971.

Charan, R. *Global Tilt: Leading Your Business Through the Great Economic Power Shift.* New York: Crown Business, 2013.

Coffey, W. *The Boys of Winter.* New York: Random House, 2005.

Cohn, J., R. Khurana, and L. Reeves. "Growing Talent as if Your Business Depended on It." *Harvard Business Review,* October 2005.

Collins, J., and M. Hansen. *Great by Choice.* Harper Business, 2011.

Cooper, T., and A. Ainsberg. *Breakthrough.* New York: St. Martin's Press, 2010.

Deloitte. *www.deloitte.com.*

Diamond, J. *Guns, Germs, and Steel.* New York: W.W. Norton & Company, Inc., 1997.

Drucker, P. "What Executives Should Remember." *Harvard Business Review,* February 2006.

Feder, B. "Quaker to Sell Snapple for $300 Million." *New York Times,* March 28, 1997.

Gabler, N. *Walt Disney: The Triumph of the American Imagination*. New York: Random House, 2006.

Gardner, J. *On Leadership*. New York: The Free Press, 1990.

Gladwell, M. *Outliers*. New York: Little Brown & Company, 2008.

Goodwin, D. *Team of Rivals: The Political Genius of Abraham Lincoln*. New York: Simon & Schuster, 2005.

Gratton, L., and T. Erickson. "Eight Ways to Build Collaborative Teams." *Harvard Business Review*, January 2010.

Grezta, T. "Spring's Nextel Network Is Finally No More." *Wall Street Journal*, July 1, 2013.

Guffey, G. *The Greatest Basketball Story Ever Told: The Milan Miracle*. Bloomington, Ind.: Indiana University Press, 2003.

Hillendenbrand, L. *Unbroken*. New York: Random House, 2010.

Isaacson, W. *Benjamin Franklin: An American Life*. New York: Simon & Schuster, 2003.

Isaacson, W. *Einstein: His Life and Universe*. New York: Simon & Schuster, 2007.

Isaacson, W. *Steve Jobs*. New York: Simon & Schuster, 2011.

ITT. *www.itt.com/about/history*.

Jensen, A. *Bias in Mental Testing*. New York: Free Press, 1980.

Kazanjian, K. *Exceeding Customer Expectations: What Enterprise, America's #1 Car Rental Company, Can Teach You About Creating Lifetime Customers*. New York: Doubleday, 2007.

Kopykoff, V. "How eBay Fared in Latest Skype Deal." *New York Times*, May 10, 2011.

Lee, Bill. *The Hidden Wealth of Customers*. Boston: Harvard Business Review Press, 2012.

Lewisohn, Mark. *The Complete Beatles Chronicle: The Definitive Day-By-Day Guide to the Beatles' Entire Career*. Chicago: Chicago Review Press, 2010.

Maccoby, M. "Narcissistic Leaders: The Incredible Pros, the Inevitable Cons." *The Harvard Business Review*, January–February 2000.

Maister, D. *Strategy and the Fat Smoker*. Boston: The Spangle Press, 2008.

Manyika, J., M. Chui, B. Brown, J. Bughlin, R. Dobbs, C. Roxburgh, and A. Byers. "Big Data: The Next Frontier for Innovation, Competition, and Productivity." *McKinsey Quarterly,* May 2011.

Markoff, J. "Company News—Visionary Apple Chairman Moves On," *The New York Times,* October 1993.

Mattel. *http://corporate.mattel.com/about-us/history/mattel_history.pdf*

Moorhead, F. and Neck. "Group Decision Fiascos Continue: Space Shuttle Challenger and a Groupthink Framework." *Human Relations* Vol. 44. Plenum Publishing Corporation, 1991.

MOSI. *www.mosi.org.uk/collections/explore-the-collections/ferranti-online/timeline.aspx.*

Peter, L. and R. Hull. *The Peter Principle.* New York: William Morrow & Company, 1969.

"Portfolio's Worst American CEOs of All Time: 19. Carly Fiorina." CNBC. *www.cnbc.com/id/30502091?slide=3.*

Protess, B. "Tallying the Costs of Bank of America's Countrywide Nightmare." *New York Times,* October 25, 2012.

Rand. *www.rand.org.*

Rand, A. *Return of the Primitive: The Anti-Industrial Revolution.* New York: Penguin Books, 1999.

Rexrode, C. "Wendy's Sells Arby's to Equity Firm." *Huff Post,* June 13, 2011.

Schein, E. *Organizational Culture and Leadership.* San Francisco: Jossey-Bass, 1992.

Seligman, M. *Learned Optimism.* New York: Free Press, 1990.

Senge, P. *The Fifth Discipline.* New York: Doubleday Currency, 1990.

Shurkin, J. *Terman's Kids.* New York: Little, Brown, 1992.

Sifneos, P. "Affect, Emotional Conflict, and Deficit: An Overview." *Psychotherapy and Psychosomatics* 56, 1991.

Spitz, Bob. *The Beatles: The Biography.* New York: Little, Brown, 2005.

Taylor, A. "How I Did it: Enterprise's Leader on How Integrating an Acquisition Transformed His Business." *Harvard Business Review,* September 4, 2013.

Tellis, G., and P. Golder. *Will and Vision.* New York: McGraw-Hill, 2002.

Tregoe, B., and J. Zimmerman. *Top Management Strategy.* New York: Simon & Schuster, 1980.

Updegrove, M. *Baptism by Fire: Eight Presidents Who Took Office in Times of Crisis.* New York: St. Martin's Press, 2008.

Verhovek, S. *Jet Age.* New York: Penguin Group, 2010.

"Wal-Mart Grapples With Its Worst Sales Slump Ever." *The Wall Street Journal*, February 22, 2011.

Wiseman, R. *www.laughlab.co.uk.*

Zanor, C. "A Fate That Narcissists Will Hate: Being Ignored." *The New York Times*, November 29, 2010.

Index

About the Author

For more than 35 years, Dr. Linda Henman has worked with executives in Fortune 500 Companies, privately held businesses, and military organizations to define their direction and select the best people to put their strategies in motion. She has helped clients in the retail, financial services, food, medical, hospitality, manufacturing, and technology industries. Some of her major clients include Tyson Foods, Emerson Electric, Kraft Foods, Boeing Aircraft, Estee Lauder, and Merrill Lynch. She was one of eight experts chosen to work directly with John Tyson on his succession plan after his company's acquisition of International Beef Products. Through thousands of hours of coaching and consulting, with hundreds of clients, Linda has observed what it takes to create exceptional organizations.

Linda holds a PhD in organizational systems, two master of arts degrees in both interpersonal communication and organization development, and a bachelor of science degree in communications. By combining her experience as an organizational consultant with her education in business, she offers her clients selection, coaching, and consulting solutions that are pragmatic in their approach and sound in their foundation.

She is the author of *Landing in the Executive Chair: How to Excel in the Hot Seat* and *The Magnetic Boss: How to Become the Leader No One Wants to Leave*, and coauthor of the recently released *Alan Weiss on Consulting*. She has also served as a contributing editor of two editions of *Small Group Communication: Theory and Practice,* has written peer-reviewed published articles, and authored numerous articles published in trade magazines.

As a professional speaker, Linda speaks about strategic leadership, succession planning, corporate culture, and mergers and acquisitions to large audiences throughout the United States. Serious about humor, Linda draws from her original research of the Vietnam prisoners of war to help others cope with change and adversity so they can emerge from setbacks more resilient and hardy.

Whether working with executives or members of boards of directors, Linda helps develop strategic leaders and solve critical problems. She can be reached at her office in St. Louis, Missouri, and by e-mail at linda@ henmanperformancegroup.com.